The UFO Report
1990

The UFO Report 1990

───────────⊙───────────

Edited by
TIMOTHY GOOD

SIDGWICK & JACKSON
LONDON

ISBN 0–283–99848–2 (Paperback)
0–283–99847–4 (Hardback)

*Set in Linotron 202 Times by
Hewer Text Composition Services, Edinburgh
Printed in Great Britain by
Butler & Tanner Ltd, Frome and London
for Sidgwick & Jackson Limited
1 Tavistock Chambers, Bloomsbury Way
London WC1A 2SG*

Contents

───────────────── ⊙ ─────────────────

Editor's Foreword

———————————— ⊙ ————————————

'Whatever anyone will say, both my son and I will *never* forget the 19th November, 1987,' wrote Mrs Barbara Forrest, in a letter to me describing a sighting at Brierley Hill, West Midlands, on that evening. 'The craft came so very low, to enable us to have a very close look. It was massive, wonderful, and frightening!'

Mrs Forrest and her son were just two of hundreds of witnesses who reported UFOs during the latter half of 1987, when a massive wave of sightings proliferated throughout the UK and in many other countries; a wave which was to continue unabated in 1988.

With a few exceptions (such as the Nullarbor case, described in Chapter 8) the national media continue to ignore these important events, or to pour scorn on the subject. 'Ladies and gentlemen, boys and girls,' began Michael Thompson-Noel in a lengthy article for the *Financial Times* in June 1988, 'believe it or not but the modern religion of Ufology today enters its 42nd year. . . . It is a religion of the space age that offers us heavenly lights, god-like aliens and flying green jellies.' Ufology, said Mr Thompson-Noel, is based on 'a rubbish-mountain of non-evidence'.[1]

Since *Above Top Secret* was published in June 1987, my travels have taken me to Australia, Brazil, Canada, USA, and the USSR. I have found encouraging signs that not all journalists share Mr Thompson-Noel's view. And in the Soviet Union, I had the opportunity of expressing my own views in an interview for Leningrad TV's *Open Door* programme in January 1989. That would have been inconceivable only a few years ago.

On 14 October 1988 a two-hour TV documentary, *UFO Cover-Up? Live*, was shown in the USA, Canada, Australia, and New Zealand. The programme included live participation from Washington DC, Gulf Breeze, Florida, and Moscow. A telephone poll conducted during and after the programme revealed that 30,835 people had experienced a Close Encounter of the First Kind (CEI – UFO seen within 500 ft); 2,482 reported a CEII (involving physical evidence); 1,477 a CEIII (alien occupants seen); and an astonishing 2,969 witnesses who claimed to have been abducted by aliens (CEIV).[2]

On the programme, Paul Shartle, former security manager and chief of requirement for the audio-visual programme at Norton Air Force Base, California, revealed the existence of an official film taken at Holloman AFB, New Mexico, which allegedly shows a UFO landing and the occupants communicating with various personnel at the base. Interviewed with Shartle was the TV producer Robert Emenegger, who obtained the film via the Pentagon in the early 1970s when he was in the process of making a documentary on the subject. He had hoped to include the film in his documentary, but permission was suddenly withdrawn.

Two alleged US Government intelligence agents, 'Condor' and 'Falcon', appeared on the documentary, with their faces blacked out and voices electronically modulated. They confirmed the existence of the so-called 'Majestic-12' committee, established under President Truman in 1947, following the retrieval of an alien spacecraft and its dead occupants in the New Mexican desert (details of which were first published in *Above Top Secret*). They further revealed that there had been actual communication with a number of extraterrestrials.

All this could be disinformation, of course. And the obtrusive synthesized background music that pervaded the entire documentary did little to enhance the agents' credibility. None the less, I have been informed that their credentials, at least, are bona fide.

Many people have written to ask me if the Majestic-12 briefing document, prepared for President-elect Eisenhower by former CIA director Vice-Admiral Roscoe Hillenkoetter in November 1952, reproduced for the first time in *Above Top Secret*, is authentic. The document (which I obtained from a CIA source) received world-wide publicity in 1987, and lengthy articles appeared in such newspapers as the *Observer* and the *New York Times*. The document's authenticity has been questioned by the Dwight D. Eisenhower Library, the Harry S. Truman Library, and the National Archives, but a great deal of information has now surfaced which tends to indicate that it is genuine.

A 1954 top secret memorandum from presidential assistant Robert Cutler to the then Air Force Chief of Staff, General Nathan Twining, makes reference to the 'MJ-12 Special Studies

Project' in connection with a meeting at the White House on 16 July that year. The memorandum was located in the files of USAF Intelligence at the National Archives, and there is every indication that it is genuine.

Dr Roger Wescott, Professor of Anthropology and Linguistics at Drew University, Madison, New Jersey, has compared the writing style on the Eisenhower briefing paper with known-to-be-authentic examples of Hillenkoetter's writings. In April 1988 he stated as follows: '. . . In my opinion, there is no compelling reason to regard any of these communications as fraudulent or to believe that any of them were written by anyone other than Hillenkoetter himself.'[3]

This does not, of course, prove that the document *is* legitimate. Further research is currently being done by Jaime Shandera, William Moore, and Stanton Friedman, and $16,000 has been appropriated by the Fund for UFO Research so that Friedman can devote several months to the project. At the time of writing, there are some positively encouraging developments.

Sightings by civil and military pilots continue to impress me. In Chapter 5, Cynthia Hind gives us details of a UFO report made by the crew and passengers aboard a Mozambique Airlines (LAM) plane, as well as air traffic controllers, at Beira, on 11 February 1988.

Two days earlier, on 9 February, an unidentified object was observed over Medellin airport in Bogota, Columbia, by several pilots and air traffic controllers. The crews of five different aircraft, including a military plane carrying Army chief General Oscar Botero, reported seeing the object, which remained in the area for half an hour. At one stage, the international José Maria Cordova airport control tower actually gave landing instructions to the UFO, believing it to be a private plane. The crew of an Avianca Boeing 727 radioed the control tower that the object was following them, and the tower ordered the plane to circle instead of landing, to avoid a collision.

Significantly, an aeronautical board imposed a news blackout on the incident, but a journalist who later succeeded in obtaining permission from the regional prosecutor to listen to the tapes of air traffic communications, reported that the object looked like a fast-moving star.[4]

Later that month a helicopter had a near collision with a 300-ft long UFO over southern England. It was established beyond doubt that no other aircraft were in the area at the time. I have interviewed the pilot and hope to publish details of this important case in the near future.

On 18 March 1988 a Xinjiang Airlines plane encountered a UFO over China. As in the Mozambique Airlines incident, the captain signalled the intruder with the plane's landing lights. (See Chapter 7.)

On 3 October 1988 two Brazilian airliners (of VARIG and VASP) were followed for fifteen minutes by a circular object, which was also detected on radar.

Another interesting revelation in 1988 was that ex-President Ronald Reagan had witnessed a UFO while he was Governor of California in 1974. 'We were flying near Bakersfield when Governor Reagan and the others called my attention to a big light flying a bit behind my plane. It appeared to be several hundred yards away,' reported Reagan's pilot, Bill Paynter. 'It began to accelerate, then it appeared to elongate. Then . . . the UFO went from a normal cruise speed to a fantastic speed instantly.'

Reagan himself described the incident to Normal Miller, then Washington Bureau chief for the *Wall Street Journal*. According to Miller, Reagan ordered the pilot to follow the object. 'We followed it for several minutes,' said Reagan. 'All of a sudden to our utter amazement it went straight up into the heavens. When I got off the plane I told Nancy all about it. And we read up on the long history of UFOs . . .'

'I didn't report the conversation at the time,' said Miller. 'Reagan didn't go into detail about the research he and his wife had done, because it was at that point that I asked him if he believed in UFOs, and he clammed up.'[5]

The year 1988 saw the passing of two great pioneers in UFO research: Donald Keyhoe, who died on 29 November, and Coral Lorenzen, who died on 12 April.

Coral Lorenzen and her husband Jim founded the Aerial Phenomena Research Organization (APRO) in 1952. Both served in the US Air Force and at one time held high security clearances. Coral was convinced that UFOs were of extraterrestrial origin and had been observing our planet for thousands of years. Her remains are interred at Arlington Cemetery, beside those of her husband.

A graduate of the US Naval Academy and an aide to Charles Lindbergh, Major Donald Keyhoe served in the Marine Corps as an aircraft and balloon pilot. He had many contacts in the Pentagon, and was the first to expose the UFO cover-up, in a series of articles and books. By the early 1950s he was convinced that the cover-up was organized by what he called 'The Silence Group'. That group, in my opinion, was the Majestic-12 committee, and this was one reason I dedicated *Above Top Secret* to him; the other reason being that it was Keyhoe's book, *The Flying Saucers Are Real*, which stimulated my interest in the subject back in 1955.

Sightings have continued in 1989 at a steady rate. The most important of these was made by the astronauts on the *Discovery* space shuttle on 14 March. The story first broke on LBC Radio on 29 March, after I had provided them with a copy of a tape which had been given to me by former NASA mission specialist, Bob Oechsler. Bob had received the recording from Donald Ratsch, a radio ham who had been monitoring the astronauts' communications, which were being transmitted on WA3NAN, the Goddard Amateur Radio Club at the NASA Goddard Space Flight Center, Greenbelt, Maryland, on 147.50mhz. At 06.42hrs EST, as the *Discovery* was over the French Polynesian Islands in the Pacific, one of the astronauts reported: 'HOUSTON, THIS IS DISCOVERY. WE STILL HAVE THE ALIEN SPACECRAFT UNDER OBSERVANCE.'

At the time of writing, NASA is denying that the incident took place. Bob Oechsler arranged for independent voice-print analyses to be made, and the results will be published in due course. Interestingly, at about 06.35hrs EST, Donald Ratsch heard (but did not record) one of the astronauts say: 'WE HAVE A PROBLEM – WE HAVE A FIRE.' According to Bob Oechsler, 'Fire' is most probably a code word. He further believes that the *Discovery* had been paced by a UFO for several hours prior to the 'Alien Space Craft' communication. A number of other radio hams heard both communications.

Finally, I would like to record my thanks to the international team of dedicated men and women who have contributed to *The*

UFO Report 1990. I would also like to thank Lord Rees-Mogg, who suggested the idea; Cyril Darbyshire, for translating much of Chapter 6; Duane Cook, editor of the Gulf Breeze *Sentinel*, who kindly supplied me with the cover photo, taken by 'Jane'; and Dorothee, who helped me so much with the typing.

TIMOTHY GOOD

London
April 1989

REFERENCES

1. Thompson-Noel, Michael: 'Wacky world of the Ufologists', *Financial Times*, 25 June 1988.
2. *UFO Cover-Up? Live* was produced by Michael Seligman and distributed by Lexington Broadcast Service (LBS). The results of the survey were published by Walt Andrus, director of the Mutual UFO Network, in the *MUFON UFO Journal*, No. 248, December 1988.
3. Letter from Dr Roger Wescott to Robert Bletchman, 7 April 1988.
4. *El Columbiano*, 22 February 1989, as reported in the *Shropshire Star,* 23 February 1989.
5. *New Truth*, Dunedin, New Zealand, 17 October 1988. The Reagan incident was first mentioned in *Landslide: The Unmaking of the President*, by Jane Mayer and Doyle McManus (Collins, London 1988, page 402).

1

A British Perspective 1988

GRAHAM and MARK BIRDSALL

Graham and Mark Birdsall have been interested in UFOs for many years, and in 1981 formed the Yorkshire UFO Society.

Despite its title, namely that of a group which operates out of Britain's largest county, YUFOS has succeeded in establishing itself as one of Europe's leading organizations, with a flourishing membership.

The Birdsall brothers both work in the printing industry, and devote most of their spare time to the society and its bi-monthly journal, *Quest International* (see Appendix).

The illustrations are by Mark Birdsall.

Britain, with a population of nearly 60 million, has the highest number of reports in proportion to the rest of the world. One of the reasons behind this extraordinary fact is the number of dedicated researchers who actively pursue the phenomenon on behalf of several organizations, one of which is the Yorkshire UFO Society.

It is here in the United Kingdom that our active investigators have found ample evidence to convince us that we are facing a genuine phenomenon that simply cannot be dismissed by this or any other government as being merely misidentifications or products of the mind. Nor do we believe that perfectly honest and respectable people, from a police officer of twenty-five years' service, through to the average man and woman with able background and character, are always mistaken in their conviction that they have encountered something that defies logic.

When one speaks with police officers, who are generally the most objective of people, and listens to their description of a UFO encounter that leaves them nonplussed and clearly shocked by their experience, one begins to question those in the UFO community and elsewhere who insist that we are dealing at all times with simple misidentifications of aircraft lights, meteorological phenomena, astronomical events, or even some form of psychic experience.

We have every confidence in our researchers' ability to get at the truth, but some UFO groups continually mock those very people who risk ridicule and sometimes their livelihood for having the courage to describe their encounters with the unknown.

As an organization, we are careful to protect the identity of all witnesses who claim to have confronted some form of UFO. It is a sad reflection on ufology that some investigators clamour to involve what is, after all, a very sceptical media. In doing so, mostly for private gain, it is at the expense of the witnesses, who suddenly find themselves thrown into the public limelight and wish they had never agreed to disclosing their information in the first place. There is intense rivalry, almost bordering on the fringes of common decency, amongst many UFO groups and self-made experts, to be the first to a UFO case, to be the first to research it, to be the first to relate details to the media, and to hell with the consequences.

British UFO research has often dealt with some of the most important events to have occurred during the last four decades. It has failed, however, to deliver much in the way of real progress, simply because it has never got its act together.

The most notable success in the UFO field of literature in recent years was *Above Top Secret*, whose author Timothy Good, a great supporter of our organization, set out to redress the balance. It is no secret that Timothy conducted much of his research practically isolated from the major UK groups. The result was unquestionably the best work ever written on this subject.

Timothy presented a calculated appraisal of the phenomenon, and in doing so proved that many governments both here and abroad were and still are actively engaged in suppressing known facts relating to their own research from the public. Using hitherto secret official documents, all relating to the UFO subject, he exposed the myth once and for all that UFOs do not interest government agencies, and therefore must be dismissed as being mere fanciful tales of imagination.

2

Our organization has centred its activities on similar areas of research. Here in Yorkshire, for example, is the ultra-sensitive Distant Early Warning base of RAF Fylingdales. This complex can detect any item in orbit around our planet, from 1,500 satellites to 15,000 items of space debris. It is known, for example, that the base can detect an object as small as a tea tray above Moscow, so one would think it highly likely that if structured UFOs are indeed entering or leaving Earth's atmosphere at will, they would know about it. Perhaps not. At this, and other key sensitive bases within these shores, personnel operate on a 'need-to-know' basis. At the top-secret listening post at Menwith Hill, close to Harrogate in North Yorkshire, and operated by over 1,000 members of the US National Security Agency, personnel come under many security classifications, none more sensitive than 'S.C.I.' (Sensitive Compartmented Information).

During his research for the book *Deep Black*, author William E. Burrows interviewed General Paul D. Wagoner, then head of the North American Aerospace Defence Command. It is to here that all data from RAF Fylingdales is sent. The General was invited to comment on the existence of a top-secret imaging satellite codenamed KH-11. He refused point blank, and then went on to explain that the KH-11 project was more sensitive than the 'Top Secret' category, and came into the classification known as S.C.I. Staff who work on such 'black' projects (the General included) come under this classification. They are given only enough access in order to do whatever is necessary to complete their task.

On his own admission, General Wagoner is allowed to know as much data about 'blacker' than top-secret projects as his immediate superiors will allow.[1] It follows therefore that officers and personnel within security agencies are themselves allowed to know only so much. How is the young RAF operator to know if the object seen over Moscow is just a tea tray?

For as long as we can remember here in Britain, the Ministry of Defence has taken the view that until such time as UFOs constitute a threat to the defence of the realm, no active research is being undertaken by Her Majesty's Armed Forces, or any other body. The MoD's official clearing house for all UFO reports within Whitehall is publicly known as AS2 (Secretariat, Air Staff 2), where public and official reports are purportedly routed, be they from the police or civilian pilots, etc.

DI55

Our organization made repeated requests to the MoD to formally admit that UFO reports also made their way to other agencies, but they persistently denied this. However, it is a fact of life that occasionally some government departments have a tendency to release information by accident that should have never been made public. Such a 'gaffe' occurred when an official document came into our hands which detailed a distribution list at the foot of a report that examined a UFO incident over Bradford, in Yorkshire, which had been telexed through to the MoD by Leeds & Bradford regional airport.

No previous documents of this kind had ever included such a distribution list. It was a major breakthrough, and revealed at a stroke that the MoD had an intricate system for analysing and actioning UFO reports within the United Kingdom and abroad. This official document listed the following organizations and departments that would have received copies of the UFO report:

Sec (AS)2 [Secretariat, Air Staff 2]
AEW/GE [Airborne Early Warning/Ground Environment]
AF/OPS/1/11 [Air Force Operations]
DI55 [?]

From this distribution list, we established definite links between Britain's Air Early Warning systems and NATO (North Atlantic Treaty Organization). We also established that the North Atlantic Defence Ground Environment (NADGE) and the United Kingdom Air Defence Ground Environment (UKADGE) would be relayed data on the report.

UKADGE is probably the most advanced air and ground defence system operated in the world today. The network includes all Royal Navy and NATO surface vessels, AWACS aircraft (Airborne Early Warning and Control System), Ground Radar bases around Britain, including Staxton Wold in Yorkshire. The data that is received from such sources enters RAF bases at Buchan, Boulmer, Ash, and Neatishead, and is then channelled through to the Air Defence Operational Centre (ADOC) at High Wycombe.

As UFO researchers, we recognized the fact that any unknown target, be it a Soviet Backfire bomber or UFO, must be pinpointed at some stage by this virtually impregnable defensive system.

Given these facts, could we really believe the MoD has no interest in UFO reports? And what of the other listing as yet not identified – DI55?

Whitehall is a vast infra-structure of various government bodies dealing with a host of day-to-day tasks affecting the Armed Forces of Great Britain and its allies. There must be hundreds, if not thousands of telephone lines intersecting the corridors of this famous establishment.

Mick Hanson, a keen and dedicated researcher for our organization, elected to solve the mystery of DI55 using guile, and a bit of cheek. He rang Whitehall and asked if he could be put through to AS2, but found himself being put through to another department. A few minutes later, he was speaking to yet another department, again the wrong one. He was being transferred all the time, but was eventually put through to AS2, although, we believe, on an entirely different and internal phone, thus raising no question in the mind of the AS2 operator that he was speaking with a civilian UFO researcher.

The AS2 operator was unable to help Mick with his request for data relating to a particular case that had been reported to him via South Yorkshire police in his capacity as co-ordinator of research in that area. He was put back to the internal switchboard, and requested that the operator put him in touch with any Whitehall department that might assist him with his research. The operator told him that if AS2 could not help, perhaps DI55 may be more forthcoming! Mick had a very fruitful conversation with a gentleman at this previously unknown department that dealt directly with UK UFO reports.

Further research concluded that the Ministry of Defence had been caught with their pants down. Letters demanded an explanation as to why the existence of DI55 had been kept hidden from researchers, but the MoD were very reluctant to admit or deny anything. We continued to delve into this deception and with the assistance of Timothy Good, finally unwrapped the most secret information of all.

RAF Rudloe Manor

As long ago as 1979 our organization knew the precise location of a base, located discreetly in the beautiful Wiltshire countryside, that had some real connection with UFO research. We knew from our source that the British Armed Forces, in co-operation with the National Security Agency, were heavily involved in something that they wished to keep secret.

This base was RAF Rudloe Manor, and without Timothy's active research, combined with information supplied by a source known only to him, and our own co-operation in revealing what we knew at the time, this base would still be operating covertly.

Several communications had been made between DI55 and Rudloe Manor, all connected with UFO sighting reports. And in *Above Top Secret*, Timothy reveals that the Flying Complaints Flight, now based at Rudloe Manor, incorporates a UFO investigation unit, staffed by personnel of the Provost & Security Services.

The Ministry of Defence denies that Rudloe Manor is involved in UFO investigations, however. According to them, one civil servant alone is employed full time at Whitehall, who amongst other duties studies UFO reports. Yet the MoD confirmed to Timothy that DI55 was also involved in investigations.[2] It is therefore untrue to state that only one civil servant is actively engaged in investigating and disseminating the bulk of UFO reports that are dispatched via Whitehall. We believe that task is too great for one individual, and are convinced we have merely scratched at the surface of our government's real interest in the phenomenon.

While other British groups involved in the UFO subject choose to research mundane reports, delve over past encounters stretching back for decades, dabble in the psychic and bizarre, our organization chose to adopt the current American UFO researchers' attitude; namely, believe your government is withholding UFO data, and strive to get at the real truth surrounding what can only be described as a cover-up of enormous proportions.

The 1988 Flap

With all this new and important data to hand, 1988 offered British UFO researchers a great opportunity to study and act upon the biggest wave of sightings to have occurred within this country for a decade.

We will now present some of the most fascinating UFO case files researched by our team of investigators, who knew full well that our current government would be keenly following developments at every stage, recognizing they were no longer dealing with a more placid UFO research group. The MoD also appreciated that our research was broadening to cover Stealth technology, the Strategic Defence Initiative programme (SDI), and hugely secretive sorties made by Remotely Piloted Vehicles (RPVs). Perhaps we had become a threat to those within the Defence lobby who wished to perpetuate the official government stance that they had no interest in UFO research.

Investigators of the UFO phenomenon have no sixth sense in determining just when a major 'flap' will occur, but when one begins to receive reports from around the country, and on a daily basis, culminating in twenty-two independent sightings on one night alone, there is ample justification for believing that something peculiar is going on, or is about to happen.

During January 1988, this organization received eighty-nine accounts of UFO activity, only four of which originated with the media. As a result, we had a mass of information about the nature of the sightings. But could we draw any conclusions?

2 January

Just before midnight on Saturday 2 January, a sixteen-year-old girl with a keen interest in astronomy thought she saw a UFO above London. When informed of the sighting, police officers based at Kensington rushed outdoors to catch a glimpse of the object. They did see it, and were convinced it was some sort of UFO. The media reported the sighting, and a headline proclaimed 'Jellyfish over London'. (Apparently when asked what the UFO looked like, one of the officers made the unfortunate 'jellyfish' remark.)

It later transpired that the 'UFO' was nothing more than a brightly shining planet, often misidentified by inexperienced observers as a genuine UFO. It is a fact that, while we all have a high regard for the abilities of police officers, very few receive basic astronomy lessons while in the service!

Ray Barron, 200 miles away, had just parked his vehicle in the driveway of his home, situated in a quiet suburb of Leeds, England's third largest city, and commercial 'capital' of Yorkshire. It was a chilly dark night, and the retired construction engineer was in a hurry to reach the warmth of indoors. What made him stop and stare into the starlit sky for the next two minutes takes us to the heart of a typical UFO report, which our researchers are constantly attempting to explain.

Mr Barron had caught sight of an object, later described as plate-shaped and coloured orange and yellow, which moved across the Leeds skyline, spinning or rolling as it did so. It appeared to descend a fraction, and it was then that he noticed some kind of smoke or vapour being emitted from the rear. Mr Barron takes up the story: 'The light was brilliant and quite large, practically half the size of a full moon. As I watched in the freezing cold, the damn thing "switched off" like a light bulb. I peered upwards and tried to find out where it had gone, but was absolutely shattered to see the spiralling smoke continue its journey! Yet it was coming out of nothing . . .'

Fortunately, the great advantage of having a network of researchers spread around the country is that we may be able to offer further data that could correlate a sighting with another report that has reached us from a completely independent source. This is exactly what occurred on this particular evening.

Mr Barron had left his vehicle at precisely 7.50 that evening. Several miles away, in the small market town of Dewsbury, West Yorkshire, Jane Marsden and her friend Vivienne O'Donnell were sitting in a parked vehicle, engaged in conversation. Suddenly, at 7.50 p.m. they noticed through the offside window of the vehicle a large ball of light passing through the night sky. Their initial reaction was one of dread, for they had no doubt an aircraft was possibly on fire and in serious trouble. However, if it were an aircraft, it was taking an awfully long time to move across the sky. Both ladies had now centred their attention on the object, and were oblivious to people and traffic passing close-by.

The object was now brightly lit, orange and yellow colours could be seen, and the definite shape of a red tail could be seen behind the main body. Both women were perplexed and disturbed. Jane later told us: 'Behind the orange "ball" was a pale blue flame, then came a long slender red tail. It was moving very, very slowly indeed.'

Two concise reports, covered in depth by our researchers – but were both objects one and the same? If the consensus is that they were, then what on earth could it have been? It has been estimated that only ten per cent of UFO witnesses actually bother to report their experiences to the media, police or local

UFO groups. If we had received a further twenty-seven reports from various people and localities, our researchers might well have been better placed to form an opinion. But with only three witnesses to an unusual event, seen over an area containing at least one and a half million people, what chance did we have? And yet . . .

Our investigators were no sooner attempting to resolve the events of that night (by the common practice of contacting the police, civil and military airfields, etc.) when we were further confounded by a reported UFO sighting that had taken place at nine o'clock that same evening in Leeds.

Mr Ted Johnson lives close to the north-west of the city. He told us of an object that had flown extremely low as it followed the contours of a nearby valley. Yet this was no aircraft, but a large orange- and yellow-coloured ball of light. Behind it came a vast stream of greyish smoke, and long after the object had disappeared to the north, this vapour remained visible. Ted is adamant that the time was 9.00 p.m., but he had no idea, of course, that three other people in the region that night had also seen some kind of strange aerial object.

During the next twenty-four hours we sought out data from our team of investigators and, as luck would have it, a report came back from the Worksop, Nottinghamshire, area. Two people, both of whom wish to remain anonymous, were close to their village on the outskirts of Worksop at approximately 7.30 p.m. Apparently, two odd-shaped 'aircraft' had flown in and around the area for several minutes. The observers noticed some unusual aspects regarding shape: very thin in terms of depth, both triangular, and each with prominent fins. (See Fig. 1:1.)

Were these aircraft or UFOs? The immediate task facing any investigation in an event like this is to discover if there are any known military exercises going on in the area of the sightings. As it transpired, there were none – officially. Yet we have recorded dozens of instances when military manoeuvres have taken place, and have invited the MoD to confirm this, yet they usually plead ignorance.

Our organization has made a thorough study of the development of so-called 'Stealth' aircraft. It is believed that the F-117A Stealth fighter has flown from bases in the UK for some years, even before being officially recognized by the US Department of

Figure 1:1. Worksop, 2 January 1988.

Defense as even existing, in November 1988. However, there is no hard evidence that Stealth craft have flown in this country. To claim that some UFO reports can be attributed to these top-secret aircraft is foolhardy, unless one is in possession of the facts. It is more reasonable to look at conventional aircraft that operate in pairs, have highly unusual designs, and fly in a manner which is calculated to confuse. Such an aircraft is the American A-10 Thunderbolt, many of which are based in Britain. These usually operate in pairs, fly at very low altitudes, and sometimes use motorway traffic as 'targets' on operational sorties. They will duck and weave among hill tops and trees, and at night such manoeuvres will always appear peculiar to the unaccustomed observer.

3 January

Just as we were discussing the merits of whether or not to place this Worksop sighting in the 'possible aircraft' category, came news of a very disturbing encounter in Humberside (formerly East Yorkshire). It was 5.00 p.m., Sunday 3 January, almost twenty-four hours after the events in Leeds.

Mrs Annette McDonaldson and her young daughter had been visiting friends in Grimsby, a fishing port on the east coast, and had just set off to return home to York. Travelling on a road just outside the town, the night had closed in, but traffic was light and there appeared to be no obstacles to delay their journey.

The bright lights which appeared in their car's rear-view mirror suggested to Annette that some large lorry was fast approaching, and she slowed down in order to let it pass. Despite relaxing her foot on the accelerator the distance between her and the lights remained the same. She asked her daughter to look behind and see what this lorry driver was playing at.

Clare McDonaldson arched round and focused her eyes on the lights, some 100 yards behind. After a while, she began to make out the surface of the road, and was shocked to realize that the lights were actually airborne, just above the ground. She could see no shape whatsoever behind the bright glare. During the course of the next three minutes, the lights bore steadily closer to the car, but suddenly vanished in an instant.

By now, confused and frightened, Annette instructed her daughter to keep a look-out for the lights. She did not have long to wait before a startled cry told her the lights were directly above their car. Panic set in, and Annette slammed her foot down hard on the accelerator, and in a short while was beyond the legal speed limit. Two more minutes passed by, and then to her horror she saw the two bright lights ahead of her and above the road. Whatever lay behind the lights was cautious enough not to allow the car to smash headlong into it. It kept an even distance between them for a number of miles. Almost as suddenly as it had appeared, the lights shot straight up into the sky at a steep angle and disappeared. [The McDonaldsons were luckier than the Knowles family, whose car was picked up and dropped back on the road by a UFO in Western Australia only a few weeks later. See Chapter 8 – Editor.]

The mother and daughter had been left in a shocked state. Their experience had so affectedd them that as soon as they had an opportunity, the police were called. Good co-operation between our organization and several police authorities ensured that we were immediately given the relevant information. Despite this early opportunity to quiz the witnesses, we were later no nearer to finding any sensible answer as to the probable cause of the incident. Perhaps some lunatic at the controls of a helicopter had decided to stage a terrifying low-level 'chase' with a passing motorist? But the two women were adamant: if it had been a helicopter, they would have said so.

As if to reinforce our growing unease that we could be witnessing the start of a major 'flap', we received a call from Pauline Russell, who had witnessed something rather odd near her home in South Leeds at nine-thirty that same Sunday evening. She had been out walking when she was attracted by a brightly lit 'egg-shaped object' moving slowly across the sky. Its design was so unusual that she stood still in order to try and fathom what it could be. There were no aircraft navigation lights visible on the object, but suddenly a real aircraft displaying its lights came into view from the opposite direction.

The aircraft and object were moving rapidly towards one another. Whatever the UFO was, it moved across the sky in a staggered motion, almost zig-zagging. The conventional aircraft came within a whisker of colliding with the unknown light, and passed just to the right-hand side of it. Pauline later admitted: 'The object was unlike anything I have ever seen in my life, and anyone on that aircraft must have seen it.' Needless to say, no one within aviation circles reported seeing anything.

4 January

This day was to prove our busiest of the whole year. In a period of just six hours and fifteen minutes, we received twenty-two reports of UFO phenomena from around the region. The events of that day are recorded by our investigator during the course of that week and beyond.

5.25 p.m. A married couple reported a massive white sphere moving just above the clouds over Harewood, near Harrogate, North Yorkshire.

7.00 p.m. A woman reported seeing a glowing white object stationary over South Leeds at a height of 1,000 ft. The object slowly moved south after some two minutes. She could see several dark points or patches on the object.

7.20 p.m. A gentleman in the small Yorkshire village of Masbrough, near Rotherham, rang to say he was observing a cluster of brilliant red- and yellow-coloured lights at a height of between 500 and 1000 ft. Local investigator Allan Petres hurried to the scene, and confirmed the sighting.

7.30 p.m. Mr J. S. Rhodes, an experienced ex-RAF officer, observed a strange-looking 'aircraft' without wings over Scholes, West Yorkshire. It glowed orange in colour, but had five darkened portholes running the entire length. He also noticed two aircraft, possibly military, near the scene. There was sound coming from them, but not from the mysterious shape which was quickly leaving the area.

7.45 p.m. Two young women were leaving their work premises in the centre of Derby when they were astonished to see three brilliantly lit white spheres directly overhead. There was absolutely no sound or movement, but as quickly as they appeared, they disappeared.

7.46 p.m. Two young men parked in the centre of Chellaston, Derbyshire, observed a large circular shaped object that looked to be made of glass, 'sewn together by threads'.

8.00 p.m. Mr Bill Moran was making his way home to Kimberworth, Rotherham, when he saw an intensely lit bright ball of light moving extremely slowly towards the north-west at very low altitude. It had two distinct colours, yellow and orange.

8.02 p.m. Mr Thomas Jordan and his son were puzzled to see a brilliant yellow sphere move slowly due north above their home in Roundhay, an attractive suburb of Leeds. Not unfamiliar with aircraft, neither could offer any explanation for what they saw. Surprisingly, three aircraft in formation appeared to head after this object shortly afterwards. Both men are very keen amateur astronomers and have always been sceptical about so-called UFOs, yet despite this they were sufficiently impressed by their experience to contact our organization.

8.15 p.m. A gentleman from York, North Yorkshire, reported seeing an object which to him resembled the old V-1 flying bomb. It flew at very low altitude and emitted sparks, debris, and flames.

8.15 p.m. An entire family was watching television in their home at Kirkhamgate, near Wakefield, West Yorkshire. Through the downstairs window they saw a large luminous green ball of light travelling slowly across the sky. They rushed to the window, then made their way outside to get a better look. The object was releasing some kind of vapour behind it which was clearly visible due to the bright light coming from the object itself. It finally disappeared out of sight beyond some hills, but apparently following the course of the nearby M1 motorway.

8.15 p.m. A woman in York was outside her home, about to call for her children who had been playing in the street, when she saw a brilliant yellow and orange sphere of light move slowly across the night sky heading west.

8.17 p.m. Mr Lee was travelling along the dual carriageway of the A38 near Shelton Lock, Derbyshire, when he suddenly became aware of a large 'lemon-shaped' object moving westwards in the sky. It was totally white in colour, but surrounding it there appeared to be a blue- or green-glowing halo. It was moving extremely quickly, and at one point Mr Lee thought the object was set to crash into the ground.

8.45 p.m. Two men travelling over the moor-tops at Blubber-houses, North Yorkshire, heading east, saw an object emitting sparks and debris at low altitude, and were convinced it was going to crash into a hillside. Both men thought the object resembled a V-1 rocket.

8.50 p.m. Several witnesses reported seeing two extremely large, glowing white spheres that flew side-by-side near Collingham, West Yorkshire. At one point, the spheres descended quite close to the vehicle in which they were travelling, causing one or two unprintable expletives! One man said the effect was like putting a brightly lit lorry in the sky.

8.50 p.m. Mr Jones of Guiseley, West Yorkshire, observed a thin green 'laser beam' that 'shot from horizon to horizon in a matter of seconds'. Being ex-RAF, he felt suitably qualified to suggest that some sort of test was being carried out in the upper atmosphere, but of what and by whom remains unanswered.

8.50 p.m. Mr Scotsman from Selby, North Yorkshire, reported seeing a thin pencil-shaped object above the area. It displayed several constant blue lights, and a number of red ones along its side.

9.10 p.m. Gordon Blake, an ex-RAF resident of Leeds, had been outdoors when suddenly a large, glowing, orange light appeared in the north-east sky. His immediate reaction was to study the light more closely, because, in his words 'it did not conform to any aircraft navigation lighting system that I had been used to'. A few seconds elapsed and then the object drew closer, finally enabling him to see that it was truly gigantic, and in his estimation, some 400 ft in diameter. It had several 'layers' and at least twelve lights flashed in or around it in formation. Mr

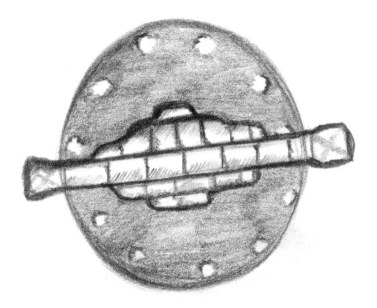

Figure 1:2.

Blake is very familiar with air-refuelling exercises that can often be mistaken for something more exotic by ground observers, but he dismisses the theory for this particular sighting. (Fig. 1:2.)

9.10 p.m. Mrs Robson and her friend had never seen a UFO before, but now they are not so sure. Close to their home in Morley, on the outskirts of south Leeds, they saw a 'rocket-shaped object' move across the sky, then downwards at high speed. Blue- and red-coloured flames poured from the rear. Without any prompting from us, they compared the object with an 'old V-1 rocket'.

9.15 p.m. Close to the A1 near Wetherby, West Yorkshire, a married couple reported seeing 'a large white light with several smaller lights within'.

9.16 p.m. Two residents at Harrogate, North Yorkshire, were disturbed to spot a large, glowing, orange-coloured object high above the town, practically stationary. It did move slowly towards their position, however, and they could make out three separate points of orange- and yellow-coloured lights within the main body, almost in cluster formation.

11.30 p.m. An elderly couple from Dewsbury, West Yorkshire, were about to retire for the night. As they were about to close the bedroom curtains, they were astonished to see a large brightly lit object, like a dinner plate, move back and forth across the sky. They managed to open the window to get a clearer look and could hear a loud 'swishing noise', presumably from the object itself. They watched, fascinated, for as long as ten minutes, before the light, which had given them the best aerial display since Guy Fawkes' night, simply 'switched off'. Perhaps this was a means of suggesting to dozens, if not hundreds of people who had witnessed the night-time events: 'That's all folks!'

This ended any further reports that night, but over the course of the next twenty-five days, fifty-six more UFO encounters would be placed in our computer files, leaving each and every one of us involved quite astonished.

11 January

One of the most intriguing encounters occurred in daylight on Monday, 11 January at 10.30 a.m. It happened on the B6265 Grassington to Skipton road, North Yorkshire. This beautiful part of the English countryside has possibly seen more reports of alleged UFO sightings than any other region of the United Kingdom over the past twenty years. Steep hills and fells overlook the area for miles around, and one needs only to progress a few yards in any direction to become virtually isolated from civilization. We could write a whole chapter on fascinating reports that have emerged over the years from this one spot alone.

Tony Dodd is head of YUFOS Research and Investigations. For twenty-five exemplary years, he served in the North Yorkshire Police Force before retiring in 1988. Based at Skipton, then later in Grassington, Tony has a high regard for the people in the area. His deep-seated interest in the subject began in the late 1970s, when he personally witnessed a number of strange aerial craft at close proximity (one of which is described in detail in *Above Top Secret*[3]). These encounters, also witnessed by several colleagues in the force, convinced him we were dealing with a 'nuts-and-bolts' phenomenon.

For the witnesses' own protection, we have used pseudonyms

in this case, which was investigated by Tony Todd, but their backgrounds and qualifications are genuine.

Dr P. T. Watkins (Ph.D. Oxon.) is a retired professor of organic chemistry, aged sixty-five. His wife, Mrs A. D. Watkins (M.A.), is sixty-seven years of age. They were travelling towards Skipton by car and were approximately one mile on from the Grassington side of the Craven Heifer public house, when an object suddenly appeared ahead of them, resembling a flat 'hovercraft' or disk. It was descending all the time from a height of 200 to 300 ft, and was 100 to 200 yards away, approximately 20 ft in diameter, and moving between 0 and 50 m.p.h. Their immediate reaction to the pulsing object was to believe some kind of partially deflated meteorological balloon was about to come down. It was travelling in a south-west to north-east direction. Mr Watkins described the object, and what happened next: 'The object seemed to have a flange or rim which undulated as it came down. It had appeared in front of us very suddenly, as though it had made a very rapid vertical descent. It then changed direction to move parallel with the ground. The front edge of the object appeared to be moving towards us initially as it passed in front of our car.'

Its edges were sharpened, and the colour appeared silvery-pink. It veered to the left of the vehicle, as if to make a landing, but then disappeared from view. Tony carried out a meticulous search of the area in question, known as the Crookrise Plantation, but found no evidence of anything untoward. He questioned the farmer who owned the land, and spoke with several workers on the plantation, but no one could add anything which might have produced an explanation. Checks with the regional police force and MoD were made, but again, Tony's investigations drew a blank. The witnesses are highly respected members of the local community, and their sighting must be considered a genuine Close Encounter of the First Kind.

That same evening, a YUFOS team in the Kimberworth valley area of Rotherham, South Yorkshire, identified several unknown 'targets' at 8.05 p.m., 8.30 p.m. and 9.05 p.m. Several photographs of the phenomena were taken using an Olympus camera and 1600 ASA film. When developed and analysed, these showed an unusual orange-coloured ball of light.

There was another sighting on 11 January, reported from southern England. According to the *Camberley News*, Mr Fred

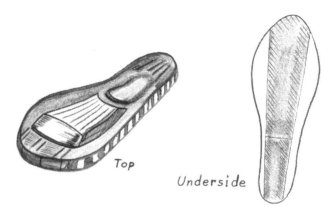

Figure 1:3. Object seen by Ivan Spenceley, 23 January 1988.

Clarke and his stepson Darryl Robson, were driving to work at 6.30 a.m. when they saw strange bright lights in the sky. On reaching Bentley, Hampshire, Mr Clarke stopped to go to a shop. 'I looked up and there was a massive object moving slowly towards Farnham,' he said. 'It was shaped like a fifty pence piece and was larger than an aeroplane.' The object had a light at opposite ends and was making a droning noise.[4]

16 January

At 12.45 a.m. on 16 January, Police Sgt Thompson and a colleague, along with numerous members of the public, watched a glowing red ball of light hang motionless above the city of Sheffield, South Yorkshire. Such was their concern that they officially notified headquarters, and questions were asked among regional military establishments if an exercise flare was being used, but the authorities denied any knowledge of the sighting. Both police officers said that the object remained hovering for at least seven minutes, until it finally vanished in an instant.

22 January

More and more reports were coming in from the region, where the phenomenon appeared to be concentrating. A highly interesting case occurred near Kettlewell, North Yorkshire, at 9.00 p.m. on 22 January. Mr and Mrs Alan Davidson had been driving north when they encountered a large triangular-shaped object directly in front of their car, moving left to right across the windscreen. In the few seconds available to them before it disappeared, they both saw that the object had a bank of lights on its base, with several more across the centre. A number of these were flashing on and off across the whole length of the 60 ft-plus structure. It was totally noiseless so far as they could ascertain.

The couple, quite understandably, had been badly shaken by this experience. They negotiated a difficult bend, then stopped the car and walked back to see if they could catch sight of the strange craft, but a search of the surrounding fields and sky proved fruitless.

23 January

Ivan Spenceley is a man of impeccable background, well educated and informed. When he first gave details of his extraordinary sighting, which took place near Chesterfield, Derbyshire, at 12.45 a.m. on 23 January, we could not fail but to be impressed by his attempts to rationalize his UFO encounter. During 1988, we had worked closely with researchers at Central Television who wanted to present a live UFO debate on the national network. We provided some material, and more importantly, witnesses who we felt would do the subject justice, such as Ivan.

He was out walking his dog late at night close to woodland, a task he had performed regularly for a number of years, when he suddenly became aware of a 'massive' oval object in the sky. On closer inspection, he could make out straight and curved lines around it. There were a series of red and blue lights constantly shining, but not in a position where you would expect them to be on an aircraft, or airship. From what appeared to be tinted windows, light was emanating continuously. The object was very low in the sky and moved at a snail's pace away from him, without any sound. (See Fig. 1:3.)

3 February

Reports continued to pour into the organization during February, and we have selected a few that typify the diversity of the phenomenon and the backgrounds of our witnesses. On Wednesday evening, around six-thirty on 3 February, an incident took place on the main Harrogate to Skipton road. This often

Figure 1:4. Sheffield, 8 February 1988.

narrow and winding route carried a coachload of forty pupils and staff who were shocked to witness an oval-shaped ball of yellow light travel alongside their vehicle. After descending to their level very suddenly, the object 'paced' the vehicle for a few seconds, moved for a while slightly ahead of it, then sped off at an estimated speed of 120 m.p.h. towards the village of Blubberhouses. Twenty seconds later, a similar object came from the rear of the coach and carried out almost the same manoeuvre.

8 February

A 23-year-old housewife from Sheffield had opened her attic window to allow in some fresh air, when she saw a brightly lit object descend through thin cloud and hover approximately 100 ft above the ground. It was illuminated by an array of beautiful, coloured, dazzling lights. These were peppermint green, ice-blue, and bright red. At the object's base she could see a massive circular white light. For a staggering twenty minutes, this young woman watched in awe as the rooftop-shaped craft remained still and quiet. A streetlight nearby dimmed during this time, and her bedroom light would flicker on and off. The object then moved away very slowly, close to housetops and trees, before quickly disappearing at an estimated speed of 100/120 m.p.h. (Fig. 1:4.)

Approximately one hour before this particular sighting, two independent reports from the Rotherham area cited a cone-shaped object displaying orange and white lights moving slowly over the town, which was only several miles from the housewife's location.

15 February

At 12.15 a.m. on 15 February, in Rotherham yet again, a father and son were returning home from an enjoyable evening out with friends. The son was attracted to a cluster of bright lights which appeared to be hovering high in the sky ahead of them. There was little traffic around them at the time, and the night sky was clear and the weather crisp. James Adams, fifteen years old, had not mentioned the lights to his father at the time, but when he saw the object descend over an electricity pylon approximately a quarter of a mile away, he frantically drew his father's attention towards it. 'My dad was amazed,' James said later. 'We could see this disk-shaped thing with a large dome on top and flashing lights around the base.' These lights were coloured red, green, yellow, orange, and white. The light on top was brilliant white. 'After twenty seconds,' added James, 'it moved away like a bullet, but we never heard a sound.'

16 February

On 16 February two separate police patrols observed a UFO over Walsall, West Midlands. According to the *Birmingham Daily News*, Sgt Stuart Griffiths and PC Michael Powell were on a panda car patrol when an extraordinary sight brought them to a halt.

'In the sky up in front of us was a very bright light,' reported Sgt Griffiths. 'I cannot be sure but the object could have been oblong in shape. It had green and red lights which were either flashing on and off or spinning around.' The officers got out of their car and were amazed to find that the craft was noiseless. 'We watched it for about two minutes and then it suddenly disappeared towards the south-east. It seemed to move much faster than an aeroplane,' said Sgt Griffiths.[5]

Fifteen minutes earlier, at 9.15 p.m., Inspector Roger Clarke

Figure 1:5A. Doncaster, 12 January 1988.

Figure 1:5B. The National Security Agency station at Menwith Hill, Yorkshire (© Timothy Good).

and Sgt Steve Godwin sighted a UFO in Darlaston when they were on patrol. 'We were driving towards Caldmore when we saw a massive object in the sky,' Sgt Godwin reported to the *Birmingham Evening Mail.* 'There were loads of lights but it was far bigger than any aircraft I've seen.'[6]

On the same evening, Mrs Margaret Brannan and her two children, together with two other young witnesses, had an extraordinary sighting near Redditch, Worcestershire. 'My brain was telling me it must be a plane,' said Mrs Brannan, 'but as I looked I realized that it couldn't be. It was the most fantastic thing I have ever seen. I still can't get over it,' she told the *Redditch Weekly Mail.* 'It was like a floating city in the sky, and the most vivid memory I have is of the tiny windows on it, which made it look like a block of flats.'[7]

24 February

Just nine days later, a Hull taxi-driver spotted a reddish-orange, spinning-top-shaped object near the Leeds Road roundabout at 4.00 in the morning. He said it was about the size of a hot-air balloon and made several changes of direction. He was sufficiently impressed to call the police immediately.

We received many reports like this during February. They came from policemen, security guards, schoolchildren and their teachers, housewives, and various members of the public. Each case was fully evaluated and judged on its merit, and where possible, comparisons were drawn with other cases that may have been somehow connected.

10 March

Such a connection appears to have occurred on 10 March. Ian Smith, a local UFO investigator for the organization in South Yorkshire, submitted a report of his sighting which appeared to tie in with another UFO report sent to us on 23 March, but relating to that night of the 10th. So we had totally independent witnesses, who had no prior knowledge of each other's sighting in Rotherham and Ossett, West Yorkshire.

Ian was driving back from Sheffield with a colleague and fellow Society member, Paul Garner. Close to the junction of the A629, Paul drew Ian's attention to an elongated object which appeared to be internally lit by some form of orange light. The entire length of the object, which was low in the sky, approximately 400 ft above the ground, appeared to pulsate. Both men could see distinct black lines running vertically around the object giving the impression that they may have been some type of windows.

The experienced investigators could hardly believe their luck – here was a possible UFO staring at them in the face! They had, of course, immediately stopped the vehicle and taken precise notes of every aspect of the object's size, colour, and shape. At precisely 8.55 p.m. the object disappeared from view travelling in a northerly direction.

Twenty minutes later, over the town of Ossett, Dianne Wild, aged twenty-eight, was closing her kitchen curtains when she noticed a brilliant yellow light approaching from the south. Although indoors, and with both windows and doors closed, she could hear a distinct humming noise. The object approached steadily, and, somewhat taken aback at the growing size and shape of the object, Dianne remained rooted to the spot. 'It was shaped like a cross, and at least the size of a football field,' she said. 'I saw a red flashing light towards the rear, and yellow lights ran along its side. I could clearly see grey and black stripes on the underside as it passed overhead, slightly to the left of our house. I have never seen anything as big or as clear in the sky before.'

Further Activity

The centre of UFO activity then appeared to be concentrated in the Midlands. Local newspapers, including the *Chase Post* in Cannock, highlighted the events, reporting no less than ninety separate UFO sightings. Amongst these were twenty-six over Rugeley, Burntwood, Boney Hay, Lichfield, Brownhills, Willenhall and Walsall. In just two hours, sixteen sightings came from Rugeley alone.

A frightened 12-year-old-girl and two friends saw a huge, oval-shaped craft hovering at 600 ft, covered with green, blue, and white lights which moved in and out of the object. Four police officers in separate towns also spotted the amazing craft. A cigar-shaped craft hovered over a Lichfield church one early morning at eight o'clock. Mr Edwards of Friday Acre said: 'It was huge and had a mushroom-shaped top which came down to a long, cigar shape underneath.' Other witnesses reported seeing a similar object rise from behind trees.[8]

Another sighting was reported by an RAF jet engine technician with ten years' service. He spotted an unusual craft in Boney Hay, and said he had never seen anything like it. He claimed to have seen a 'brilliant white, smoke ring at nine o'clock in the morning.' Above it was an object with a small rotating blue light. It hovered at the spot for a full minute before moving off at great speed, leaving what looked like a vapour trail coming from the object's left side. Within a minute or two it had disappeared completely. A radar operator was reported to have disclosed to the *Chase Post* newspaper that he could confirm something unusual had been seen, but could not go into detail.[9]

When ordinary men and women encounter UFO phenomena, and are brave enough to speak about their experience with investigators or the media, their description of events offers a valuable insight into this hugely complex, but fascinating subject.

10 April

On Sunday night, 10 April 1988, David White, head of Artwork and Illustration Studios in Oxford, was driving home after a visit to Blewbury. In the sky a red glow followed his car travelling several hundred feet above. When he stopped at a crossroads, the light stopped too. He wound down his window but could hear no sound from the mystery object.

'I thought I was going crazy. Just for my own peace of mind, I drove back across the Downs to see if I could get closer to it. I drove off towards Wantage and it moved with me again. I kept flashing my car lights and when I stopped again, it stopped and was just sitting stationary above me.

'I went through Wantage and I could still see it as I drove towards Faringdon. Then, two or three miles on that road, it disappeared. Just like that! I first saw the object at precisely 11.00 p.m. When it vanished – it was 11.41 p.m. – I looked at the car clock. It could not have been a plane as no plane could just stop still in the sky without a sound.

'The second time I stopped, I could see that it was a red light and at the centre it was white. There was no shape to it and as I kept looking at it, it was zig-zagging up and down. I knew everyone would say I was potty, or that some RAF pilot was having a damn good laugh at my expense, but it was really weird and I have never seen anything like it.'

Despite calls to the police and local RAF bases, no one could satisfy Mr White with a rational explanation.

Another equally interesting account of a UFO encounter during April came from Cwmdare, South Wales. John Rees was out walking his dog when something caught his attention in the sky. He saw a luminous object moving along a spiral path in a north-easterly direction towards Neath:

> 'I would not have bothered to take a second look if it had not been for the spiral path and the intense luminosity – and two downwardly directed parallel beams. It had a cylindrical shape, like a lager can. The clouds were pitch black on the horizon, but the moon was above the cloud line and it was very bright. Fortunately, the object stayed above the cloud line and I was able to keep it in view. It moved towards Neath and then back, in a southerly direction towards the Meardy mountain. I was watching it for about three-quarters of an hour.
>
> 'I usually meet a teacher when I am out walking the dog between 10.15 p.m. and 11.00 p.m. I was hoping he would come by, so I could have someone to verify the sighting, but unfortunately he did not turn up this time. I was shocked I can tell you. I have never seen anything like that before. I thought it was a plane out of control at first. Planes do fly over the Cynon valley at that time of night. I have never believed in UFOs but there is no doubt that I saw something out of the ordinary. There was no noise from it.'

John is closely linked with local operatic groups in the area and is warden of Cwmdare Youth Club. A respected member of the local community, he is foreman at Enghart Fans, a large industrial firm where several workers have remarked 'Beam me up Dr John!'[10] He has nevertheless stuck to his account through all the ridicule and is typical of thousands of witnesses to UFO phenomena who brave the critics and speak the truth.

24 April
Some people, however, prefer to remain anonymous, like the Elsecar man who was driving home after finishing work in Ecclesfield, just north of Sheffield, on 24 April. Just after 10.00

26

p.m., he spotted a hovering UFO over Hoyland and Elsecar. He stopped the car twice so he could study the silent object more carefully.

'It was really very strange. Although it was dark I could see it was a vague box-shape and there were big green, white, and red lights on it which stayed lit-up all the time. It was huge and absolutely still, and what really surprised me was that it did not make a sound. I thought it must be some sort of aircraft, but it was so still and quiet it could not possibly have been.'

The 38-year-old man drove home keeping his eye on the object, but by the time he drove into his driveway, it had disappeared from view. A next-door-neighbour was out walking her dog, so he quickly mentioned what he had seen. They both set off walking down the road to see if it was still there, but there was no sign. Later, he went indoors and told his wife what he had seen. He kept returning to the window to see if it had returned, and was rewarded. 'I couldn't believe it when I saw it there again, so I called my wife to have a look.'

Together they watched the object move slowly across the sky until it disappeared for the last time.

'We even opened the window to see if we could hear a noise, but it did not make a sound. I could not believe how big it was. Then it suddenly disappeared. Neither of us have ever experienced anything like it before, and I don't particularly want to ever again, although we were not frightened – just inquisitive really.

'I don't want people to think we are crackpots. I know it sounds stupid, but I know what I saw and I'm glad my wife witnessed it too. It's just a pity that we didn't have a film in our camera. If we had managed to take a picture of it, people would have to believe us!'

29 April

Since the beginning of the year, when it became apparent that UFO activity was much higher than normal, our researchers had devoted many long hours during bitterly cold nights attempting to photograph the phenomena throughout the region. On some rare occasions we had been successful, but none more so than on the night of 29 April, around nine o'clock.

YUFOS investigators Paul Garner, Ian Smith, and Allan Petres had been called out to the Kimberworth area of Rotherham, South Yorkshire. Several witnesses had reported seeing an unusual light and contacted our South Yorkshire Co-ordinator Mick Hanson, who quickly organized a team to investigate. Our three-man team had begun their journey full of optimism that perhaps this would be the night when they would arrive at the scene in time to see a UFO.

Armed with three cameras and films of various speeds, they reached a high vantage-point known as Fenton Road. At exactly 9.00 p.m., the men noticed a distinct yellow and orange, glowing ball of light approaching their position. They estimated the first point of reference in terms of distance was approximately five miles. The men described the object as long and oval-shaped, but no sound could be heard. Allan Petres, using Konicacolour very fast SR-V3200 ASA film, managed to take a series of photographs when the object came within a mile of their position.

Figure 1:6 is representative of many similar photographs that have been taken of UFOs. One finds an unusual shape, pretty colours, but little else. On the other hand, by adopting computer-enchanced techniques, one is able to compare such images with those of conventional craft. These scientific methods have been used by some UFO groups for many years, but as yet we have not received the completed findings for this particular shot. The apparent vapour image on the Kimberworth photograph was not visible to ground observers, yet the camera recorded it. This could prove to be highly significant.

Military Activity?

A common feature of many UFO reports that appeared throughout the summer months of 1988 was that of a large triangular-shaped object displaying bright, illuminated lights. Two of these appeared together over Stafford during May. One witness, Mr John Teasdale, felt sure that the objects were no more than VC-10s flying from RAF Brize Norton in Oxfordshire. Checks with the base revealed two such craft had taken off from the

Figure 1:6. The yellow and orange, glowing ball of light seen at Kimberworth, Rotherham, photographed by Allan Petres (© YUFOS).

base on the night in question and it was possible they may have flown over Staffordshire.

However, another witness, Enid Turner of Uttoxeter, disagreed. 'I don't believe they were VC-10s, no way,' she said. 'I would know one if I saw it. I often used to go to air displays, and they definitely weren't that.' She said the objects were very low, silent and slow-moving, with a lot of very bright lights.[11] Other witnesses reported seeing a strange cluster of orange and red lights. This brings us to an area of UFO research which few groups in Britain become involved with: the role of the military, and as a consequence, the government.

The public have a fair conception of what is travelling on our roads, on the railways, and at sea. It has less idea of what is flying overhead. In Britain, there are numerous military airfields, as well as test sites for experimental craft, some of which are used to fly remotely piloted vehicles (RPVs) that are later used in Northern Ireland and along the Soviet border, for example. Combine these with flight-refuelling exercises, and it is easy to understand how many people can be forgiven for thinking they are witnessing some form of UFO activity. During the miners' strike of 1984, hundreds of people reported seeing a cluster of lights over East and West Yorkshire. Headlines next day pronounced the visitor was a UFO; something the Ministry of Defence were happy to go along with, adding they had no idea what the object may have been. Our research proved that it was in fact a military helicopter using a 'Nightsun' searchlight that had been used to pinpoint several power plants and coal mines in the event that it would be needed by the police to hurry to a precise location. This had happened in Nottinghamshire, where pickets had appeared from woodland to confront men who had defied the strike call and were heading for work. The police had used helicopters to illuminate the area, thus depriving the pickets of their cover.

The government at the time insisted that the Armed Forces were not involved in the strike, but we eventually uncovered the truth. The *Bradford Telegraph & Argus* newspaper received our findings, conducted their own research, and on New Year's Eve splashed a front-page story confirming our analysis. The MoD would not comment, nor would a number of airport spokesmen who were actively involved in the episode.

Frightening Encounter
During the winter of 1988–89, four young women had set out in a car for a night out in Wisbech, Cambridgeshire. It was after 7.30 p.m. and their journey would take them through dark, remote country lanes. Suddenly, two of the women became aware of a large star-like object to their right which was airborne and keeping pace with them. They frantically alerted their companions when the huge diamond-shaped object shot towards the car. On its top was a large, red light, and around the centre were red, blue, green, orange, and mauve lights.

The driver panicked at the close proximity of the object, which was brilliantly illuminated. She accelerated to a dangerous speed in an effort to put some distance between them and the craft. The women became more terrified when it came to within feet of the car, sped past them and descended, stopping suddenly at ground level 100 yards ahead of them. As the driver braked, and the car went into a skid with wheels locked, the object 'flipped' over and came down to land on the side of the road. All four women briefly observed some form of dome on the craft.

The car had come to a halt, but had spun round facing the

opposite direction. All the women were hysterical and frantic with fear. The driver put her foot on the accelerator and raced away, leaving the UFO behind. Not daring to look back, they sped up a slight incline and were horrified to see flashing blue lights in the sky above it. All thought another UFO was waiting for them, but when they reached the top of the incline were surprised to see four police vehicles parked on the side of the road, which had not been there before. They slowed down but did not stop, for although they all felt relieved to see the cars, and six police officers who were moving into nearby fields and woodland, they somehow didn't trust them and sped away. The officers were carrying some kind of equipment, and a couple of the women thought that at least two were armed with rifles. All the women reported hearing the distinct sound of a helicopter after passing the police vehicles, but the UFO was *not* a helicopter, they agreed, and in any event it was enormous and silent.

The women took another route back home, cancelling their night out, and were comforted by their parents.

This case is under investigation by our organization. We find it significant that four police vehicles should converge in such a remote area, and hope to be able to throw more light on this aspect of what is clearly an important case.

The summer months saw a familiar crop of reports, but clearly there had been a marked downturn in the number of sightings. Some areas, however, experienced a burst of activity, notably in the Midlands, around Stafford. The Member of Parliament for Stafford, Bill Cash, requested that witnesses contact him directly in order that he could raise the matter with an appropriate minister at the House of Commons.

Reports continued to come to our attention until the end of the year; some good, others indifferent, but each given our attention – from the Merseyside cinema manager who left his premises on 17 October and saw a silver disk-shaped craft descending over the area, hover and then depart – to the Sheffield couple who watched in awe as a Mexican hat-shaped object illuminated the sky just 600 ft above them, its dazzling light spinning continuously.

We also ended the year with a spectacular night-time 'fireball' event which was seen over much of northern England. On 21 December, reports began to reach local police authorities and the media that a large glowing ball of light had passed across the sky around midnight. By contacting civil and military authorities, coastguards, and witnesses, we built up a picture of the event that satisfied us we were dealing with either space debris or satellite re-entry, which disappointed a number of journalists who thought a UFO story was about to break.

Whilst no single UFO case in Britain drew national or international front-page headlines during 1988, we still witnessed a greater increase in the overall number of sightings than in recent years. The Ministry of Defence received approximately 400 reports, a figure not exceeded since 1981 (600 reports). And at the same time, 1988 provided us with the largest public gathering for an organized UFO conference here in Britain for a decade, when 420 people attended our annual event.

We were happy that so many witnesses to the year's phenomena had come forward to divulge their experiences, but disappointed that no real breakthrough had been made in our efforts to identify the true nature of UFOs. Much of the progress in that field has come from the United States, where researchers have access to documentation through the Freedom of Information Act, the media is more responsive than in the UK, and the public are more positive in their attitude.

The reports we have gleaned throughout the year, and last decade, tell us that we are dealing with a very real phenomenon that demands scientific study and greater interest shown by politicians, who must begin to appreciate that not everyone who claims to have seen a UFO is always mistaken. Until that takes place, it is left to organizations like ours to maintain vigilance, and to apply pressure on those key personnel within the government who prefer the *status quo* to remain – perhaps for ever.

REFERENCES

1. Burrows, William E.: *Deep Black: The Secrets of Space Espionage,* Bantam Press, London 1988, pp. 22–4.
2. Good, Timothy: *Above Top Secret: The Worldwide UFO Cover-Up,* Sidgwick & Jackson, London 1987, pp. 120–22.
3. Good, Timothy: op. cit., pp. 115–16.

4. *Camberley News*, Surrey, 29 January 1988.
5. *Birmingham Daily News*, 18 February 1988.
6. *Birmingham Evening Mail*, 17 February 1988.
7. *Redditch Weekly Mail*, 26 February 1988.
8. *Chase Post*, Cannock, 17 March 1988.
9. *Chase Post*, 7 March 1988.
10. *Aberdare Leader*, 28 April 1988.
11. *Stafford Newsletter*, 27 May 1988.

2

UFO lands in Suffolk – and that's Official!

RALPH NOYES

Ralph Noyes was born in the tropics and spent most of his childhood in the West Indies. He served in the RAF 1940–46 as a navigator, engaging in active service in North Africa and the Far East.

He entered the Civil Service in 1949 and served in the Air Ministry and subsequently the unified Ministry of Defence. For nearly four years he headed Defence Secretariat 8 (DS8) which among other tasks logged UFO reports from members of the public.

Ralph Noyes retired in 1977, leaving in the grade of Under Secretary of State. He has since pursued a writing career, and has written a number of articles and science fiction stories. *A Secret Property* (Quartet Books, 1985) deals largely with UFOs, including – in fictionalized form – the Rendlesham case. In 1989 *Country Life* published several articles by him on the mystery cornfield circles.

'UFO LANDS IN SUFFOLK – AND THAT'S OFFICIAL!'

These were the words in which a British Sunday newspaper told us, in October 1983, of one of the most remarkable UFO cases in British history. The events they were reporting had taken place nearly three years before, in December 1980, in Rendlesham Forest in the English county of Suffolk. Now, almost a decade after these events, much more has come to light, and we have had time to draw conclusions. No apologies need be offered for retelling this extraordinary story: it encapsulates many of the central problems of ufology.

I call these incidents 'The Rendlesham Case', after the pine forest in which the events took place (see Figure 2:1). Other commentators have used other names, including 'The Bentwaters

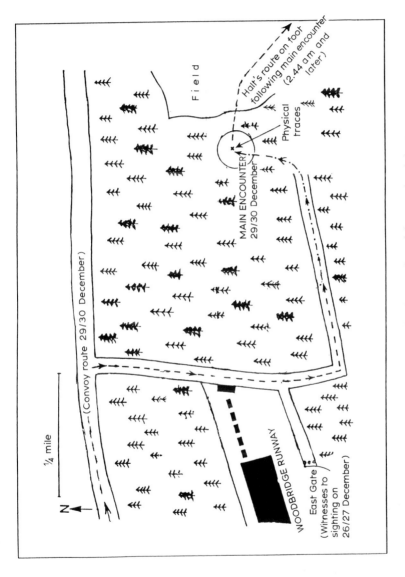

Figure 2:1. The Rendlesham Forest landing. Adapted from a sketch by Dr Jamison.[4]

Case' and 'The Woodbridge Case'. A glance at the references at the end of this article will remove any doubts about which case is meant.

Why is the Rendlesham Case Important?

In most UFO cases we have nothing more to go on than what a witness is able to tell us, often some days or weeks after the event and not infrequently after the lapse of months or even years. If we are lucky, there may be two or more people who claim to have seen the same event. At the end of the investigation we are left with our notes of what the witness(es) have told us, supplemented perhaps by a rough sketch of the site and an artist's impression of whatever 'entities' and/or 'vehicles' formed part of the narrative. Increasing shrewdness, painfully learned over several decades, forces us to reduce most of these laboriously gathered stories to the probable misperception of something quite ordinary (or, rather rarely, to hoax). What remains when these 'IFOs' (Identified Flying Objects) have been eliminated makes up the hard core of our 'great cases', those bizarre and puzzling reports for which no conventional explanation seems possible and which continue to interest those many of us who suspect that behind all this 'smoke' there must be some important 'fire'. But the hard evidence which might convince our critics – or even persuade ourselves! – tends to remain woefully absent; as elusive, indeed, as the clinching facts which, for more than a century, have been sought by those engaged in psychical research in pursuit of their own (surprisingly similar) dreams, hunches and El Dorados.

The crucial importance of the Rendlesham case is that we have the signed statement of a relatively senior officer of the United States Air Force, Lt.-Col. (now Brigadier General) Charles I. Halt, the then Deputy Base Commander of the important USAF complex at RAF Bentwaters/Woodbridge in Suffolk, submitted to the British Ministry of Defence shortly after the alleged events occurred. The receipt of this document by the British MoD has been formally acknowledged in the British House of Commons by the responsible Minister (even though it took more than two years to wring out this statement, following a long period of denials and prevarications). And Colonel Halt has repeatedly confirmed that it was indeed he who signed it. Whatever interpretation we care to place on this document, and much of this article will be concerned with interpreting it, there can be no doubt that it was officially issued by an officially appointed US authority to an official British governmental agency.

The importance of this fact can hardly be exaggerated. It is unique in British ufology. Although diligent research by ufologists has turned up some interesting cases in which the British MoD were undoubtedly involved, for example the Bentwaters/Lakenheath incidents of August 1956 and the occurrences at RAF West Freugh in April 1957 (of which good accounts are given in *Above Top Secret*[1] and have since been supplemented elsewhere), no definitive statement has ever been issued about them, and I doubt, as a former official of the Department, that anything ever will be. The Halt memorandum is altogether special in being an official – *and officially authenticated* – statement. Few other documents match it in this respect. I can think of nothing except certain of the releases made in the United States under the American Freedom of Information Act and reproduced by Lawrence Fawcett and Barry Greenwood in *Clear Intent*,[2] and, to a greater extent, by Timothy Good in *Above Top Secret*.

As that Sunday paper put it, 'UFO Lands in Suffolk – *And That's Official*'. It was those last three words which persuaded me, for the first time in my life, to buy that particular scandal-sheet. Having bought it, I knew that the case was crucial.

What Happened at Rendlesham?

Great difficulties have dogged all students of this case, partly as the result of deliberate obfuscation by the USAF, the Pentagon, and the British Ministry of Defence; partly because the wide range of alleged witnesses (many of them demanding anonymity) have told an equally wide range of conflicting stories; partly because UFO-sceptics have strenuously sought to distort facts in favour of their own views; and partly, alas, because some serious research-ers have allowed their prejudices and suspicions (and, in some cases, sheer lack of judgement) to introduce wholly unnecessary complications.

Credit must always go to the authors of *Skycrash*[3] for the immense efforts which they devoted to this case and for producing the only full-length book we yet have: nothing can detract from the dedication with which they pursued an exceptionally difficult investigation. But the book remains irretrievably marred by the attempt of the authors to combine their account of the case with a travelogue of their researches and to report a number of irrelevancies which range from the naïve to the unwittingly comic. (The ladies' pursuit of the unfortunate Col. Halt and his teenage son – see, for example, Chapters 16 and 30, and pages 186–9 and 194–7 – is the stuff of which high farce is written. To take merely one example, I doubt that any of us has much to learn from the account on page 35 of the unfortunate mishap which two of the authors suffered while driving their car along a rutted, dirt-track road at a considerable distance from the supposed UFO landing-site more than a year later.) The book remains a mine of potential information – but also a minefield of dubious speculation, without so much as an index or an attempted calendar of events.

The most convincing attempt to give us a connected narrative, while at the same time fully exposing the difficulties which beset us, is given by Timothy Good.[1] This is indispensable reading for anybody coming fresh to the case.

Since *Above Top Secret* was written, we have had the interesting research undertaken by Dr Jamison of the State University of New York.[4] It is surprising that Jamison fails to indicate any awareness of Good's book or of the highly significant investigations undertaken in the United States by Raymond W. Boeche,[5] but his article is useful in clearly establishing the USAF chain of command at Bentwaters/Woodbridge at the relevant time, and in placing beyond reasonable doubt that it was Halt – the fourth down in that top echelon – who led a party of his subordinates into Rendlesham Forest on 29/30 December 1980. This provides further collateral for those of us (myself included) who have always held, since the release of Halt's Memorandum was secured under the US Freedom of Information Act in June 1983 (two and a half years after the events it reports), that Halt was an eyewitness to the events of 29/30 December and that his memorandum is the key document. In answer to the question which heads this section, 'What happened at Rendlesham?', I believe that we are right to take Halt as the one and only first-hand source whose report is on the official record. All else, important though much of it is, rests on hearsay and requires the caution with which we must always approach the second-hand.

DEPARTMENT OF THE AIR FORCE
HEADQUARTERS 81ST COMBAT SUPPORT GROUP (USAFE)
APO NEW YORK 09755

REPLY TO
ATTN OF: CD

13 Jan 81

SUBJECT: Unexplained Lights

TO: RAF/CC

1. Early in the morning of 27 Dec 80 (approximately 0300L), two USAF security police patrolmen saw unusual lights outside the back gate at RAF Woodbridge. Thinking an aircraft might have crashed or been forced down, they called for permission to go outside the gate to investigate. The on-duty flight chief responded and allowed three patrolmen to proceed on foot. The individuals reported seeing a strange glowing object in the forest. The object was described as being metalic in appearance and triangular in shape, approximately two to three meters across the base and approximately two meters high. It illuminated the entire forest with a white light. The object itself had a pulsing red light on top and a bank(s) of blue lights underneath. The object was hovering or on legs. As the patrolmen approached the object, it maneuvered through the trees and disappeared. At this time the animals on a nearby farm went into a frenzy. The object was briefly sighted approximately an hour later near the back gate.

2. The next day, three depressions 1 1/2" deep and 7" in diameter were found where the object had been sighted on the ground. The following night (29 Dec 80) the area was checked for radiation. Beta/gamma readings of 0.1 milliroentgens were recorded with peak readings in the three depressions and near the center of the triangle formed by the depressions. A nearby tree had moderate (.05-.07) readings on the side of the tree toward the depressions.

3. Later in the night a red sun-like light was seen through the trees. It moved about and pulsed. At one point it appeared to throw off glowing particles and then broke into five separate white objects and then disappeared. Immediately thereafter, three star-like objects were noticed in the sky, two objects to the north and one to the south, all of which were about 10° off the horizon. The objects moved rapidly in sharp angular movements and displayed red, green and blue lights. The objects to the north appeared to be elliptical through an 8-12 power lens. They then turned to full circles. The objects to the north remained in the sky for an hour or more. The object to the south was visible for two or three hours and beamed down a stream of light from time to time. Numerous individuals, including the undersigned, witnessed the activities in paragraphs 2 and 3.

CHARLES I. HALT, Lt Col, USAF
Deputy Base Commander

Figure 2:2. The Halt Memorandum.

Is the Halt Memorandum a Truthful Account?

Halt's statement to the British Ministry of Defence, signed on 13 January 1981 (see Figure 2:2) reports the following, roughly a fortnight after the events it describes:

(*a*) In the small hours of the morning of 27 December 1980 three USAF patrolmen encountered a 'strange glowing object' of not inconsiderable size in a part of Rendlesham Forest adjoining the 'back gate' of the Woodbridge airbase. [This 'back gate' can be confidently identified as the East Gate in the Figure 2:1.] The object possessed some of the characteristics of a structured 'vehicle': it was 'metallic in appearance and triangular in shape', two to three metres across the base and roughly two metres high. As the patrolmen approached it, it manoeuvred away from them and disappeared. An hour later, however, it was briefly seen again outside the back gate.

(*b*) 'The next day', three depressions in the ground were discovered where the object had been sighted. ['The next day' could conceivably mean the daylight hours of 27 December, or possibly the day of 28 December. Some commentators have made heavy weather of this ambiguity. My own view is that it is wholly unimportant.]

(*c*) On the night of 29 December, Halt and 'numerous individuals' took radiation readings in the area of the sighting; and later (over a period extending into the small hours of the morning of 30 December) they saw a succession of complex light-phenomena, both within the forest and subsequently in the sky.

This, in essence, is all that Halt tells us. There are strong indications that other, much stranger, things were taking place on the night of 29/30 December, and that the memorandum is, to say the least, deliberately tight-lipped and low-key. This has interesting implications on which I shall comment later. Immediately, however, we have to consider two possibilities which have been much discussed: first, that Halt seriously misperceived something quite ordinary (or was even the subject of hallucinations); second, that he wrote his memorandum as a deliberate piece of misinformation for the concealment of some wholly mundane accident or military embarrassment.

Those who want explanations of this kind have sought either to explain away the events which Halt describes or to discredit the memorandum on some other grounds. Let us consider these ploys in turn.

Attempts to Explain Away the Memorandum

Over the night of 25/26 December 1980 the re-entry of space debris, and subsequently a bright meteor, were seen by many people in the eastern counties of England. Bright meteors and space debris are sometimes mistaken for UFOs. It is always convenient for those who abominate UFOs to discover that there has been something of the sort in the immediate (or even rather remote) neighbourhood of an alleged UFO sighting. It has therefore suited some sceptical commentators (for example, Ian Ridpath at a meeting of the British UFO Research Association on 10 December 1983 and again in the *Guardian*, on 5 January 1985) to argue that the first event reported by Halt (item (*a*) in the above summary) took place in the early hours of 26 December, when there was a brief but conventional bright light in the heavens, and not on 27 December, as Halt tells us, when there was, alas, nothing important of an astronomical nature going on.

Efforts have been made to sustain the 'meteor hypothesis' by references to an entry in police records in the neighbouring village of Woodbridge on the morning of 26 December, recording a telephone call from the Woodbridge airbase to the effect that they were anxious about 'a light in the forest'. And at least one television documentary has dropped the broad hint (by way of visual innuendo) that the consequent arrival in Rendlesham Forest of a police car with flashing lights a little later that Boxing Day morning accounts for at least the first paragraph of Halt's memorandum.

A long chapter could be devoted to untangling this peculiar story, in which one commentator after another has repeated, apparently without much checking, whatever was last printed by his predecessors, and in which many allegations have been made on little documentation. Suffice it to say that the police found nothing on their two sorties into Rendlesham Forest on 26 December (according to the report which Ian Ridpath very creditably obtained from them in 1983); and that, even if Halt had made the extraordinary error of mis-dating his 'first event' (and Service officers, if nothing else, are well trained to be meticulous about dates and times), a police car can hardly be mistaken for a 'strange, glowing, triangular object, two to three metres across the base and two metres high', skittering about a pine wood. Finally, the 'meteor hypothesis' leaves utterly unexplained the occurrences which Halt felt it was his duty to report to the British Ministry of Defence as having taken place two days later on 29/30 December 1980.

This 'second event' has proved something of a problem for

most commentators. Even those of us who are inclined to take Halt's memorandum at its face value find it surprising: UFOs, like lightning, rarely strike twice at the same place. But sceptics are faced with a far greater difficulty. If they are to seize upon that bright meteor as the likely trigger for some flight of hysterical hallucination among a sizable number of American servicemen, they then have a strong temptation to cook the books in favour of assuming that both the first *and* second events reported by Halt took place on the *same* night, preferably 25/26 December (or, less plausibly, 26/27 December) when there was not only a recent meteor and/or police car but also, perhaps, some spirits of the season acting in support of them!

But very tortuous arguments are needed to sustain this approach. A thoroughly blinkered view has to be taken of the strong collateral which exists for the occurrence of events on two separate occasions (there is ample material in *Above Top Secret*[1] and *Skycrash*[3]). And Halt has to be assumed as totally incompetent about dates and/or as possessed of an inexplicable wish to mislead the British Ministry of Defence in a document intended solely for them. Sceptics have accordingly tended merely to toy with the 'single night' view and to pass rapidly to a search for some additional 'trigger' which can be invoked for the second occasion.

The front runner in this somewhat breathless search has been the Orford Ness lighthouse (though the hazard-lights on a nearby MoD establishment have also sometimes been invoked). The lighthouse, which is roughly five to six miles from the likely site of the events of both 26/27 and 29/30 December and on a bearing of between 90 and 100 degrees or so, can certainly be glimpsed through the pine trees of Rendlesham Forest – so readily, indeed, that it must seem like an old friend to anybody who has served at the Woodbridge airbase for more than a few days. Its colour is white; it makes one revolution per minute; its flash is five seconds long; it is as regular as clockwork. The theory of those sceptics who wish to invoke it as an explanation is that Lt.-Col. Halt and 'numerous individuals' misperceived this cosy old acquaintance as a complex series of remarkable light-phenomena, including 'a red, sun-like light' which 'moved about and pulsed', threw off 'glowing particles', broke into 'five separate white objects' . . . etc. (see Figure 2:2).

Much ingenuity, verging on the deceitful doctoring of television film, has been used by those who see the lighthouse as their refuge against the marvellous. Connoisseurs of tormented explanations should read the enjoyable account of these follies (or dishonesties) given by Randles *et al.*[3] and Good.[1] One only regrets that Charles Fort, that assiduous collector of the ridiculous statements made by 'experts', was not alive to see these choice specimens of his favourite indoor sport.

Attempts have also been made to explain away the concluding sentences of Halt's memorandum in which he describes some prolonged phenomena in the sky at a very late stage in the morning hours of 30 December 1980. I happen to share at least some of the doubts of the sceptics about these relatively unexciting events towards the end of Halt's unusually busy night. It seems possible that these belated celestial objects were, indeed, bright stars. . . . Perhaps Halt and his 'numerous individuals', emerging from the most momentous occasion of their lives, were somewhat conditioned to see wonders in the skies where possibly none existed – just as I, groping my way into Piccadilly from a Royal Academy exhibition of the Post-Impressionists a year or two ago, continued for a while to see trees and even buses pulsating with the extraordinary energies which Vincent van Gogh had, on behalf of us all, perceived in Provence a century before. But in conceding this point (if concession it is) I think it should be stressed that, at this point in their argument, our worried sceptical colleagues have already had to advance an extraordinary hotch-potch of explanations: space debris, a bright meteor, a police car, drink and drugs, a lighthouse, other lights on the coast, dear old Sirius . . .

Occam, you will remember, urged us to cut away unnecessary complications in our attempts to explain phenomena and to look for the simplest explanation. The simplest explanation of Halt's memorandum is that he was reporting – as precisely as wondrous events permit – what he and 'numerous individuals' encountered on 29/30 December, together with such facts as he had been able to ascertain from his subordinates about the occurrences of 26/27 December.

But if you cannot 'explain away', the next most useful step is to discredit – a process somewhat analogous to that old lawyer's saying, 'No case; abuse the plaintiff's attorney'. Let us consider the discreditors.

Attempts to Discredit the Memorandum

In June 1985 I attended a meeting of the Committee for the Scientific Investigation of Claims of the Paranormal (CSICOP) held at London University in Gower Street. It has done sterling work in exposing fraud, gullibility and misperception in many areas of superstition, and it is greatly to be valued on this account. It also has its own shabby record of cooking the books when faced with anything truly remarkable which appears to breach the 'continuity of nature', as understood in its own curiously nineteenth-century terms.

At that June meeting I discussed the Rendlesham case with a notable UFO-sceptic (whose name I won't mention lest it involves him in a suit for damages!). 'Halt', he said, 'is an overgrown boy scout. Everybody knows that you cannot trust a word he says once he's got involved with some freaky obsession.'

This was not my first encounter with attempted character-assassination: former Whitehall officials (of whom I am one) are familiar with this kind of thing among politicians, journalists, and even civil servants. What struck me on that CSICOP occasion was that not one word was uttered by my informant which bore directly on the Rendlesham case; he rested himself entirely on seeking to discredit the unfortunate officer who had the glum responsibility of recording the facts as he saw them. The attempt struck me as crude – but probably effective. How many others, I wondered, had now written off the Rendlesham case on nothing more than this? As it happens, I have every reason to believe from many other sources that Halt is a reliable USAF officer and a valued colleague: his promotion to full Colonel in November 1983, while still serving at Bentwaters/Woodbridge, is testimony enough. I mention the CSICOP incident merely to convey how perilously easy it is to get damaging innuendo about the place if one's motive is to rubbish remarkable reports. Naturally, I discounted the innuendo entirely, and I continue to do so.

Other, less crude, attempts have been made to discredit the Halt memorandum, and by people who are genuinely seeking the truth (and who must therefore be forgiven!). The following are the main contenders, selected from the references at the end of this chapter. In each case the Halt memorandum is interpreted by the 'discreditors' as intended to conceal some non-UFO event by way

44

of offering a cover-story plus disinformation. On this theory, Halt (perhaps under instruction) was trying to divert attention from:

(*a*) Something *nasty* which the military had lost in Rendlesham Forest (nuclear? chemical? biological?).
(*b*) Something *secret* which the military had lost in Rendlesham Forest (a new quick-descent helicopter? A pilotless drone of astounding new abilities? Space-gear/space-specimens? Or the Stealth aircraft?).
(*c*) Something *intrusive* from the 'Other Side' (a crashed Bear or Badger? A crashed pilotless probe?).

As a former Defence official, who had responsibilities for designing and frequently reviewing the procedures for handling major mishaps (e.g. the possible loss of nuclear contraptions, the crash of aircraft, the 'going-spare' of other troublesome items), I have no doubt at all that we and our American allies would never have been so foolish (or irresponsible) as to conceal our problems by propagating peculiar stories of a kind hard to believe. We would either have kept the whole thing secret (if the public hadn't heard of it and we were also satisfied that no public damage would ensue), or we would have conspicuously cordoned off the area and braced ourselves for the inevitable questions. In neither case would we have engineered the release of some strange narrative to, for example, the authors of *Skycrash*[3] by way of anonymous airmen in local pubs.

But there is a far more convincing argument than anything which can be uttered from the suspect throat of a former Defence official! Halt's memorandum was sent to the Ministry of Defence; it was not given any public circulation; it was clearly never intended for public release; and it was more than two years before it leaked into the public domain. It can, therefore, never have been intended as a piece of disinformation. (And I cannot resist adding that if good officials had really wanted to conceal something, the last thing to cross their minds would have been to stimulate the susceptibilities of over-excitable ufologists!)

So I reach the conclusion that Halt's memorandum was not designed to serve any ulterior purpose; that it was the carefully considered document of a wholly competent USAF officer; and that we must take it at its face value.

The Halt Tape

Late in 1984, more than a year after the Halt Memorandum had been made public via the US Freedom of Information Act, the officer who succeeded Halt in the chain of command at Bentwaters/Woodbridge, Col. Sam Morgan, released a copy of a tape-recording which he said had been made by Halt during the events of 29/30 December 1980 and which had subsequently come into his (Morgan's) possession. Morgan chose to send this tape to a ufologist – Manchester solicitor Harry Harris – who had, from time to time, associated himself with the investigations made by the authors of *Skycrash*. Harry Harris, in turn, made this tape-recording available to the public. Copies of it have been on open sale ever since. The publicly obtainable copy is of poor audio quality, but a written transcription of it, made by Ian Ridpath and Harry Harris, is also on sale.[6]

There has been much speculation about this tape, including, inevitably, many guesses about the possible motives and reliability of the several hands through which it has passed. Those who are doubtful about its authenticity have tended to adopt one of two theories. The first, favoured by those who regard the Halt Memorandum itself as deliberate disinformation designed to divert attention from a military mishap, tends to argue that the tape is 'more of the same kind', that is, that it has been put into circulation by Defence authorities, using as their channel the relatively low-level (and therefore, if necessary, disavowable) Sam Morgan, together with a ufologist who could be counted upon to give it further currency among ufological colleagues. The second (somewhat scurrilous) view is that a person or persons unnamed saw some possible gain to themselves in disseminating this irresistibly interesting electronic article.

Both of these views imply, of course, that the tape is a fake. And any serious commentator would be failing in his duty if he neglected this possibility. I, personally, dismiss the 'disinformation' theory on much the same grounds which persuade me that Halt's Memorandum was not intended as a cover-up. By the time of the tape's release into the public domain the events of December 1980 were already nearly four years past. The British MoD, the Pentagon and the USAF had weathered without difficulty the minor rumpus attending the publication of Halt's Memorandum in mid-1983. Who in their senses on the official side – whatever the motives – would have wanted to risk stirring up a renewed row in late 1984 by putting into public circulation a sensational new piece of information, whether faked or not? The theory strikes me as simply absurd.

Excluding the Defence authorities on these grounds, did somebody else fake the tape? Ufology (like psychical research and, indeed, many other fields) is open, alas, to the depredations of practical jokers, of a wholly terrestrial kind, even when monetary gain is not in question. We know, for example, thanks to the diligent researches of Jenny Randles and others, that a reputable astronomer chortled quietly in his study for three decades after putting into circulation under a pseudonym an account of a close encounter in Scotland which fazed quite a number of ufologists. We also know that whoever faked the remnants of the Piltdown Man went to his grave with nothing more to reward him than whatever perverse satisfaction he may have felt at diddling the palaeontological establishment. We need not look for monetary gain in suspecting a possible hoax; human nature is quite enough to be going on with. It is far from ridiculous to wonder whether somebody, somewhere, faked the 'Halt Tape'; and the fact that some small profit may have been made by selling the alleged copies has understandably reinforced the critical observations of at least some commentators.

In the circumstances, the best we can do with the 'Halt Tape' is to use the well-tried methods of research historians and investigative journalists, that is, to ask ourselves two questions: first, is the tape internally consistent?; second, how does it relate to any primary document (in this case the Halt Memorandum)?

As for internal consistency, two points must immediately be stressed. The first is that the tape made available to us on public sale cannot possibly be a full recording of any original. It runs for only about eighteen minutes whereas the events it describes – on the time-readings which it distinctly records – extend over several hours. The second, somewhat daunting, fact is that the tape is interrupted by two short passages, one of piano music (!) and one of a voice uttering (as far as I can judge) the cryptic words, 'He took *this* long to dock', both of which differ greatly in their acoustic quality from the rest of the recording. I can understand the position of anybody who considers that these

47

points are sufficient grounds for dismissing the tape from further consideration. My own view, however, is that the second of them is, if anything, paradoxical evidence that the tape is genuine: any committed faker could easily have eliminated these traces that the tape he was using for reproducing Halt's original had been employed earlier for other purposes (including the recording of some favourite piece of piano music!). The first point – the abbreviation of the tape – could well be explained by some understandable decision on the part of those who released it that there is a limit to what listeners will put up with! My own suspicion, however, is that the abbreviation was made, possibly by Halt himself, to exclude material which, though honestly perceived (not only by Halt but by other witnesses), was far too bizarre to be left on record (and I shall return to this point). But whichever of these views you take, the abbreviation does not in itself discredit the tape.

As for compatibility with the primary document, Halt's Memorandum, the tape seems to me to stand up to any test one cares to apply: it covers about the same time-span (taking the time-readings it contains); it deals with the same events; and it describes them in the same sequence. It has the kind of messy, half-audible quality which one might expect from the 'electronic notebook' which any sensible officer takes with him to the scene of an incident on which he may later have to make a written report (and which he never expects will be listened to by anybody except himself). And – apart from the two brief interruptions discussed above – it has what BBC engineers describe as 'exterior acoustic', that is, it was manifestly made in the open air (together with a large supporting cast). Those who wish to regard it as a fake will have to envisage a very elaborate piece of deception and to explain why they think it was undertaken.

Having exercised the caution due to evidence which lacks the official stamp given to Halt's Memorandum, I personally accept the tape as authentic. It adds useful details to our knowledge of the events of 29/30 December 1980, and it puts beyond reasonable doubt that Halt was following up occurrences which had been reported to him from the night of 26/27 December. My only reservation is that I suspect the tape has been deliberately abbreviated to exclude the weirdest part of the encounter.

Other Witnesses, Other Allegations

Shortly after the publication of *Skycrash* in the late summer of 1984 I made a visit to the Rendlesham area and talked with several of the local characters which the book identifies. Halt, of course, had already departed, and so had his RAF counterpart, Squadron Leader Moreland (technically the resident British 'landlord' of the Bentwaters/Woodbridge complex and the officer who transmitted Halt's Memorandum to the British Ministry of Defence).

I found that USAF families on the base had only a dim and hearsay recollection that something odd had happened on those December nights of nearly four years before. (Such is the speed of turn-over of military personnel and the shortness of human memory.) Mrs Boast, whose family live on a farm quite close to the likely site of the UFO visitation and who are described in *Skycrash* as 'frightened people', terrorized into silence by 'strange' visitors, told me that she and her husband had little to tell except the memory of something bright in the sky, which could well have been the meteor of 25/26 December. She said that she was not frightened and had never been persecuted except by ufologists. Later, in the pub at Butley, I chatted with the two elderly brothers (a pair of friendly and entertaining 'characters') who are described in *Skycrash* as having suffered mysterious disturbances to their television in December 1980. I gathered that they were still having the same sort of problem from time to time, the TV set being in the nature of a much prized vintage article.

I came away from Suffolk with only two vital pieces of information: first, a vivid impression of the Rendlesham area from which, helped by Halt's Tape, I feel confident in marking on the map (Figure 2:1) the route probably taken by Halt on 29/30 December 1980; second, the recollection of some superb oysters in the village of Orford. I cannot subscribe to any view that local residents saw much of significance in December 1980 or that they live under obscure threats from obscure authorities (without so much as mentioning the matter to their lively and energetic Member of Parliament).

Much more important are the many accounts of the events of 29/30 December 1980 which have been given to investigators by a range of alleged USAF witnesses.[1,3] These accounts are, of course, wholly without the official stamp carried by the Halt Memorandum, and it is impossible to apply to them the kind of analysis which persuades me that the Halt Tape is authentic. They tend, moreover, to contradict each other on points of detail. In total, however, they add up to a formidable body of testimony to the occurrence of highly bizarre events which none of the witnesses had anything to gain by describing – and probably something to lose.

We are told by these witnesses of interferences to the functioning of military vehicles and equipment; of a dense yellow mist or semi-substantial disk which formed in the forest (like a 'transparent aspirin tablet', said one witness with inadvertent whimsy); of the sudden transformation of this 'proto-form' into a large domed or saucer-shaped structure following a spectacular display of lights (one account calls this new object 'tremendous' and expresses surprise that it was able to fit into the clearing); of silver-suited entities suspended in a shaft of light; of a local distortion of perception which caused shadows to appear to move independently of the objects casting them . . .

This sensational scenario, which reads like a drug-induced nightmare, is not mentioned in Halt's Memorandum and forms no part of his tape-recording. Its absence from the latter in particular has been thought by some to be damning evidence against its 'real' occurrence. But the tape, as already mentioned, is greatly abbreviated. It also moves from one time-check to another (recorded in Halt's voice) at a very uneven rate. There is, in particular, one passage of nearly an hour – from 1.48 a.m. to 2.44 a.m. – which passes in a mere three to four minutes and contains an extraordinary discontinuity. At one moment, which can be put at roughly 2 a.m. or a little earlier, Halt reports a remarkable object:

'. . . It looks like an eye winking at you. Still moving from side to side. And when you put the starscope on it, it's like this thing has a hollow centre, a dark centre, like the pupil of an eye looking at you, winking. And it flashes so bright . . . that it almost burns your eye.'

There follows what the transcribers of the tape call 'a garbled security communication' and then Halt immediately resumes, in a remarkably steady voice, with relatively unexciting information that has nothing to do with the breathless wonder of that great winking 'eye'. He says:

'We've passed the farmer's house and across into the next field . . .'

Half a minute later Halt gives a time-check of 2.44 a.m. For the rest of the tape, events are reported in somewhat low key. All are of the kind which determined critics have interpreted as the inadvertent – or even deliberate – misperception of the Orford Ness lighthouse and of the bright stars in the sky (and which I, personally, would not go to the barricades to defend against that suggestion).

Some of these other witnesses have given us not only their extraordinary UFO visions but also the suggestion that General Gordon Williams (the Bentwaters/Woodbridge supremo) hastily joined Halt's posse in the small hours of 30 December; that he communicated with the 'silver-suited entities'; that members of US Intelligence were also present; that cinefilm was taken; that this film was flown immediately to USAF headquarters in Germany; that exceptional steps were taken to swear all witnesses to silence.

No collateral has ever been obtained for these other allegations, despite inquiries which I (and more significantly Lord Hill-Norton, former Chief of the Defence Staff) put to the Ministry of Defence, and notwithstanding the determined attempts of Ray Boeche[5] to secure information through Senator Exon, a member of the Senate Armed Services Committee. Nor has any of us been able to verify the persistent rumour that radar traces exist of the Rendlesham events. On all these matters I think we are bound to remain reserved – noting, however, that the Defence authorities, both here and in the USA, have given unmistakable signs of unease, prevarication and downright dishonesty.

So What Really Happened at Rendlesham?

My own conclusions are as follows.

On two occasions in late December 1980 USAF personnel serving at Bentwaters/Woodbridge came face-to-face with the UFO phenomenon in its most dramatic form. The Halt Memorandum and the Halt Tape put this among the few cases which cannot be denied.

The events encountered were weird almost beyond belief – though quite consistent with many other reports we have had of the UFO phenomenon. These events were only partially 'substantial', but 'real' none the less. Something 'manifested' which was absurdly large for the forest clearing in which it appeared and the spacing of the pine trees among which it skittered. We have little evidence of serious damage to the environment but every indication of a profound effect on the humans involved.

The authorities – as often before – had no idea what to do with this startling intrusion into human affairs. Perhaps photographs were attempted; perhaps they were sent to Defence authorities 'up the line' – but the only trace we have subsequently had[5] is that they were probably 'fogged' and that nobody will acknowledge them! The tree-damage and radiation traces have long since disappeared.

The unfortunate Col. Halt, faced with the burden of having encountered the miraculous, and conscious of having caused a rumpus on British territory (a fact about which he has shown himself to be courteously concerned), consulted his British 'landlord' (Squadron Leader Moreland). After the lapse of a fortnight he cleared his yard-arm by sending a curtailed report to the British Ministry of Defence (via Moreland). (He may, of course, have sent other reports to his own superiors, but I doubt that we shall ever see them.)

The MoD, as often before (I speak with feeling as a former member of that troubled Department of State!), were merely embarrassed by this latest outbreak of ghostly occurrences and/or the evidence that USAF colleagues had gone out of their minds. They filed a report and forgot it. In 1983, some clerk in the department, quite unaware that anybody might care (because nobody had ever seemed to attach much importance to this kind of thing) released Halt's report to American friends who seemed to be interested for obscure reasons of their own.

British officials and Ministers – with their accustomed genius for evading embarrassing matters – have stalled ever since. Senator Exon in the United States (far more responsive to questions from the public) took a hard look at the matter but was horrified by what turned up: members of the USAF, and even the denizens of the Pentagon and the Intelligence community, had clearly gone soft in the head about ghost stories. Goodness knew what damage this might do if the Russians (or, worse, the American public) got wind of this evidence of vulnerability to superstition. Better check out that Boeche fellow . . . Better clam up . . .

But the US is a more open society than Britain. Not only were the Citizens Against UFO Secrecy (CAUS) able to force out the Halt Memorandum (a step inconceivable in the UK), but some members of the USAF were determined that the events of December 1980 should not remain buried. Witnesses were prepared to tell their stories; a few senior officers took the responsibility of uneasily backing them; and one of them, Sam Morgan, released the Halt Tape. Perhaps some last-minute failure of nerve led to the serious expurgation of the tape (as I have conjectured above); and perhaps somebody may now take courage and give us the tape in full. But more has already been provided to us in this case than in most others.

What does the case tell us? Not much more, perhaps, than many other 'high strangeness' occurrences – but with the fairly rare collateral of an authenticated document and a much wider range than usual of witness reports. It confirms what some of us have long felt – that the UFO phenomenon is utterly 'real', but something other than wholly 'nuts-and-bolts'; that it is, indeed, a phenomenon at the very edge of human comprehension, more analogous to the apparitions and poltergeists of psychical research than to the space-vehicles and space-brothers which (some decades ago) I would have been glad to welcome. If I have been unkind to the authors of *Skycrash*, may I now make amends by quoting their conjecture [page 93] that the UFO experience is possibly some 'incomprehensible meeting with an alien phenomenon which the mind can only embody in symbolic terms'.

The Rendlesham case also confirms, at least for me, that governments and their official agencies are undoubtedly engaged in concealment and obfuscation – but that the cover-up is of ignorance and unease. (This was certainly the game which I felt it necessary to play, myself, during my own term as an official of the Ministry of Defence from 1949 to 1977.)

Finally, I draw the conclusion that even very sensible ufologists are capable of utterly confusing their own inquiries by pursuing dark suspicions of anybody with a uniform or an official title, rather than examining the strange facts which come their way. They might be surprised to know how expert and well informed ufologists look to unfortunate officials sitting behind a Whitehall desk with the job (competing with many others) of responding to the public about inexplicable events!

Whatever 'intruded' at Bentwaters/Woodbridge in December 1980 has possibly done so often before in human history. It will probably continue to do so – in its own time and according to its own inscrutable purposes. It seems to have been manifesting with increasing frequency and increasing elaboration in recent years; it is, indeed, nearly shouting its head off . . . and it may be important to our species to come to terms with it. If Col. Halt has done nothing except to draw attention to it in undeniable form, we shall probably have to put up a statue to him some day in some leafy square.

REFERENCES

1. Good, Timothy: *Above Top Secret*, Sidgwick & Jackson, London 1987, Chapter 4 (pages 78–95).
2. Fawcett, Lawrence and Greenwood, Barry: *Clear Intent*, Prentice-Hall, New Jersey 1984.
3. Butler, Brenda; Street, Dot and Randles, Jenny: *Skycrash*, Neville Spearman, 1984.
4. Jamison, Benton: 'A Fire in the Forest: New light on the Rendlesham Landing', *International UFO Reporter*, Vol. 13, no. 5, September/October 1988.
5. Boeche, Raymond W.: 'Bentwaters: What do we know now?', *MUFON 1986 UFO Symposium Proceedings*, June 1986.
6. A copy of the Halt Tape and transcript is available from Quest Publications International Ltd, 15 Pickard Court, Temple Newsam, Leeds, LS15 9AY.

3

The English Corn Circles in 1988

GEORGE WINGFIELD

George Wingfield was educated at Eton College and Trinity College
Dublin, graduating in 1966 with an M.A. Hons. degree in Natural
Sciences.

He worked briefly at the Royal Greenwich Observatory, Herst-
monceux, on stellar spectra and the Earth's magnetism. He currently
works for IBM UK Ltd in the field of Systems Engineering.

George Wingfield became interested in the Corn Circles phenomenon on 8 August 1987, after visiting Westbury, Wiltshire, where a
number of Circle formations had recently appeared. This also led
to an interest in the related subject of Ufology.

During 1988 the strange phenomenon of the English Corn Circles
developed once more in the most unexpected fashion. Since the
early 1980s when the press first drew public attention to the Circles,
a furious controversy has raged as to their cause. There were those
who considered that they had to be hoaxes. There were those who
thought they must be caused by the downwash of helicopters, and
others who were convinced they were made by animals chasing in
circles in the crop. Some insisted that they were meteorological
effects. And, naturally enough, there were those who suggested
that they were made by UFOs.

The more serious investigators of the phenomenon in this country
got together to form a Circles investigation group a few years ago.
Among the five original members were Colin Andrews, an electrical
engineer from Andover who works for the Test Valley Council;
Pat Delgado from Alresford, Hampshire, who once worked for
NASA in the USA; and Dr Terence Meaden, a prominent meteor-
ologist who runs the Tornado and Storm Research Organization
(TORRO) from his home in Bradford-on-Avon, Wiltshire.

To these researchers it soon became abundantly clear that the Circles could not possibly be produced by helicopters or wild animals, and that their sheer numbers, going back over the years, precluded hoaxing as an explanation, although just a few Circles were recognized as hoaxes. Certain features of the Circles which were regularly seen would moreover be impossible to hoax. So what then was the solution to this mysterious problem?

There were certainly no easy answers. From the outset, Dr Meaden was convinced that the Circles were caused by atmospheric vortices of wind, and he has maintained that view until recently. Although he has propounded this theory at great length in *The Journal of Meteorology*,[1] it is fair to say that there are many meteorologists who do not support his standpoint.

None of the other four members of the Circles investigation group agreed with Dr Meaden's meteorological explanation, and subsequently the group split away from him in 1988. Colin Andrews and Pat Delgado now head a larger team, Circles Phenomenon Research (CPR), and their book, *Circular Evidence*,[2] was published in 1989.

Their approach to the Circles phenomenon is much more widely based. In addition to a wealth of conventional scientific data which has been amassed, they have researched evidence of a UFO connection and also investigated the possibility that the Circles are caused by 'Earth Energies', a concept that has been developed by other scientists and archaeologists. This subject is often referred to as 'Earth Mysteries'.

Unfortunately, serious study of the Circles along these lines is frequently ridiculed by the ill-informed and by those who are anxious to rubbish explanations which conflict with their own. Their usual method of avoiding discussion of uncomfortable facts about the Circles which do not suit their theories is to try discrediting their adversary with charges like: 'But he is a UFO believer.' This is, of course, intended to invoke the public's preconceived idea of UFOs – that peddled by the tabloid press – as solid circular spacecraft flown by little green men. This is a cheap trick. The UFO phenomenon is something far more complex and subtle than this simplistic concept, and it would be a foolish man indeed who maintained that the UFO phenomenon, whatever its nature, was nothing but an illusion.

Certainly the Circles remain as much of an enigma as ever, but

1988 brought many new clues which gave considerable support to both the Earth Mysteries interpretation and to the UFO connection. Quite possibly these two approaches have much in common, and there readers must make their own judgement.

Circle Characteristics

The Corn Circles may have been with us for many years, but they have hardly been a regular feature of agricultural life in this country. They appeared in small numbers in the late 1970s and early 1980s, and we have a few reports from earlier years, although some farmers claim to have seen Circles in their fields as long ago as the 1930s and 1940s. A woman whose husband farmed in Hampshire forty years ago remembers seeing Circles then; the country people would not hand-reap them, since they thought them 'uncanny and of devilish origin'.[3] But unfortunately such reports cannot be verified since there is no photographic evidence to confirm that this was indeed the same phenomenon.

Since 1980 the number of Circles found each year has risen slowly but steadily to nearly 100 reported in 1988. The Circles themselves vary in size from about five to sixty feet in diameter and the crop within is flattened in a spiral swirl. The crop in question is usually wheat or barley, though some Circles have been found in rye, oats, rape-seed, and occasionally long grass. The Circles occur between late May and September when the crop is growing and has reached a fair height. Most strikingly, the flattened corn is laid with an almost geometric precision, leaving the standing crop at the perimeter upright and virtually untouched. The plants are almost invariably bent, but not broken, so that they lie flat and continue to grow horizontally. Sometimes, though, the force is such that a few plants are ejected from the ground and flung out of the Circle. Very often the swirled corn is layered, with the lower plants pointing at different angles to those above; an effect that would be very hard to produce artificially. Most of the Circles are slightly elliptical in shape, although this is rarely apparent to the untrained eye. And one never finds indentations in the ground indicating that any solid object has landed, though a Circle found at Childrey, Oxfordshire, in September 1986, exhibited a clean-cut cylindrical hole, nine inches deep and a foot across, from which the soil had vanished.

The most noticeable feature of the English Circles, unlike the few which have been reported from abroad, as far as we know, is that they occur frequently not only in multiples, but in elaborate formations. There have been doublets, triplets, quadruplets, and quintuplets, some of which are illustrated in the accompanying diagrams. There are also ringed Circles and double-ringed Circles. But let us deal with what was found in 1988.

The Meteorological Explanation

Shortly before the first Circles of 1988 appeared at the end of May, a conference of meteorologists in Oxford was told by Dr Meaden that he had 'solved the mystery of the Crop Circles'. They were caused by 'descending atmospheric vortices' or 'stationary whirlwinds', the mathematics of which were well understood. This claim was reported in the national press and no doubt widely believed by many people. It was said that Dr Meaden was quite adamant that his explanation of the Circles was correct. Nevertheless it is fair to say that his claim will most likely come to be seen as ranking with the 1956 declaration of the late Astronomer Royal, Professor Richard Woolley, that space travel was 'utter bilge', not long before artificial satellites and astronauts in orbit round the Earth became routine.

Dr Meaden stated that the Circles are formed by the action of atmospheric vortices or 'stationary whirlwinds' and it is quite easy to see why he should think that was the case[14]. The swirl of the flattened crop in the Circles carries the unmistakable signature of a rotational force, and if a rotating column of air is artificially produced in a wind tunnel fitted with equally spaced woollen strands, similar swirl patterns to those seen in single Circles in the cornfields can be produced.

Unfortunately, that is just about where the similarity ends, and there are very good reasons for believing that the force which acts on the corn is not atmospheric at all. First, the precise geometry of the Circles, which often consists of patterns of considerable complexity, is unlike anything produced by meteorological effects. All other rotational winds, such as whirlwinds and tornados, move across the countryside leaving a swathe of destruction and, usually, anything but neat markings.

Second, even if one could produce a stationary rotating column of air, it seems certain it could not produce the effect which is observed. The precise patterns indicate that some force has acted directly on the plants themselves causing them to bend through ninety degrees. If one uses normal manual force to make such a bend, the result is either that the stalk buckles (so that the upper part of the plant dies) or else the plant returns to its original vertical positon without any permanent bend being effected. In the Circles the plants remain bent, growing horizontally. One has only to see the effect of a strong atmospheric force, such as the downdraught of a helicopter, on corn or grass, to realize that high-speed air simply would not produce this effect on plants, even if it could be manipulated like a precision drill, as one is required to believe.

Third, why did these 'stationary whirlwinds' seemingly reappear around 1980, and occur in increasing numbers throughout this decade? This is hardly indicative of a meteorological effect. There is also the fact that the Circles without any doubt whatsoever have evolved over the last few years in a way that is totally unlike any other natural phenomenon. The increasing size and complexity of the patterns cannot be dismissed merely by saying that we only see all these now because we are looking for Circles, which was not the case in previous years. That simply is not true, as I hope to demonstrate in this chapter.

The First 1988 Circles

On the morning of 4 June the first set of 1988 Circles appeared, overnight as usual, in the middle of the great punchbowl below Cheesefoot Head near Winchester. Clearly visible from the road above, three thirty-foot-diameter Circles, all swirled clockwise, had formed in a neat equilateral triangle in the barley crop. This was a formation seen just once before at Bratton, Wiltshire, in 1982. At Cheesefoot Head, Circles had appeared regularly each summer since 1981 in varying formations, with the sole exception of 1984. The landowner, Lieutenant-Commander Henry Bruce, and his son Peverill had doggedly believed that the Circles were the work of hoaxers, but although one Circle found here in 1986 was proved to have been a hoax, this belief has become increasingly difficult to sustain. The 1988 triple set was in barley which had no 'tram-lines' (the usual parallel paths made by the tractor wheels) that could allow intruders or hoaxers access without trace. The Bruces had zealously excluded all potential trespassers, and no visible tracks through the crop could be seen leading to these Circles.

Four days later an identical triple Circle formation was found six miles away in barley at a remote location near Corhampton, although it is possible that these were formed up to three weeks earlier. These Circles proved even more remarkable. They were not visible from the nearest road, and were accidentally discovered by Mr Hall, who farms this land, when he walked into them (along a 'tramline') while inspecting his crop. Two of these Circles were located in such a way that they were exactly tangential to adjoining tramlines on both sides, with the third Circle centred exactly on one of the tramlines, as can be seen from Figure 3:1. The 'locating' of Circle formations like this is frequently found and gives reason to believe that the referencing of the Circles to artificial features, such as 'tramlines', has been intelligently contrived. Although there are no set rules which govern this aspect of the Circles, it is definitely something that cannot be ignored.

The most remarkable thing about this Circle set only became apparent some days later. The crop, which had originally been swirled flat, grew upwards again to almost its previous level; but in doing so, it appeared to undergo some peculiar sort of change which is apparent only in the aerial photograph (Figure 3:1). Each of the three Circles could be seen to be 'imprinted' with markings which divide it into seven concentric rings and forty-eight separate sectors. This was a major new CPR discovery, and at the time the effect seemed totally inexplicable. But it did strongly suggest that whatever force had caused the corn to fall might remain *in situ*, producing other more subtle effects under certain circumstances. And it seemed quite impossible to explain in terms of 'stationary vortices'.

The Double-ringers

In August 1987 there had appeared near Bratton in Wiltshire a double-ringed Circle which was unique. It consisted of a circle, fifty-five feet in diameter, in which the wheat was flattened in a clockwise swirl, surrounded by two concentric flattened rings,

Figure 3:1. Triple Circle formation at Corhampton, June 1988 (© Colin Andrews).

each about three feet wide. These rings were separated from each other and from the central circle by belts of standing wheat about eight feet wide that were quite untouched. Most remarkably, the corn had been flattened anticlockwise in the enclosed ring, and clockwise in the other one. Nothing like this has been reported previously anywhere in the world and this served to confirm the evolving nature of the Corn Circles.

In June 1988 three of these double-ringers, of similar size and configuration to the 1987 one, appeared in Hampshire within a fortnight. Again the mysterious and extraordinary nature of the Corn Circles was exhibited, for anyone who cared to look, in a way that left little doubt in the minds of most open-minded people that these things were intelligently produced. The very precise geometric pattern showed nothing of the randomness which we associate with natural phenomena, yet the obvious alternative that the Circles were man-made seemed untenable too.

The first of the 1988 double-ringers was found on 11 June on the Longwood Estate in barley, about three-quarters of a mile south-east of the Cheesefoot Head triple. Besides the large double-ringer there were five additional single Circles (of fifteen feet diameter or less) nearby, seemingly scattered about a line running north-west to south-east through the main Circle (Figure 3:2). Circles had been found here in the previous year, but nothing quite like this prodigy, which was only the second of its kind ever seen. Then, some days later, the Army Air Corps at Middle Wallop contacted Colin Andrews to inform him that another double-ringer had appeared in a wheat field at Charity Down, thirteen miles north-west, not far from their airfield (Figure 3:3). As with quintuple Circles which had appeared at Charity Down in 1985, this had been spotted from the air, and from that time one has been aware that the military maintain an interest in the Circles, which they regularly photograph from their helicopters.

On 27 June I flew, together with Timothy Good and Ralph Noyes, in a light plane piloted by Leslie Banks with a view to photographing the 1988 Circles which we knew about. Our first target was, naturally, Cheesefoot Head, where we expected to find just the triple set of Circles which had been the first of the season. We were amazed to find not only that set but a huge new double-ringer Circle which had appeared in the punchbowl two days earlier and which we had not heard of (Figures 3:4 and 3:5). This was of similar size (100 feet in diameter across the outer ring) to the other two, and had formed in that part of the punchbowl nearest to the main road (A272) where some of the research group had kept vigil on various nights earlier in the month. Needless to say, nothing had been seen on those occasions.

Eye-Witness Accounts

The elusive nature of the Circles has always been one aspect of the mystery which is most frustrating. Despite the increasing number of Circles that are found, no one ever seems to have seen one actually being formed, with two notable exceptions. This would appear to indicate that most Circles are formed at night, and also that they form extremely rapidly, within, say, ten to twenty seconds. On the two occasions when witnesses claim to have seen a Circle form, nothing was visible in the air above the site, though in one case a high-pitched humming sound was heard.

In the summer of 1983, Melvyn Bell, who lives near Bratton, says that while out riding a horse at dusk near there, he saw frenzied agitation in the corn some sixty yards away, and saw

Figure 3:2. Double-ringer Circle on the Longwood Estate, near Cheesefoot Head, together with five single Circles, June 1988. Wind damage is also visible (© Timothy Good).

Figure 3:3. Double-ringer Circle at Charity Down, Goodworth Clatford, June 1988 (© Timothy Good).

Figure 3:4. Double-ringer at Cheesefoot Head, June 1988 (© Timothy Good).

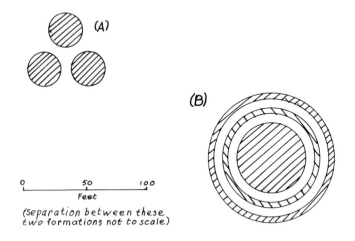

Figure 3:5. Cheesefoot Head Corn Circles: (A) a Triple, 4 June 1988; (B) Double-ringer, 25 June 1988. (The separation between the formations is not to scale.)

a thirty-foot Circle being flattened out. No noise was heard at that distance. The witness is an associate of Dr Meaden, so it was perhaps inevitable that this event was described by Mr Bell as a 'stationary whirlwind'. Despite subsequent reference to 'dust, dirt and light debris spiralling into the air',[4] which was not mentioned to Colin Andrews when he was first told the story, it does not seem that one can draw much conclusion as to what caused this Circle.

The only other reported observation of a Circle being formed in this country was when many people apparently saw one appearing in daylight. This was when a Circle formed in grass near Warminster, 'just like the opening of a lady's fan', and was observed by about fifty people skywatching for UFOs at a time when that town was the Mecca of UFO hunters in the 1960s and 1970s. 'A perfect circle was accompanied by a high-pitched humming sound.' This event was reported by Arthur Shuttlewood in the magazine *Now!*[5] It is highly ironical that the meteorologists who are anxious to debunk any UFO connection with the Circles should pick Shuttlewood's report to substantiate their case. That what they saw was caused by a whirlwind was most certainly not Arthur Shuttlewood's interpretation of the event, nor that of the other skywatchers. Sadly enough, many UFO researchers have rejected as too unbelievable much of what he reported from Warminster during that period, and it is high time that this was reappraised.

For some unknown reason we seldom now receive reports of Circles in grass in this country, but nearly always of Circles in cereal crops. Nevertheless, it would be reasonable to suppose that the phenomenon described by Shuttlewood is the same as that we are dealing with today. More significant is the fact that it is in just those places where we find the Circles today that Arthur Shuttlewood and the skywatchers of yesteryear were observing UFOs twenty years ago. And also some reports of close encounters with landed UFOs and their occupants – that rarest of UFO events – during the 1970s, are in exactly the places where today's Circles occur.

UFOs and Circle Sites

This correlation is very remarkable. During that particular flight in June we flew over and photographed a quintuple set of Circles in a barley field between Upton Scudamore and Cradle Hill,

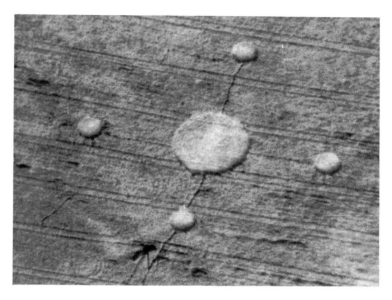

Figure 3:6. Quintuple set of Circles at Upton Scudamore, June 1988 (© Colin Andrews).

near Warminster. This 170-foot formation appeared on 14 June and was, we mistakenly thought, the first set of 1988 Wiltshire Circles. (see Figure 3:6). It was of interest in that the main circle of this quintuple was swirled in an anticlockwise spiral, unlike any in the quintuple Circle sets that have been found before or since. It was also exceptional in having opposite pairs of clockwise and anticlockwise satellites, which had then never been seen before. With the sole exception of another quintuple that had appeared in August 1987 in a field just a few hundred yards away from this one, all quintuple Corn Circles previously reported displayed clockwise swirl in all five circles. Once more the Circles had given a clear indication of their evolving nature.

Now consider the following account which Arthur Shuttlewood was given by a prominent local businessman and Justice of the Peace. The J.P. was driving with his wife and son from Warminster towards Westbury when he rounded a sharp bend past the first turning off to Upton Scudamore. It was on a clear bright August night at about eleven o'clock. He continued:

I saw a huge red ball, fiery and glowing, which rolled slowly over a clump of trees and above a hill on the right. It hung suspended for a time in the air, the rolling motion ceased, and I drew to a halt to watch more closely. It drew me like a magnet, that shining light!

Gradually the large ball commenced to turn on its axis, revolving and changing colour as though cooling down from immense heat. It was now a fluorescent egg, flattened out somewhat, a brilliant orange in the sky. A deep crimson band spread along or through the centre of the egg, jutting out slightly from either end.

We looked on amazed as four small red balls of light shot out of the main scarlet beam and protruded into the air for what we estimated to be twenty feet or so. At no time were these smaller spheres disconnected from the main object. They seemed to be linked to it by a slender thread of paler red light that swayed like the tentacle of an octopus! They remained in that position dancing vaguely from side to side, for about two or three minutes. Then they quickly shot back into the larger shape and disappeared from sight.[6]

This extraordinary description of a UFO near Upton Scudamore coincides rather remarkably as regards shape with that of the quintuple sets of Corn Circles, which have been found in just that place in 1987 and 1988. And yet the episode described above took place in 1966! Can there possibly be some connection?

A similar object was sighted near Charity Down in August 1985 by Mrs Joan Simms of Over Wallop, about seven days after a quintuple set of Circles had appeared there. This UFO consisted of five lights positioned like the five spots on a dice, and the outer lights repeatedly entered and left the central light. Mrs Simms said that the UFO was so bright that it hurt her eyes to watch it for too long. A BUFORA investigator subsequently suggested that what Mrs Simms had seen was the planet Venus, which surely deserves some sort of prize for silliness.[7] Nevertheless, it does prove difficult to establish a direct connection between particular sightings and the formation of a set of Circles. However, the coincidence of place between UFO sightings and the actual Circles remains inescapable.

Close Encounters

Besides UFO sightings, it was intriguing to find that it was in the lane running beside that very field near Upton Scudamore where the Circles now appear, that German parachutist Willi Gehlen had a close encounter experience in September 1976. While sleeping in his estate car which was parked in the gateway to a field, he found that the car's hatch-back had apparently unlocked itself and opened. After this happened a second time he heard a strange humming sound like a swarm of bees, and then saw a very tall figure, which he assumed was the farmer, standing near the gate. This figure did not reply when Gehlen excused himself for parking there, but shone a light at him then went away. Shortly after, he heard the humming noise again, and saw a large shape lift off from the ground. There was a 'pink, pulsating glow' coming from it as it flew into the sky at an angle of 45°.[8] All this was recorded well before people became aware of the Corn Circles mystery, or that the Circles were appearing where these events had happened.

Mrs Joyce Bowles of Winchester claimed to have had four separate close encounters with 'aliens' in 1976 and 1977. These were at Chilcomb, where Circles have been found (see Figure 3:7), two miles east of Winchester and a little over a mile from the punchbowl at Cheesefoot Head, and also near Headbourne Worthy, just north of Winchester, where Circles first appeared in the summer of 1976 close to where one of her encounters occurred during the same year. On each occasion she was accompanied by a second witness who supported her story. During one encounter she was taken inside what seemed to be a landed UFO. 'Lights were blinking and flashing everywhere,' she said. 'The man told us this was his field, whatever that meant. One of his colleagues pulled out a paper which had all sorts of lines on it. In the middle was a circle with rings round it.'[9]

Again, all of this was reported and published well before the Corn Circles became known. And it is not as if reports of close encounters with aliens were so common in this country that the coincidence of their extremely close proximity to principal sites where the Circles are found can just be shrugged off. Although the nature of the two UFO phenomena (those observed near Warminster and near Winchester in the 1960s and the 1970s) seems to have altered, there would appear to be very strong indications indeed that the Corn Circles of the 1980s are part of the same mystery. It is easy then to see why some have suggested that what we are looking at may well be 'time-travellers' from either beyond this planet or from the Earth's own future. But obviously in our present state of knowledge such an explanation can only be treated as wild speculation.

Figure 3:7. George Wingfield standing in a Circle at Chilcomb, August 1987 (© Lord Haddington).

The Yatesbury Circles

At the end of June an aerial survey by the Circles Phenomenon Research group revealed no less than thirteen Circles in several large fields of barley at Yatesbury, just two miles west of the famous Stone Circle at Avebury. Many of these had been discovered earlier by local farmers, and they were all plain circles swirled both clockwise and anticlockwise in groups of two or three. Several other Circles were found a mile away near Beckhampton.

Further inquiries in the area led to some surprising new information which was volunteered by Mr Roy Lucas, a farm worker. He had been cutting verges near Yatesbury between 7 and 8 a.m. on 16 June, which was an overcast day, when he observed in an adjoining field about 400 yards away something like a 'puff of smoke' rise from the ground and drift slowly upward. When about ten feet high it had suddenly billowed and swirled about. The centre of this column of vapour then appeared grey and dense, and twisted very rapidly. Then, all within a few seconds, the 'smoke' dispersed completely. Mr Lucas said that his first impression was that a tramp had lit a small fire in the field. Then a few minutes later the same thing happened again further across the field, and five minutes later the sequence was again repeated. When he went to investigate there was, needless to say, no tramp, no fire, and nor for that matter any holes in the ground. But neither were there any Corn Circles, although some of these were found later that day in an adjoining barley field. Mr Lucas admitted that the 'smoke' could well have been steam, fog, or any white vapour for all he knew.

Naturally, Dr Meaden interpreted this as a 'descending atmospheric vortex', despite the fact that whatever was observed appeared to have risen up from the ground. Whether or not this phenomenon is what caused the Yatesbury Circles, we cannot tell, but it does sound very similar to what was observed near Trowbridge, Wiltshire, in 1979. Here the witness saw 'smoke' coming through the hedge as he drove along the main road. 'Whatever it was,' he said, 'I don't want to see it again. Six feet of it came into the middle of the road. It stopped and tilted on end. I thought it was going to hit the van.' The smoky column travelled ahead of the van, which was moving at about 35 m.p.h., for a short distance, then it 'just went into a gateway'.[10]

Distribution of the Circles

Besides the English Corn Circles, there are various reports of single Circles in Australia, Canada and Japan, and a very few in the USA. Photographs of some Australian ones show that we are dealing with the same phenomenon, but there is no indication that the foreign Circles display anything like the complexity of pattern and the frequency of occurrence of the English Circles.

Those who regard the Circles as meteorological phenomena maintain that they are most likely widely distributed throughout the British Isles. The fact that the great majority of those reported in Britain during the 1980s have been clustered in Wiltshire and Hampshire, with just a few in adjoining counties, is solely because that is where the Circles investigators have been looking, they say. This supposition is patently untrue. In the last few years an increasing number of pilots have become aware of the Corn Circles, and many first reports come from them. It is almost certain that the vast majority of Circles do not go undetected. Not only do they occur mainly in very specific parts of Wiltshire and Hampshire, but at two principal sites, Cheesefoot Head and below the White Horse at Westbury, they have also returned to the very same fields with annual regularity since about 1980. This is more reminiscent of a rare bird's nesting habits than of a meteorological effect! And when they do appear, they often proliferate like mushrooms, as at Yatesbury.

In June 1988 I photographed the luxuriant green wheat field below the ancient Westbury White Horse, which is carved in the chalk hillside. No wind damage of any kind was to be seen in the crop. I knew with complete certainty that the Circles would soon return to this field, and indeed they did so on 30 June. The 'loose' triple set and the linear triple which appeared that day can be seen in Figure 3:8. Each set consisted of a small (20-ft), medium (30-ft), and large (50-ft) circle which were swirled both anticlockwise and clockwise. They reappeared within yards of the positions where Circles of different configurations had been found in 1987, and also in previous years.

71

Figure 3:8. 'Loose' triple and 'Linear' triple below the Westbury White Horse, July 1988 (© George Wingfield).

The Oadby Circle

So consistent are the Circles with regard to places and the sort of places where they appear – usually in the immediate vicinity of prehistoric sites or tumuli – that it is of great interest when one is found outside the usual area. A few have been found in previous years in Sussex, and some near Wantage in Oxfordshire, but nothing of this kind had ever been found north of Wantage.

On 26 June I wrote to my brother, a geologist living in Leicestershire, on the subject of the Circles. I concluded with the sarcastic remark that if he really wanted to see what I was talking about he would have to travel to Wiltshire or Hampshire, since I could not possibly arrange for a 'stationary whirlwind' to travel to his part of the world. Rather curiously, just one day after he received this letter, he saw a report on the local Central Television news that a mysterious ringed circle had appeared in a cornfield at Oadby, just outside Leicester. At this point, let me hasten to disclaim any credit for this strange occurrence, which had in fact been first discovered about a week earlier! This flattened circle of wheat was about fifty-three feet in diameter and surrounded by a

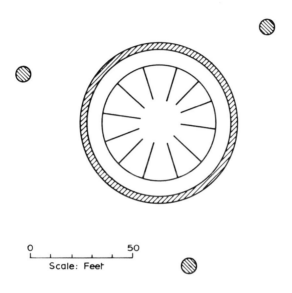

0   50

Scale: Feet

Figure 3:9. The Oadby Circle, June 1988.

narrow concentric ring. Symmetrically disposed about this were three small satellite circles (each of four feet diameter) which were approximately at the apexes of an equilateral triangle (see Figure 3:9).

Members of the Circles Phenomenon Research group, who examined this, were cautious at first, but finally decided that it was indeed the genuine phenomenon. The configuration was not the same as any seen previously, and the plants in the main circle had been flattened radially with hardly any swirl and as if by tremendous force from the centre.

On the night before the Oadby Circle was found, a lay preacher from Fleckney, who asked to remain unnamed, was driving near Oadby with his wife and son, when they saw a very bright, white light apparently hovering over the field. The family were alarmed and stopped. After a time the object vanished upwards into a cloud at great speed. It was later established that there had been no night flying from the nearby airfield on that night. The lay preacher, who was apparently disturbed by what they had seen, said: 'It was weird, but we know what we saw.'

A Mrs Hudson, whose house in Oadby overlooks that field, said that although she does not usually draw her curtains on that side, she was overcome with a panicky feeling at 11 p.m. and felt she had to draw them. Her neighbours, who were having a late supper at the time, saw a bright, white flash from the field, followed a few minutes later by a second flash.

A local resident subsequently made a number of tape-recordings in the Oadby Corn Circle. Some of these, which I have listened to, have picked up distinctive repetitive noises which are similar to noises that registered on tape-recordings made in Circles in Hampshire and Wiltshire. When BBC Television were making recordings for the *Country File* programme, screened in October, they too picked up this sort of noise when interviewing Colin Andrews in a Circle, and there were also 'ghost voices' on one of their tapes. At Oadby the recorder was left to run while those present withdrew a good distance to ensure their sound would not be heard. Recordings were made at various times of day with different tape-recorders to eliminate instrument faults. At no time are the recorded noises heard directly by anyone in or near the Circle. In view of this, it is possible that what is picked up is caused by sharp variations in the magnetic field, since the recording medium is magnetic. In particular, there is a hollow tapping noise with a beat of about 100 per minute. Its slightly irregular variation gives the impression of, say, a heartbeat rather than anything of mechanical origin.

Tracks into the Circles

Despite the widely differing theories as to the origin of the Circles, most serious researchers are unanimous in agreeing that the Circles phenomenon is not a hoax. Over the last five years or so there have certainly been several hoaxed Circles, which usually looked neat and impressive to the unititiated but could always be seen to be fake by those who were familiar with the phenomenon. This was because genuine Circles almost always show fine details which would be extremely hard for a hoaxer to replicate. First, the swirl patterns are mostly in the shape of an elaborate spiral and not just concentric rings, such as would result from the drawing round of a chain or rope attached to a central post. Second, the corn is usually laid flat with a kind of 'veining' effect, in that it is alternately bunched together and thinned out on the ground (see Figures 3:8 and 3:9). And third, the Circles are nearly always slightly elliptical, which is indicative of a rotating force, and not something that a hoaxer would find easy to reproduce.

The 'tramlines' in the crop almost always intersect the Circles and allow access on foot without any treading down of the crop. For quite some time this led people to believe that hoaxing could still be the case. But with an increasing number of Circles to inspect it was soon apparent that satellite circles, or smaller ones not intersected by tramlines, were very often without any tracks through the corn to or from them, in the case of fresh Circles. Naturally, unless one was first on the scene, it was not possible to make much in the way of sensible judgements about tracks, since the tendency of visitors is to go into every Circle in the group, and where there is no tramline access, to push through the standing crop.

But the Circles investigation group did find that unvisited Circles occasionally had thin tracks to them even though the Circle was ostensibly fresh. Initially it was assumed that these tracks were made by animals, such as deer or hares, which were sometimes seen in the Circles. On a few occasions a single, thin track, whose direction was indicated by the way the corn was bent, led either into or out of a satellite Circle without a return track. This looked strange indeed! Could they have been made by birds which had landed in the Circle or had flown out of it? There seemed to be no reason why not, since gamebirds, in particular, often run through the crop rather than fly.

Footprints in the Corn

Then came new indications of visitors to the Circles which proved even more puzzling. After the appearance of the double-ringer Circle at Cheesefoot Head, all further Circle activity in Hampshire ceased. All new Circles were to appear in Wiltshire during July, and again this strange phenomenon moved into a new phase. After the first six Circles below the Westbury White Horse were found, we naturally expected many more just there, as

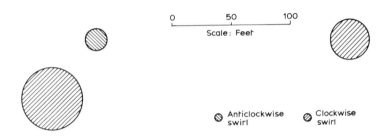

0   50   100

Scale: Feet

Anticlockwise swirl   Clockwise swirl

Figure 3:10. The Upton Scudamore triple, 8 July 1988.

had occurred in 1987. But this was not the case. The next group was formed during the night of 7/8 July in a field beside the Warminster to Westbury road just beyond the turning to Upton Scudamore, exactly next to where the J.P. had stopped to observe that bizarre UFO many years before.

The farmer, whose land it was, saw the Circles in his field from his farmhouse at an early hour. There was a 'loose' group of three similar to one of the earlier triples at Westbury. He telephoned Colin Andrews, who drove over at once from Andover. The farmer had inspected the crop in his wheat field late on the previous night, when there had certainly been no Circles. Since they were not visible from the nearby A350 road, he assumed that he alone was aware of them, and was therefore very surprised when a white helicopter appeared in the sky and hovered low above the Circles, presumably photographing them. Possibly this was the military from Warminster, though a white helicopter is unusual.

When Colin Andrews arrived he went straight to the field with the farmer, and they both felt certain that they were the first to reach this set of Circles. But in the standing corn between the Circles he could see small tracks, mostly along the seed-line, which seemed to have been surreptitiously made. In places, what appeared to be a small shoeprint could be detected, such as one might expect to belong to a woman or a child. These prints were even found under the flattened wheat in one or two places, which seemed to indicate that they either preceded or were contemporary with the formation of the Circle.

These tracks and the occasional 'shoeprint' were to be found again and again in all of the Circles which appeared in the vicinity of Silbury Hill within the next month. Everyone who was aware of them suspected initially that some sort of hoax was being perpetrated. But the later conclusion was that, otherwise, these Circles gave every indication of being genuine.

So what possible interpretation can be put on these tracks? Possibly we were mistaken, and persons unknown had entered the Circles before the investigators, on each occasion. But it did not seem that way. Possibly these particular Circles were formed using some kind of human involvement of a sort at which we can only speculate. Possibly the tracks and the 'shoeprints' were not of human origin at all.

Alas, one cannot be served up with Circles in the way we might like to have them. Each new feature we discover brings with it more doubt and more bewilderment. Each aspect seems capable of different interpretations. One wonders what the meteorologists will make of Circles which come with built-in footprints, though no doubt they will have an explanation. The only lesson which can really be learned from this odd development is that a rather less dogmatic approach to the whole phenomenon is advisable.

The Silbury Hill Circles

In mid-July a completely new chapter opened in the Circles saga. We were first aware that an enormous quintuple set of Circles had been found very close to Silbury Hill on 15 July. This formation was far larger than anything previously seen, measuring about 290 feet across. Its situation beside the main A4 trunk road meant that no passing driver could avoid seeing it. Large numbers of cars stopped and their occupants went into the wheat field to visit the Circles, or climbed Silbury Hill to view this great imprint, which resembled the five faces of a giant dice. Naturally, this mystery received extensive local TV and newspaper coverage.

Figure 3:11. The first quintuple set of Circles at Silbury Hill, July 1988 (© George Wingfield).

Figure 3:12. Satellite in Silbury Hill quintuple set, July 1988 (© George Wingfield).

Apart from its size, the most remarkable thing about this Circle was its proximity to Silbury Hill, which is the largest prehistoric artificial mound in Europe. This 130-foot, flat-topped, conical barrow was constructed in elaborate layers in about 2600 BC for an unknown purpose. A ley line which runs through Avebury Stone Circle and Silbury Hill also crossed the position where this new set of Circles had appeared.

The central fifty-five-foot Circle was swirled in a clockwise spiral, and its satellites, each about twenty-one feet in diameter, were anticlockwise but for the clockwise northerly one, which was nearest to Silbury Hill. Shortly afterwards a further quintuple set was found a mile to the west near Beckhampton. This was of similar size, but with smaller fifteen-foot satellites, three of which were clockwise and one anticlockwise. This completely new feature – the asymmetric disposition of the satellite circles' swirl – tempted one to think that these new Circles presented some coded clue as to their origin or purpose. Quite apart from this, the sheer size of these quintuples, in which the satellites were roughly 100 feet distant from the main circle, was unprecedented.

On 24 July we discovered a third huge formation in a remote area nearly three miles west of Silbury Hill, and well away from the road. It is known as 'Rupert's Circle' (after discovery by my son, Rupert). This was of similar size to the first two quintuples, but completely lacked one satellite, the most northerly. The east and west satellites were both twenty-four feet in diameter and were swirled anticlockwise and clockwise respectively. The southernmost satellite was only twenty feet in diameter, anticlockwise, and separated by a record 140 feet from the main Circle. The distortion of the regular quintuple set shape was unexpected, but not inexplicable in the light of subsequent investigation. And here, once more, despite being first on the scene as far as we could tell, we could see the small tracks between the satellites and the main circle, which characterized all of these large quintuples.

Curiously, all three of these large quintuples lay close to the line of an ancient Roman road. So too had the Oadby Circle. Most likely this was purely coincidental, but such is the strangeness of this phenomenon that it is perhaps worth bearing in mind. And in each case one of the two axes of the formation was exactly parallel to the tractor 'tramlines' in the

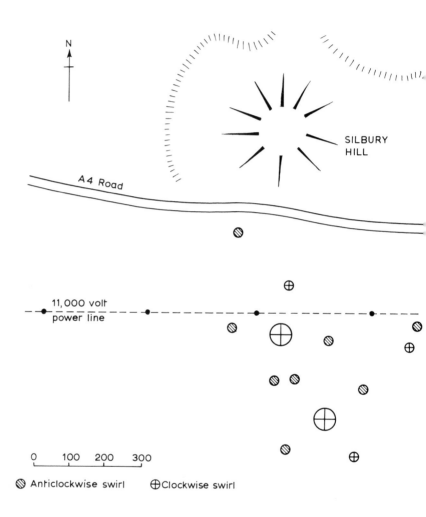

Figure 3:13. Diagram showing location of the Silbury Hill Corn Circles.

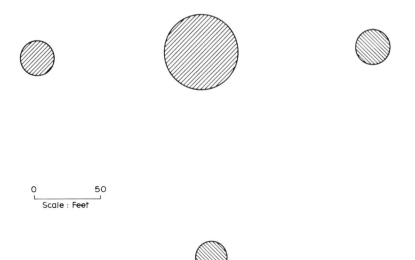

0 _____ 50
Scale : Feet

Figure 3:14A. 'Rupert's Circle', a huge formation in a remote area nearly three miles west of Silbury Hill, July 1988.

Figure 3:14B. Silbury Hill from the air (© Timothy Good).

81

field. This could hardly be mere chance, and this 'locating' of the formations can immediately be seen from the photographs (Figures 3:11, 12 and 17). To any objective observer, one thing was by now abundantly clear: the Circle formations were not just randomly positioned, as one might expect of a completely natural phenomenon, but appeared to be intelligently located with respect to linear features of the landscape – not something necessarily requiring high intelligence, but intelligence nevertheless.

The Avebury UFO

On 22 July the local *Marlborough Times* led with a headline story entitled 'Strange Sighting at Silbury Hill'. This featured a large photograph of the Circles opposite Silbury Hill, but also made brief mention of the fact that an unnamed woman from Marlborough had witnessed a bright object in the sky near Avebury a day or so before the first Corn Circles appeared there.

This story, in conjunction with the tracks and 'shoeprints' in these recent Circles, naturally aroused the suspicions of those in the Circles investigation group. 'Footprints means hoax' was the obvious conclusion to be made, though the elaborateness and scale of such a production was unbelievable. If this was the case then surely the UFO witness's account must also be bogus. It was with this in mind that Colin Andrews and I went to interview Mary Freeman, whose name we had discovered by inquiries. Much later that evening we left, sure that this was not the case, and impressed by her detailed and convincing account of what she had experienced.

On the evening of 13 July, perhaps twenty-four hours before the first Circles were formed at Silbury Hill, Mary Freeman had had dinner with a friend near Avebury, and was driving home along the A361 road through that village, which is a mile north of Silbury Hill. (See Figure 3:15A.) She followed the road through the great Stone Circle and turned left into the 'Avenue' (so-called because it is partly lined with ancient standing stones) to go towards Marlborough. No other cars were about. Over to her right she caught sight of an intense golden/white glow in the clouds. The source of this light, which she said was much, much brighter than the full moon, was enormous, silent, and stationary

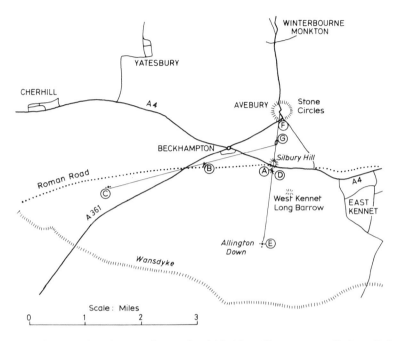

Figure 3:15A. Map showing the roads which Mary Freeman travelled on 13 July 1988, when she was attracted by an 'energy beam'.

Figure 3:15B. The Avebury Avenue (© Timothy Good).

just above the ceiling of low cloud. Since it was New Moon that day, no moon was visible.

She glanced back at the road, and when her eyes returned to the object she then saw a long, narrow beam of white light shining obliquely downward at the ground. Her immediate impression was that this was an 'energy beam', or that it was 'channelling energy'. She did not know why she had this thought. The beam was directed south over the top of Silbury Hill or, at least, where she knew Silbury Hill must be, since it is not visible from that point on the road. Her instinct was to drive on and turn towards Silbury Hill to find the place where the beam touched the ground.

Within seconds of her seeing this immensely bright object, there was a further strange occurrence. Various things, such as a booklet and a cigarette pack, which had been left on the front shelf of her Renault 5, suddenly flew into her lap for no apparent reason. She drove on slowly, watching the UFO and its beam, and turned right on to the A4 road towards Silbury Hill. There were still no other cars on the road. But before she reached Silbury Hill, her view was briefly obscured by trees, and when she next looked there was nothing to be seen. When the things had flown off the shelf, she noticed that the dashboard digital clock read 11.13 p.m. The whole episode lasted barely three minutes.

The object which Mary drew for us was an elliptical shape, and from the centre of its base shone a thin beam of light at 45° to the vertical. Since it was in cloud, its edges were not sharply defined, but the clouds did not appear to affect the beam. I asked whether the beam diverged downwards, indicating that the UFO was its source, or diverged upwards from the ground, suggesting that car headlights or a searchlight was shining on the clouds to produce this effect. Mary indicated that the beam of light was parallel-sided; indeed, there was no way of telling whether it shone down from the UFO, or up from the ground towards it. It could not possibly have been a car's headlights or a searchlight; the object in the cloud was far too bright, and moreover the base of the cloud, through which the beam projected, was not lit up. Mary said she was not frightened by this strange and silent spectacle; perhaps more awed, or 'honoured', as she put it.

Clearly this experience had a deep emotional effect on Mary Freeman. She returned home by midnight and told her flatmates, whom I met and talked to, and, later, her mother and brother,

Figure 3:16. The two quintuple sets of Circles at Silbury Hill. August 1988 (© George Wingfield).

what she had seen. It was not until six days later that she was told by Richard Martin, whose story subsequently appeared in the *Marlborough Times*, about the Circles at Silbury Hill. The possibility of a connection between these and her UFO sighting then seemed inescapable. Despite a gap of at least twenty-four hours between Mary's sighting and the appearance of the Circles, the UFO beam had touched the ground where the Circles had formed.

Further Circles at Silbury Hill

On 26 July farmer Roger Hues discovered that a new quintuple set of Circles had formed in his wheat field opposite Silbury Hill, immediately adjacent to the original set. This configuration was identical to the first set and virtually the same size. And, as can be seen from Figure 3:16, this new quintuple has two sides of the square whose corners are the centres of its satellite circles, exactly parallel to the 'tramlines'. Its orientation was 135° different from the first formation in that its single clockwise satellite pointed roughly south-east, towards West Kennet Long Barrow. Even though it lay in full view beside the main A4 road, no one had reported seeing a thing. A night-long vigil on Silbury Hill several days later, using an infrared night-sight through which the Circles were clearly visible in the dark, failed to give any sign of who or what was producing them. There were no nocturnal visitors and nothing was seen to move.

Again, the *Marlborough Times* lead story headlined these events: 'Circles Mystery Intensified by Further Sighting'. But this referred to the new Circles rather than to any further UFO sighting. And at some stage in the following days a further three single Circles appeared in the field close to the two large quintuples. They now seemed to be spreading like a rash!

Significant Alignments

On 4 August yet another large quintuple set of Circles – the fifth – was reported to have been found in a remote wheat field on the slopes of Allington Down, about a mile and a half south of Silbury Hill (see Figure 3:17). This quintuple was of similar size to the others but had adjacent pairs of clockwise and anticlockwise satellites. For once, the formation was not aligned with the 'tramlines' through the corn, which was surprising. However, when I first reached the main circle, I found that large sections of this particular field displayed long parallel striations in the crop where the wheat was more lightly coloured. One axis of the quintuple was aligned precisely parallel to these features.

If this alignment merely reinforced the unmistakable indication of intelligent 'location', another significant alignment was now quite apparent. A line drawn through this latest quintuple and through the position of the other two at Silbury Hill also runs through Silbury Hill itself as well as Avebury. Moreover, the position of the UFO seen by Mary Freeman just south of Avebury, as indicated by her, lay, so far as we could be sure, right on the line. The 'energy beam' which she had seen was, it then appeared, directed along this imaginary line.

Quite apart from this, one could see from the map (Figure 3:15) that another line drawn through the two western quintuples near Beckhampton intersected the first line in just the position where the UFO had been seen. Surely this was more than coincidence?

Further investigation soon led me to think that the first line described above was indeed a ley line. It additionally passed through other ancient sites including that of a Stone Circle, of which no trace now remains, at O.S. Grid Ref. SU098671. It was after writing an article for *Flying Saucer Review* on the Silbury Hill Circles, in which I referred to this as a ley line,[11] that I went to consult John Michell on the subject. While with him, I was looking through his copy of Paul Devereux's book, *The Ley Hunter's Companion*,[12] when I chanced on an aerial photograph of Avebury and Silbury Hill on which was imposed an oblique white line. Such was the position of this line that my initial reaction was that this an artist's impression of the beam shining down from Mary Freeman's UFO. It was in fact a representation of the ley line which passes through Avebury and Silbury Hill, and is described in great detail by the author. This corresponds very closely with our first line, described above.

Earth Mysteries and the Circles

Evidence of a connection between UFOs and ley lines is examined in some detail in Paul Devereux's book, *Earth Lights*,[10] which explores the thesis that UFOs are basically an Earth phenomenon associated with Earth energies, but does not exclude the idea that the phenomenon interacts with the human psyche in some way, giving the impression of a living thing, or even intelligence.

Without entering into detailed consideration of this analysis, it is instructive to look at the Earth Mysteries interpretation of the Circles, although there are many conflicting points of view. The basic thesis is that there exists an as yet undefined force, or Earth energy, that is associated with many of the ancient sites such as stone circles, henges, dolmens, barrows, and tumuli. Such sites are very often found to be in alignments, and the straight lines connecting these sites are known as leys, or ley lines. The ley lines, it is suggested, are channels along which this energy flows, or else the sites, which define the leys, have been specifically positioned as markers along such channels, which were known to their prehistoric architects. Taking this argument further, some protagonists of this theory maintain that the Corn Circles are indeed caused by manifestation of this Earth energy; it is the rotating force, coming up out of the ground, that causes the corn to fall. Many researchers are breaking new ground currently in their efforts to understand more about the nature of the leys, and their mysterious Earth energy.

Although many orthodox scientists would react to all of this with derisory snorts of 'Pseudo-science!', there is an accumulating body of evidence to support this particular approach. The primary method of detecting this Earth energy is by means of dowsing, using metal rods, but much work has been done recently at various ancient sites using standard scientific instruments to measure electrical currents and magnetic fields that appear to be associated with the Earth energy. In particular, significant results have been produced by the Dragon Project, in which lengthy investigations were carried out at the Rollright Stones and other sites.

CPR has carried out extensive tests with dowsers in the Circles and in positions where Circles have been. Almost invariably, very strong dowsing reactions are observed, which have proved extremely consistent. Results in the Hampshire and Wiltshire Circles show a force that acts on the dowsing rods which is generally in the same direction as that in which the corn is swirled. The force is also detectable in the standing corn, and varies in direction and strength depending on distance from the centre. This force can be frequently detected flowing to the Circle along an energy path from a nearby archaeological feature such as a tumulus, which may be situated on a known ley line, and this energy path may distort the formation or cause a quintuple's satellite not to form, if it crosses such a position. Quite apart from the dowsing experiments, electrical measurements have shown consistently anomalous values in the Circles and their vicinity.

Although it is too early to assess the results of this work, there is a strong indication that whatever force causes the corn to be laid flat, it persists in and around the Circle for long after the Circle forms, and can usually be detected in that place weeks after the crop has been harvested and the field ploughed. In fact, a good dowser can, without too much difficulty, pinpoint the position of a previous year's Circle in a field, without having been told where to look. The dowsers also sometimes detect definite changes of polarity in this force long after the Circle has been formed and the crop harvested. Visually observable changes in the direction of swirl of the corn, and even the size of some Circles, have been noted in a very few cases, such as two formations near Westbury in August 1987.

All this serves to confirm something which has long been suspected: That whatever 'agency' produces the Circles, it is not only invisible, but is most likely present for some time before and after the corn is found to have been laid flat. This would explain why various effects such as 'electrical crackling' noises, humming noises, beating noises, bright flashes, recurring flashes, and indeed, UFOs, have been reported, sometimes before, and sometimes after, the Circles have formed. The true nature of this 'agency', whether it involves Earth energy or electromagnetic energy or something else, remains, for the time being, a mystery.

A Religious Perspective?

There is also another perspective to the Circles that deserves mention, even though most people will consider such an approach quite beyond the pale. This is the interpretation given by religious groups such as New Era, which believe that the Circles portend the coming of the New Age. Associated with this group, though not part of it, is the medium Isabelle Kingston.

In March 1987, when she had been working with a group of students on Silbury Hill, she channelled messages which purported to come from 'The Watchers', a higher intelligence referred to as 'beings from other areas'. It should be stressed that similar messages from supposedly extraterrestrial entities known as 'The Watchers' or 'The Guardians' are not new and have been reported for many years.

Isabelle Kingston's channelled message indicated that the building of the Hill of Sil (Silbury Hill) was originally commandeered by these beings. 'Sil' is apparently derived from the word meaning 'Shining Being'. Temples such as Silbury Hill were allegedly built with the intention that they should last until this time in history to help humanity. The Avebury Sanctuary, in particular, was apparently alive with a pure energy that links all places of power around the globe.

Two weeks before the Circles appeared at Silbury Hill, Isabelle Kingston says that she was told that 'they' would appear there, and she then channelled a further message addressed to her group of healers, who had asked about the meaning of the Circles. They were told that these had made them aware of the presence of 'The Watchers', and that these guardians had been linked with humanity in order to bring the power necessary 'to build the new Jerusalem'. 'The Watchers' had been coming here for many years but until now Man's awareness did not recognize the signs. England lay at the centre of the great 'Pyramid of Light' that will be guiding humanity's understanding. 'The Watchers' was the name of a collective intelligence guiding human mortals. It was an intelligence from outside the planet, not linked to angelic beings, but part of the 'cosmic consciousness'.

The symmetric pattern of the Circles allegedly indicates where the power enters the Earth's magnetic field. Silbury Hill draws such cosmic power. There were ley lines running through the Earth, and at various points lines of power were energized. 'You are witnessing the coming of the New Age', the medium was informed.

It is difficult to see why there should be any connection between the presumably pagan ancient sites of Salisbury Plain and the Christian religion, from which derive the references to the 'new Jerusalem'. But perhaps one should not quibble over minor details. Clearly, acceptance of channelled messages like this requires an act of faith, and equally clearly they will be dismissed as pure fantasy by those who are guided solely by orthodox Western science of the 1980s. Nevertheless, I think that omission of this part of the story of the 1988 Circles would be a mistake.

Besides New Era, there are other groups that claim to summon up Earth energies by various methods and which use dowsing to detect certain symbolic patterns of religious significance on hillsides in Wales and Cornwall. These would presumably be visible, like the Circles, had the places where they are found been sown with suitable crops. One cannot help wondering whether these people, if they have the power they claim, are those who made the mysterious footprints on the Silbury Hill Circles or indeed whether they were in some way involved in the creation of these Circles.

Certainly one should not overlook the symbolism that the Circles embody, and this is most apparent in the final part of the 1988 Circles story. This episode is just as curious as the Silbury Hill saga, and once again the reader will have to decide whether this, too, might have a religious dimension.

The Celtic Cross

After the discovery of a sixth huge quintuple Circle in wheat near Hungerford, fifteen miles east of Silbury Hill, on 16 August, things seemed to go quiet. By this time most barley had been harvested and within a week or two the combine harvesters were at work in the wheat fields. It seemed natural to assume that the 1988 Circle season was over.

At the beginning of September, Colin Andrews mentioned on several occasions a Celtic Cross, which fellow CPR researcher 'Busty' Taylor had discovered in 1985 in the churchyard at Goodworth Clatford, not far from his home in Andover. He showed me photographs of this, and speculated that we might get Corn Circles of this pattern – something that I thought most unlikely, since the only Circle remotely like this had been an ordinary ringed one, but with four small satellites outside the ring, on the Longwood Estate, Hampshire, in 1986.

The churchyard Celtic Cross at Goodworth Clatford commemorates various members of the Thornton family including Herbert Thornton, Canon of Winchester, who died in 1923. It bears a fair resemblance in shape to the magnificent High Crosses of Ireland, which were carved between the eighth and tenth centuries AD, and of which there are particularly fine specimens at Clonmacnois and Ahenny. The Thornton's Cross, like these, has a central circle in the cross, and four smaller circles on the positions where its large concentric ring intersects the arms of the cross. The ornamentation on the central circle even has a distinctive clockwise swirl. Colin had become so interested in this cross at that time that he even took a Canadian TV crew, who were making a programme on the Circles, to see it.

A week later, on Saturday, 10 September, Colin received a telephone call from the farmer on whose land the double-ringer Circle at Charity Down had appeared in June. 'Do you want to look at another one?', he said. 'If so, you've got just four hours. I've got men standing by, and the field has got to be cut today.'

Two days earlier, on the Thursday evening, Colin had visited the double-ringer and had made certain electrical measurements. He had noticed then a significant increase in energy at this Circle, which had been more or less dormant since June. The new Circle

91

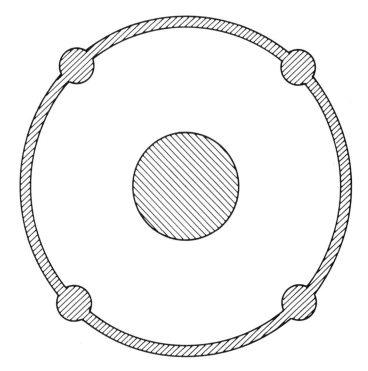

Figure 3:17. A 'Celtic Cross' at Charity Down. September 1988.

formation, which had appeared since, was less than 100 yards away. Its shape was that of an enormous Celtic Cross.

The central circle, in which the corn was swirled in a clockwise spiral, was about forty-seven feet across. Surrounding this at a comparatively great distance, unlike any other ringed Circle, was a vast outer ring, measuring 153 feet in diameter and four feet wide. Equally spaced around the ring were four satellite circles, each of about fourteen feet diameter and clockwise. These lay on top of the flattened ring, since one could see that the corn in these had been laid down later, if only perhaps by a few seconds. And instruments showed higher electrical readings in this formation than in any previous Circle.

Nothing quite like this extraordinary and elaborate hieroglyph imprinted in the corn at Charity Down, just two-and-a-half miles from the stone Celtic Cross in the churchyard, and four miles from Colin's home, had ever been seen before. It was recorded on video from both the ground and the air that day, and a photograph of it appears on the front cover of the book, *Circular Evidence*.[2] In view of Colin's earlier obsession with the Celtic Cross, one might be forgiven for assuming that 'they' had read his mind – or else that he had read 'theirs'. Sceptics who are unable to assimilate such a bizarre conjecture would probably insist that he must have faked this Circle. But this was undoubtedly the genuine phenomenon at work, and for anyone who knows Colin, there is not the remotest possibility that he could have done such a thing.

During that afternoon on 10 September the crop was cut, and so ended the 1988 Corn Circle season. But the fallen corn is merely an outwardly visible sign of what is at work here, and the 'Circles' are undoubtedly with us even after they are harvested. The episode of the Celtic Cross Circle had a curious sequel some weeks later.

On 14 January 1989, Colin went with Pat Delgado and George de Trafford (another researcher) to visit Isabelle Kingston for the first time. After discussing the Circles, he drew her attention to a small Celtic Cross ornament which she possessed, just as they were leaving. Three hours later, while watching TV with her family, the set turned itself off and a similar Celtic Cross, composed of many red and blue dots, appeared on the TV screen, despite the fact that the set was unplugged from the mains supply. This was witnessed by Isabelle's mother and by her neighbours. Isabelle says that she was aware of 'exceptionally high energy levels' in the house, during and after the visit.

How can one possibly interpret what happened here? Clearly some agency of which we only have the haziest perception seems to be at work. Perhaps more of the enigma will be revealed in the coming months. If the Circles run true to form, they will return to perplex and amaze us once more in the summer of 1989. [Indeed, they have! – Editor.] Most likely we will see more Celtic Crosses, in the same way that 1987's unique double-ringer was thrice replicated at the start of the 1988 season. Whether or not we come any closer to understanding what lies behind this mystery is anybody's guess. But there seems little doubt that quite a few people will have to set aside their prejudices and preconceived ideas, and look once more at this strange phenomenon with rather more open minds.

REFERENCES

1. *The Journal of Meteorology*, Vol. 6, no. 57 (1981), Vol. 7, no. 66 (1982), Vol. 8, no.75 (1983), Vol. 9, no. 89 (1984), Vol. 10, no. 87 (1985), Vol. 11, no. 109 (1986), Vol. 12, no. 116 (1987), etc.
2. Delgado, Pat and Andrews, Colin: *Circular Evidence*, Bloomsbury Press, London 1989.
3. Anecdote from a correspondent of Ralph Noyes (January 1989).
4. *Journal of Meteorology*, March 1985.
5. *Now!*, 29 August 1980.
6. Shuttlewood, Arthur: *Warnings from Flying Friends*, Portway Press, Warminster 1968, pp. 78–9.
7. Fuller, Paul and Randles, Jenny: *Mystery of the Circles*, BUFORA, 1986.
8. Blundell, Nigel and Boar, Roger: *The World's Greatest UFO Mysteries*, Octopus Books, London 1983, p. 131.
9. Ibid., p. 129
10. Devereux, Paul: *Earth Lights*, Turnstone Press, Wellingborough, Northants. 1982, p. 209.
11. Wingfield, George: 'Did Avebury UFO Produce the Silbury Hill Corn Circles?', *FSR*, Vol. 33, no. 4, 1988.
12. Devereux, Paul and Thompson, Ian: *The Ley Hunter's Companion*, Thames & Hudson 1979, pp. 132–3.
13. *Kindred Spirit*, Vol. 1, no. 5, November 1988. P.O. Box 29, Warminster, Wiltshire, BA12 9YD.
14. Dr Meaden has now modified this theory. See his new book, *The Circles Effect and Its Mysteries*, Artetech Publishing Company, 54 Frome Road, Bradford-on-Avon, BA15 1LD.

4

So You want to be a Ufologist?

PATRICIA GRANT

Patricia Grant was born in Zanesville, Ohio, in 1922. She was educated in Ohio, California, and Massachusetts, and obtained a B.Sc. degree in architecture from the University of Cincinnati.

She came to the UK in 1958 as a civilian architect with the US Navy. Her interest in UFOs began with the Kenneth Arnold sighting in 1947, and has continued unabated to the present day. Now retired, she is no longer engaged in active investigations, but continues her research into UFOs and related subjects.

The *Portsmouth Journal*, Cosham, of 11 December 1988, gives us the latest 'gen' on UFO statistics. An 'expert' has told the Journal that 99.9 per cent of UFO sightings can be *easily* explained. One must point out that these odds are slightly better than those the United States Air Force gave us nearly forty years ago when they announced that 100 per cent of sightings could be explained if there were sufficient information to hand.

These latest statistics advise us that one must investigate 100 cases of UFO sightings per year in order that one tenth of one UFO sighting will have any significance whatsoever. One would assume that the *Portsmouth Journal*'s 'expert' has a doctorate in statistics. He does not: he is a photographer's technician. However, appearances can be deceiving. In our community there was once a dairy man who entertained his customers by reciting excerpts from Lucretius, Catullus, and Horace, with a bit of Virgil thrown in. Rumour had it that he crooned the fragments of Euripides' *Phrixus* while milking his cows. It transpired that he was a classics scholar with a respectable Ph.D. and had opted for the 'good life'. It follows that the *Portsmouth Journal*'s favourite son very well may be a mathematics whiz kid who cares naught for academe.

The point being made here is that your profession, craft or occupation will not disqualify you from becoming a ufologist or even an 'expert' ufologist. You may be a scientist, artist, teacher, policeman, lorry driver, machinist or a dustman. Journalists, postmen, housewives or stockbrokers are all welcome. In seeking new outlets for your energies and creative instincts you need have no hesitation in entering this field of study. As Dr Jacques Vallée was once overheard to remark: 'In ufology, we are all beginners.'

If you decide to become an adept in this arcane occupation, you will want to know where to begin. Burning with enthusiasm for the subject, you probably have read a great deal about it. *Read more.* There are two major rules in ufology – although many ignore them – and the **first rule** is this: *Collect and catalogue as much data on the subject as you can.* The **second rule** is more difficult for some: While engaged in the pursuit of scholarship, *try to develop a lot of good old-fashioned common sense*, because you will certainly need it. As for recommended reading material, *FSR (Flying Saucer Review)*,[1] the oldest remaining and internationally acclaimed UFO forum is a *must*. Subscribe to it, and as a companion, the purchase of *The Encyclopedia of UFOs*[2] is a valuable investment as a source of information. Apart from these indispensable guides, read everything else on the subject that you can lay hands on.

When you think you are prepared to take the next step (sighting investigations), you may want to join a UFO group. There is a plethora of these about, some large, some small, but each of them fall more or less within one of the following four categories:

Contactee Cults (CCs)
Sceptical True Believers (STBs)
Pseudo-Scientific Activists (PSAs)
Serious Scientific Approach groups (SSAs).

Only *you* can judge which type best suits your temperament. If you feel uncertain, let us look at them all, one at a time.

Contactee Cults

Your short-cut to Arcturus or Vega may be found in almost any Contactee cult. All CCs have one thing in common: a 'Master' who is in close contact with loving, helpful Alien Beings of high intelligence from Zeta Reticuli, Tau Ceti, or wherever. (So far nothing has been heard from the Crab Nebula, but word may come any day now.) When the 'Master' receives the messages he will transmit them to all and sundry who have joined his cult and paid the subscription fees.

A surprising number of initiates join these groups. One 'Master' rented Caxton Hall for an evening to announce the latest Cosmic Communiqué and the auditorium was packed. Unless rent-a-mob was on hire, there were an awful lot of eager would-be emigrants to Jupiter on the scene.

Having joined the Common Market, England is presently playing host to a branch of a European CC which promises to 'demystify' the human body. This cult came into flower when its 'Master' met small aliens from a silver spaceship which hovered near him as he walked in the old volcano country in France. Claiming to have spent an entertaining evening with Jesus and Buddha, he has recruited, among others, a charming Quaker lass as spokeswoman for his movement in Britain.[3] Her attendance at one of the cult's camps in Europe unveiled a lot, literally. Putting it baldly, there was a lot of nudity and 'everyone did their own thing'. Of course everyone was *terribly responsible* about sex, 'with the AIDS problem and all that'.

It is self-evident that the CCs do not really investigate UFO sightings. Membership is 'no work and all play' and 'follow the leader'. Although the United States has the largest number of CCs in the world, Great Britain does not do badly considering its size and population. In order to understand how they operate it is not a bad idea, if you can afford it, to join several of them. Apart from the pathetic footnotes they engender, you may find them highly entertaining, but they do much to hinder serious research.

By following the two major rules of ufology you can do something to counteract the highly publicized antics of the groups. For one thing, you can repeatedly point out that the Contactee cult must not be confused with the *individual* who claims to have had contact. That person is an alleged *witness* and seldom has a following of any sort. In this exercise, however, we are not examining witnesses, we are looking at UFO groups.

To return to the main theme, finding the type of group that best suits you as a budding ufologist, do not despair if the CCs fail to inspire you. *You have learned something*, albeit nothing about investigating UFO sightings. For the time being, *apply rule one, apply rule two, and keep on reading.*

Sceptical True Believers

This cult consists of individuals and a few groups with their various hang-ups, and to become one of them you must support their dictums and recite a few idiocies of your own, ever remembering that all witnesses are to be denigrated, ridiculed, or patronized. Let that hubris of yours really all hang out!

Your STB colleagues will be highly vocal individuals who *truly believe* that all sightings of UFOs are (*a*) misconceptions, (*b*) hoaxes, or (*c*) hallucinations. They *truly believe* that they know better what the witness or witnesses saw than the witness does. This category includes men and women with completely open minds: whatever they hear goes in one ear and right back out the other. Since they *truly* believe they know best in all things, they manufacture any data to support their hypotheses. This method of research is hardly acceptable in scientific circles, but this does not bother them in the least. They *truly believe* that anything they do not know is not worth knowing. When there are UFO photographs that have been painstakingly authenticated, they declare the same to be fakes. By the same token, pilots have eyeball floaters and experienced radar operators are ignorant. To prove their commitment to the faith, they descend to near-libel against the serious scientist who studies the UFO phenomenon.

There is now evidence that some STBs are in the employ of the government, and of course, those who are jolly well know that people are seeing odd things in the sky. Learn to recognize an STB because there have been efforts by one or more of them to infiltrate genuine UFO study groups. The accomplishment of this aim spelt disaster for one group.[4] And learn to distinguish between the STB and the reputable scientist, who through lack of time or inclination has never studied the UFO problem. The latter will be a sceptic because he knows nothing of the subject and will freely admit it.

With an enquiring mind and a healthy curiosity about life, you will not wish to be associated with the STBs and their ostrich philosophy. Do not despair yet. *You have learned something*, albeit mostly about the vagaries of the human psyche. As we prepare to move to pastures greener, *apply rule one, apply rule two and keep on reading.*

Pseudo-Scientific Activists and Serious Scientific Approach groups

Most groups, other than the CCs and STBs, genuinely try to adopt a serious scientific approach to the solution of the UFO problem. Since most ufologists have had little or no training in the disciplines of science, one must make allowances for the members who fall by the wayside through excessive zeal. The major responsibilities of ufologists are investigations of reports of sightings, and analysis of the data for each sighting report. The work of these groups, large or small, is extremely valuable because they investigate mountains of UFO reports.

The priority in each case is to discover whether or not there is a mundane explanation for the sighting. In spite of the depressing statistics given by the *Portsmouth Journal*'s blue-eyed boy, around 15 to 20 per cent of sightings are unexplained after thorough investigation and analysis. Both the PSAs and the SSA groups are usually very good at sorting the wheat from the chaff. However, on occasion one of the PSAs will publicize a 'mundane' explanation that is so utterly ridiculous that it makes our STBs look like Nobel candidates.

These groups have the most far-reaching interests. Not only are UFO sighting reports investigated, much attention is also given to space travel and secret weapons, humanoids, contactees and abductees, brainwashing, and ball lightning. You will enter the world of time travel, parallel universes, and the ten or twenty-six dimensions other than the three-plus space/time we can understand. (Few will mention the heterotic string theory on which the theory of these dimensions has been conceived, nor will there be much discussion of the fact that if they do exist, they are pretty small . . . one million, million, million, million, millionth of an inch!⁵) You will hear much about certain curious apochrypha of science: poltergeists, Nessie, Bigfoot, tulpas, monsters, fairies, ley lines, the pendulum, dowsing, Earth lights, fungus-ingesting owls, and fair-weather whirlwinds. Any one or all of these may or may not be related to the UFO phenomenon. They are all unexplained and *nobody knows* where they fit into the picture.

Anyone who has lived as long as I have probably will realize that there are many unexplained things in life. The only time I was privileged to meet the late Dr Allen Hynek, he made the comment to me that a certain witness was a 'repeater'. (As with all new 'ologies', one must become acquainted with a special glossary. In ufology, a 'repeater' is a witness who has had more than one sighting of a UFO.) By Dr Hynek's demeanour I was unable to tell whether he was inferring that this witness had been lying or whether he thought a different significance should be assigned to the case.

Weeks later, while walking my dog through a Kentish meadow, I thought about Hynek's remark at some length. It suddenly occurred to me that when a child, in a different meadow, I had known a 'repeater' of quite a different sort. A little playmate of mine, hereafter to be known as Nancy B., had a genius for finding four-leaf clover. During one happy summer, she and I and several other little girls spent hours roaming through a Connecticut pasture looking for these good-luck charms. *Nancy found one or two every single day!* I had no luck at all and the rest of the girls found only one or two during the entire holiday. While preoccupied by these thoughts, involuntarily, almost unconsciously, I bent down and plucked . . . *a four-leaf clover!* I was astonished; I remain astonished. I cannot understand it, nor the significance of it, if there is any. What I *do* know is that that *did* happen to me, that Nancy B. *did* find four-leaf clover day after day, and that in all cases the clover were certainly not figments of the imagination: they were real. By the same token, it is probable that people see UFOs because UFOs are real and are there to be seen. Why some witnesses have more than one UFO experience is another question. It may be simply that they happen to be in the right place at the right time, or it may have a significance which evades our reason. *Nobody knows.*

There is no harm in forming hypotheses that incorporate these mysteries into the UFO problem. Of course the bulk of this 'esoteria (to coin a new word!) is as unexplained as is the UFO. When a hypothesis is confused with a *soli on*, the trouble begins. Some ufologists become so enamoured with one or another of their own pet theories that they convince themselves they have found the answer. It is usually the pseudo-scientist who commits this *faux pas*. When whole groups become orientated toward one or another theory, hostilities are formed between rival groups and research is damaged. A recent article by Pieter Hendrickx of Belgium in *Quest* magazine,[6] calls for various groups to end their differences and co-operate with one another, and one can support Hendrickx whole-heartedly. Of course, dissension is nothing new in scientific pursuit. Isaac Newton was an irascible old codger and Paracelsus was not noted for a friendly disposition. Nevertheless, the UFO is such a complex problem that it will require a genuine team effort to solve it.

For the purpose of this exercise it is assumed that the many drawbacks discussed have not diminished your interest in ufology and that you wish to soldier on. As you sit leafing through the latest batch of news cuttings, you will find much to interest and amaze. Here, a book review in the 26 January 1989 issue of the *Cambridge News* begins: 'Jacques Vallée claims in DIMENSIONS that he has been abducted and experimented upon by humanoid aliens.' Having read the book with care, you will probably return to its pages and read it again and again in search of this claim. You will not find it. *Never mind*. If the Schonnel Reading Scale is valid, that poor journalist has not reached the proficiency of age nine yet. And in the *Essex Chronicle* of 10 February 1989, you will see a photograph of a teacher and his pupils holding up a tissue paper and cane hot air balloon. Having sent several aloft, these happy pranksters are delighted that members of the public have mistaken the balloons for UFOs. *Never mind*. The glee will soon turn to grief when Farmer Brown's barn is set alight. And in at least half a dozen of these scribblings you will find mention of little green men, to say nothing of the queries of the witnesses' bibulous habits . . . Best of all, here are pictures of Stealth aircraft, looking no more like Stealth than a wolfhound looks like a chihuahua. And although the Stealth bomber has not been flown outside the United States as yet, you will be told that this craft accounts for many sightings in Great Britain. If you shrug and yawn at this rubbish, you have become a good ufologist.

You will know that disinformation, including this garbage, is THE VIRUS IN THE UFO COMPUTER. Now you can help programme.

Carry on! *Apply rule one, apply rule two, and continue to study with diligence.* In ufology, no one yet has reached the Pons Asinorem,[7] much less crossed it. You well may be the first – and the best of British luck to you!

REFERENCES

1. FSR Publications Ltd., P.O. Box 12, Snodland, Kent ME6 5JZ.
2. *The Encyclopedia of UFOs*, edited by Ronald D. Story, New English Library, London 1980. (A new edition is planned for 1990.)
3. *Herald Express*, Torquay, Devon, 19 November 1988.
4. Good, Timothy: *Above Top Secret*, Sidgwick & Jackson Ltd, London 1987.
5. Hawking, Stephen W.: *A Brief History of Time*, Guild Publishing, by arrangement with Bantam Press 1988, pp.162–3.
6. *Quest International*, Quest Publications International Ltd, 15 Pickard Court, Temple Newsam, Leeds, LS15 9AY.
7. *Pons Asinorem* ('The Bridge of Asses'), Euclid, *Elements*, Book 1, Proposition 5 – 'Too difficult for asses or stupid boys to get over.'

5

Testimony from Africa

CYNTHIA HIND

Cynthia Hind was born in South Africa and studied at Cape Town University until World War II, when she served with the South African WAAF. She then moved to England, where she lived for eleven years.

She has written numerous short stories for radio, including the BBC, as well as many articles on a variety of subjects. She has been interested in UFOs for seventeen years, and is the author of *UFOs – African Encounters* (Gemini, Zimbabwe 1982).

Cynthia Hind has travelled all over the world as a UFO researcher, and is the MUFON Co-ordinator for Africa. She lives in Harare, Zimbabwe.

It has always been important for me to prove that Africa is an excellent example of the evidence for the existence of UFOs. The reason for this is that so many people have had interesting experiences and reported case histories, when I know that the vast majority are totally unexposed to media influence or interpretation.

It is true that although television is affordable only by the more affluent, neighbours, friends, and family do share the viewing. My domestic staff of three, for example, whom I have provided with a TV set, will often have ten or twelve persons to watch with them. Nevertheless, it is a very limited audience out of the eight million people in my country (Zimbabwe) alone, and the choice of programme veers more towards *Mavengwevengwe* (local music) or *Makadoka* (a sit-comedy) than, say, *Star Trek* or *V*. And even then, the viewing is limited to the towns and not the rural areas.

With regard to radio broadcasts, the listening public is divided

103

between a station broadcasting continual pop music and programmes in the vernacular. The English language programmes,
although including sophisticated science programmes from the
BBC as well as some locally produced, are seldom listened to
by the rural population, who obviously prefer programmes in
their own dialect.

I have kept a watching brief of programmes over the past few
years. Astrology, UFOs, and some paranormal subjects are dealt
with on an irregular basis but always in English only.

With reference to UFO books, there is an absolute dearth of
these in Africa – perhaps with the exception of South Africa. Most
African countries are in tight economic straits, and although some
countries do import books from abroad, I can almost guarantee
that no allocation will be made for the purchase of books dealing
with UFOs. It would be an interesting exercise to find out from
British publishing houses what percentage of the most recent
UFO books ever found their way to English-speaking Africa.

On examination of the evidence, I want to make it clear that
although people are never liberally exposed to UFO lore or its
case histories, there is always the off-chance that people *might*
hear something in this connection. Thus, even though I have
stated that UFO witnesses are never exposed to pre-knowledge
of the UFO syndrome, there is always the remote possibility
that some type of contact has been established. I say all this in
deference to the more sceptical students of Ufology.

Like the Brazilians, the African people have in their culture
many references to *vadzimu* (spirits), such as *shave, Mudzimu,
Ngoza*, all of whom must, to them, emanate from 'somewhere
above'. Therefore, it should not be difficult for the people to
relate to entities from other worlds, be they physical planets or
even another dimension.

But it is the concept of 'outer space' which is daunting. With
the rural African people, measurements relate in terms of the next
village or the nearest big town. To explain 'overseas' is difficult;
to explain 'outer space' even more so. Many have never viewed
the open sea and the largest expanse of water they have seen is
an inland lake, where the opposite shore is often clearly visible,
for example, Lake Malawi, Lake Kariba, Lake Victoria. As to
visiting the moon or other planets, 'Only God can walk on the
moon' they say.

If one stops in the country to ask one's way, your informant will look at you first. If you appear tired and weary, dripping with perspiration and fatigue, he will say, 'It is not far, a few more turns in the road', despite the fact that your destination might be many kilometres away. On the other hand, if it is a beautifully cool, brilliant day, and you are fit and eager, he will describe in minute detail every turn of the road, every identification on the way, happily wishing you a long and rewarding journey. It is in the African culture to say what pleases you most, so one has to be especially careful during investigations to put your question in such a way that you can elicit an accurate reply, as opposed to what the witness feels you want to hear.

Another point I find significant is the short memory of the rural people about matters which they deem unimportant. *UFOs are unimportant.* The African, on the whole, does not understand the concept of UFOs nor their impact on civilization. It does not matter to him that the entities emerging from strange machines might be from another world. They are not part of his culture. He does not relate to them, and aside from his immediate fear of their strangeness, they are entirely irrelevant to his life style.

I feel that, unlike a UFO experience for an average British family, who would probably recall events in terrifying detail for the rest of their lives, the rural African is more involved with production, procreation and possible promises of a better life. And indeed, who can blame him?

In Dr Roberto Pinotti's excellent paper *Contact: Releasing The News*, which he presented at the IAF Congress in Brighton on 15 October, 1987, he gives his reasons on why governments have not informed the public of the existence of UFOs.

He speaks of 'ET and Culture Shock', and to me this would be a deciding factor, certainly in relation to the African continent. We all relate to our own particular culture. Although we know that we are not the centre of the Universe, 'we are central in essence', he says. Anything widely divorced from our own familiarities, our own dreams of what and who we are, is foreign; more so to the unsophisticated who are barely aware of the greater and lesser societies on our own Earth. Pinotti says:

'from the cultural point of view, their contact with Europeans castrated African and pre-Colombian societies, destroying most of their original age-old characteristics: from their practical everyday life to their version of the world and its existence. It was culture shock they had to face; and their technology, their science, their economy, their religion, their philosophy and their ethics, disintegrated against the structure of the European civilization.'

How true that is.

Although I cannot always be sure that the rural African people I interview have never heard of craft from outer space, at least I know that whatever they have heard, it would be extremely superficial, with a lack of understanding; a mere peripheral acknowledgement that there may be something untoward coming from out of our skies.

Abductions

Whilst abductions are the current enthusiasm of ufologists, I am finding that whatever abductions are – whether a psychological subconscious concept or an absolute reality – they are certainly occurring in Africa. Unfortunately, I have not come across any cases where brown-skinned Africans are involved. Indeed, this would be a tremendous breakthrough. However, even with the few cases I now have, it still shows that UFO events occur in waves.

When there were lights in the sky, lights in the sky were visible in Africa. When craft landed on the ground, some of the best CEIII cases occurred. And since my return to Africa from the MUFON/Fund for UFO Research Conference in Washington, DC in June 1987, I have interviewed several abductees. I must admit that my first reaction was that of ambivalence: how come the abduction reports from the sixties and seventies were almost totally unacceptable (Elizabeth Klarer/Edwin of Durban) and now suddenly in the eighties, they were genuine physical affairs?

On the other hand, Budd Hopkins's investigations were thorough and professionally conducted with positive reports from psychologists. The psychological implications, according to Hopkins, had been carefully examined and he had been assured that the abductees were not suffering from some mental aberration; they were not schizophrenic nor paranoic. If they were reacting to an abnormal experience, it was because the experience *was* abnormal.

But whereas in Great Britain, Australia, Europe, and America, books such as *Intruders* by Budd Hopkins, *Abductions* by Jenny Randles and *Communion* by Whitley Strieber, must stir the imagination of their readers, in most of Africa such books are not available.

I have found that when dealing with witnesses in abduction cases in Africa, there is an innocence to their awareness; they are embarrassed by the story they are telling me because it is not like anything they have heard before. They know no one has experienced what they have experienced and they are afraid of the ridicule, and a little ashamed of repeating it aloud. They have never heard of Budd Hopkins, Kathy Davis or Whitley Strieber: they would never apply the term 'abduction' to their experience, nor are they sure it is a UFO case.

In December 1988 I interviewed Janet from Bulawayo in Zimbabwe. For me, her experience, which occurred in 1982, was an exciting one. It came to her in the form of a dream where she dreamed she was in a large room made entirely of metal – the floors, the walls, the ceiling. The room was filled with rows of tables on which were lying many medical instruments. Janet cannot recall being examined except that she could feel the people in the room putting something on her head, something like a cap. They were normal people except that they were dressed in one-piece suits of a shiny white or silvery colour.

When she awoke the following morning there was a lump the size of a five-cent piece on the right-hand side of her head. She showed the mark to her mother. The mark is now very much reduced but still visible. I did see it, but frankly, it could be anything. However, the importance of this case is that Janet was not aware of people having pellets implanted into their heads, and when I mentioned such a possibility at the end of our interview she did not appear to be particularly interested.

Since the dream, Janet has noticed many different things. She now has an adverse reaction to anything electrical. When she uses her hairdryer or curling tongs, the surge of electricity is unpleasant and her head is painful where the mark is. During thunderstorms, frequent in summer in tropical Zimbabwe, she experiences a disturbing tingling sensation whenever lightning strikes.

In 1984, while working in a London office, she was sitting at her desk and moved backwards (she is not sure for what reason she did this!) when a string of neon-tube lights fell and broke on her desk. On another occasion, in her dining-room, a neon light bulb fell and shattered on the table, barely missing her. More recently, while in her kitchen, a similar incident occurred, when an ordinary light bulb and its light shade fell and shattered a few centimetres from where she was standing. She commented that in each instance she recalls moving away from the spot where she had been standing, seconds before the lights fell, thus avoiding injury.

Apart from some recurring astral travelling dreams, she records only one other psychic experience. She was in the garden of her home when she saw two creatures she describes as 'fairies'. They were very small, about six centimetres perhaps, dressed in long, flowing white gowns and with gossamer wings. As Janet told me this, she laughed and appeared embarrassed. I felt she did not really want to talk about the 'fairies' to me; she parted with the information reluctantly. They were stationary just above some golden nasturtiums and she saw them only briefly. One moment they were there, and the next, they were gone.

With regard to her 'dream', I asked whom she thought the people were and what they wanted from her. She did not know, she said, but she has become increasingly afraid that they are coming to take her away. And yet, she added, if they want her to go with them, she would do so. She would like to go somewhere else; to another planet, perhaps. She feels there is little on Earth that can make her happy. She also had an emotional problem at home (she did not clarify this) and has not found a satisfying relationship for herself although she is a very attractive young woman; slight, small in build, with wide blue eyes and blonde hair. She told me she was a 'loner' and really prefers her own company.

A second Bulawayo witness was Jenny. Briefly, her story is the retelling of a dream which she has had at various times of her life going back some twenty years. The significance of the dreams was that they were precognitive and involved a man dressed in white who would take Jenny to places prior to her going to live there; in fact, without any knowledge on her part that she and her husband would be moving. She would only recognize the area when her husband was posted there (he was in the British Army at the time). She was convinced that these dreams were different from ordinary dreams. The reports on the whole were not particularly out of the ordinary except for one incident.

Jenny recalls being taken over a choppy sea towards an octagonal building with large windows, floating on top of the water. She was taken inside where there was a hive of activity monitored by people dressed in blue. A beautiful woman (obviously humanoid) came to Jenny and explained that 'they' were watching our Earth. A young man, to whom she pointed, was monitoring an earthquake condition about to occur in Turkey. Jenny was distressed. She says, 'Although they were very kind, some sort of manipulation was going on, in our own interests, they said, and helping with the over-population of our planet.'

An extension of the abductee's own thoughts on the matter? After all, even the most uninvolved in Africa must realize the basic problem of the population explosion among our people. Or indeed, is there some form of manipulation really going on by an alien civilization older and wiser than we are?

MB of Masvingo, Zimbabwe, had a less explicit experience. Her alleged abduction was rather vague, with humanoid beings of great physical attributes. Again, in this case there was no exposure to contemporary UFO reading matter, nor to media reports of small beings with slanting eyes and sexless appearance.

With MB, the interesting feature of her report was the sudden appearance, during the night, of a round, silvery object humming 'like a swarm of bees'. The object appeared a second time two years later when she was taken inside the craft.

She described flying in the craft and being so close to the ground that she could see small pebbles on the Earth and the furrows of ploughed fields. At one time she found herself in a corridor with a choice of doors. (Some emotional indecisiveness in her personal life?) When she realized 'they' were taking her back to Earth, she panicked. She pleaded with them to keep her there – wherever 'there' may be.

Janet of Durban, South Africa, says she was drinking coffee late one night when she saw a man step out of her wardrobe, which appeared to change into a long, endless tunnel. The man beckoned to her but she was determined not to go to or with him, and clung to the sides of the bed. She found that she had no free will and subsequently felt herself dragged down the tunnel.

In the morning she had difficulty in raising her bruised arms and was unable to comb her hair. (There is no corroborative evidence for this as Janet was divorced and lived alone.) She recalls being taken to a room with a table (examination table?) and a strange smell.

Caroline of Chipinge, Zimbabwe, has the most interesting story of all. She was lying on her bed awake when she saw a ball of light shoot through the ceiling and come down to the floor. The following then occurred:

(*a*) Caroline was paralysed by the object.

(*b*) The light, which was extremely bright, beamed downwards.

(*c*) Caroline felt 'they' wanted to take her up in the beam.

(*d*) She was able to see through the ceiling of her bedroom to the trees and sky outside.

(*e*) She tried to call out but no sound came from her throat.

(*f*) When the object had gone, she rushed to call her mother, putting on the lights as she moved through the house. (During our War of Independence most farmers used extensive security lighting in the immediate vicinity of their homes. This has been retained despite the end of the war, owing to terrorist attacks.) *All the lights went out.*

(*g*) A whirring sound accompanied the movement of the object.

(*h*) When Caroline was talking to her sisters after the event, they maintain that her words were confused and distorted. She also noticed that her sisters, when speaking to her, were slurring their words. (This slurring of speech occurred in the Nullarbor Plain case in Australia, 1988. See Chapter 8.)

I am surprised at the number of reports I have received in the space of a year. And why now and not before?

Overall the average number of cases of all types varies from one or two per month to about five or six per month in a busy period. But most of these used to be misidentified lights in the sky, which Dr Willy Smith, an able and respected colleague, would soon identify for me: a bolide; part of a meteorite shower (all so clearly visible in the unpolluted skies of Africa); space debris; or a satellite.

But abductions are different. There can be no misidentification as the story is so clear: the witness is aware of what is happening and is taken aboard or away by, presumably, alien beings. And although on occasions the witness admits that it occurred during a dream, why does *this* dream stand out so clearly from all others? Abductions don't happen every night, or even once a month. They usually occur once in a *lifetime*, sometimes twice. Only in the case of Jenny did meetings happen more frequently. The witnesses do not speak readily or eagerly of their experience, and because they usually don't know who to turn to, some stories don't come to light for years. And how many hundreds are never revealed?

With me, at least the witnesses know that I am sympathetic and understanding: they know they can talk to me, and that in itself is a release. But I cannot answer their questions: *Why* did this happen and *why* to them?

Of course, there is a pattern, but with wide margins. I know, for example, that the abductions happen mostly to women: they are all good-looking – some exceptionally so. They were young when it first happened, although not in terms of Budd Hopkins's seven-year-old syndrome. There are other major factors, but they do not apply to everyone, and with only five or six cases I cannot formulate a distinct enough pattern. So I will just have to wait and see.

As far as I know, the psychologists have not yet provided an answer either. Thus the enigma remains, and it grows on a psychological level. When UFO events were all physical, it was interesting but remote. Now that there is interference with the mind and control of the will, should not our voices be more clearly heard?

Airline Crew Sighting, 1988

My most recent report of a UFO is a well-observed pilot and crew case that took place over Beira, Mozambique, on 11 February 1988.

Commandant Simplicio Pinto of Mozambique Airlines (LAM),

111

was Chief Pilot on a flight from Quelimane to Maputo, the capital of Mozambique, in a Boeing 737. As there was no fuel at Quelimane, Pinto made a short stop-over in Beira, landing at 18.09 hrs. At the end of the runway there is a turn-around area, orientated to 170° magnetic. As he entered this area, Pinto could see a strange object in the sky.

'It looked like a wing parachute or something like a flying mattress, and appeared to be in layers,' he said. 'The object had a fluorescent light, like those mercury lamps which give off an intense, very white light; the hotter the lamp gets, the whiter and more intense the light . . . something like that.'

Captain Pinto reported that the object seemed to be stationary or moving extremely slowly and he had no idea of its altitude. It was like nothing he had ever seen before. 'Just to make sure, I asked my co-pilot, Jamal, to enquire of the control tower whether they had sent up a weather balloon. They replied with the questions: "Why are you asking? Is it because of that object up above? We began to see it at about 15.00 hrs and the Air Force radars have also picked it up. So far, we don't know what it is, but it seems to be positioned about 125 kilometres from Beira."'

Pinto remarked that for an object to be seen so clearly at 125 km distance, it would have to be a very large object; a Jumbo would not be seen at such a distance, he added. Also, it would have to be metallic to be detected by radar.

The stop-over in Beira was short. Three passengers left and fourteen boarded the plane. When the Chief Stewardess, Isabel Lobo, opened the door of the plane, she saw many people looking up at the sky, and running up to the flight deck she asked: 'Did you see it? What is it?' Pinto confirmed that they had also seen it.

Half-an-hour later Captain Pinto asked the control tower for permission to take off. Meanwhile, the object still hovered over Beira. The control tower asked Pinto if he was prepared to take off with the object right above him. He replied that of course he would take off – why should he not? Apparently, the control tower had reservations about this, but finally the plane took off southwards towards Maputo. At this stage, the object was also to the south. Said Captain Pinto:

'As soon as I was up, I could see the object from much closer. I had no further doubts. It was not a plane, it was

112

not a weather balloon, it was not something ejected from an aircraft or satellite. It was like nothing I have ever seen in my twenty-two years of flying.'

Pinto then continued heading south to identify the object. This was at about 18.40 hrs and it was getting darker on land, although in the air it was much lighter. The sun was on Pinto's right and it was not difficult for him to see.

'I saw the thing. It was simply enormous. It seemed to be stationary south of Beira, but did not seem to be as high up as I had originally calculated. I climbed above 11,000 feet (3,300 metres), but had to veer right a bit as the lights were so intense, they blinded me. There were three, like searchlights, placed in a triangle.'

The 'searchlights' emitted so much light that it became difficult to focus or judge distances. Positioned behind Pinto, Isabel Lobo could not take her eyes off the object. The Captain asked her to find out discreetly if anyone in the cabin had a camera so they could take a picture of whatever it was. She had seen a Japanese passenger with one, but he had disembarked at Beira and nobody else had one. Pinto did not inform the passengers about anything untoward: with 114 people on board he was afraid that there might be some panic.

'I then decided to switch on the two landing lights on the port side to see whether there would be any response from the object. But because of its powerful lights, it was difficult to distinguish anything. I had thought of climbing above the object but as much as I tried, it was always above us. I called the stewardess to witness what I was about to do. Then I switched the lights on and off twice.'

Suddenly, the object started to climb vertically, its lights becoming weaker as the distance increased. Captain Pinto turned the plane back to its original course. The object was still in sight and he kept in touch with the control tower, wanting them to have a complete record of what went on. He tried to locate the object on his radar but no image showed. He climbed again but the object remained much higher, still on the port side.

'By this time we were flying at about 24,000 feet and it seemed stationary above the mouth of the Save River, near Mambone. I continued to climb but it appeared to be very far away, even when we reached our cruising height of 31,000 feet.'

Meanwhile, it had become dark, although for a long time they continued to see the UFO with its triangular lights. Then they flew into storm clouds and it was lost from sight.

The following day (12 February), Captain Pinto flew along the same route on the Harare (Zimbabwe) flight, at about the same time of day. Though he searched the sky carefully, there was nothing to be seen – not even a star or planet.

'What was the object we saw? I don't know, but I would really like to find out. I think that with more sophisticated instruments, there would have been enough time to obtain more detailed information. I saw the object for forty-five minutes while people in Beira saw it hovering for more than three hours. I keep on asking myself: what could it be? Why did it suddenly climb higher? Was it in response to our signal with the landing lights? Did their instruments perhaps signal that our plane was getting too close?'

Captain Pinto said that two days before his sighting, an object with similar characteristics had been observed above Medellin Airport in Colombia, South America (see page ix). Two days later, another was seen over Madrid. Commented co-pilot Jamal:

'There are always reports of UFOs, but I have never seen one until this time. Commandant Pinto called my attention to the object, saying "Do you see that thing over there?" I looked and saw a long object, bigger than our plane, without windows and with a metallic look about it. It seemed to hover above the mouth of the River Save. I asked the control tower, "I thought you said there was no traffic around: what is that thing doing above us?" They replied, "We see it but we don't know what it is . . ."

'When we asked for permission to take off, the control tower gave us clearance: that is, they said we could go but at our own responsibility. So we took off and went to have a closer look.

114

It had very powerful searchlights. Then, when Commandant Pinto switched on our landing lights, the object slowly drew away, as if letting us overtake it. Yes, we all saw the object very clearly, but nobody could explain what it was. One thing I know for certain: it was like nothing I have ever seen before.'

Chief Stewardess Isabel Lobo added:

'When our plane stopped in Beira, I looked up and saw the object. It looked like a very large star but it did not twinkle. I asked the pilot if he had seen it and he said he had. It was a very large and powerful light. They told me it had been detected on radar, therefore it was no star.'

Isabel Lobo said that the Captain then climbed as quickly as possible and she could clearly see the searchlights in a triangular formation, almost like those of a football field. Even at ground level, the light hurt one's eyes. She said she was not afraid when the Captain switched his landing lights on and off, but the object then moved away suddenly in the opposite direction. 'I think that if the plane had not had so much cargo and so many passengers, the Commandant would have gone in closer,' she said.

When the object moved away, she likened it to a diamond ring with all the little lights shining. She was not sure if it was stationary or not, but it seemed to be moving very slowly, almost as though it was hovering. 'The truth is that in my twelve years as an air hostess, I have never seen anything like that, whatever it was,' she concluded.

My first reaction was that either NASA or the French space agency were involved with further balloon experiments (such as those in 1985 and 1987, which led to UFO reports in Zimbabwe), but there has been no verification. There are also many peculiarities that do not fit. How does one establish the truth, one way or another?

Speculations

I ask myself – not unreasonably I feel – what in Heaven's name have I achieved in all these seventeen years? From 1972 I have been involved with UFO investigations in Africa. I have travelled thousands of miles, been in often unhealthy areas and even dangerous situations. I have also been invited to speak at numerous international conferences, UFO group meetings, men's and women's groups, schools, and sometimes in remote places where only four or five people were able to attend.

There are those who are resentful to me, disbelieving of me and who perhaps intensely dislike me and what I am doing. On the other hand, I have believers from the abysmally ignorant, to respected pilots, policemen in high standing, and university students.

It is an exacting and tiring task where abuse and praise are given liberally; where TV shows and radio broadcasts, despite the hard work and research involved, rarely pay.

I live in a country where foreign exchange is a very precious commodity and while some people are sure that UFO lecturing is a lucrative occupation, I do not find it so. My travel allowance of 300 US dollars per annum covers very little.

Leo Sprinkle, Psychology Professor at Wyoming University in Laramie, once said to me, 'Serious UFO investigators are not only dedicated people, they are chosen people.' Well, whoever chose me, I wonder if they really did me a favour?

I have never seen a UFO although I have stood for many hours in Zimbabwe watching the marvellously clear, star-studded skies of Africa. I have sat in the Karroo, South Africa, on a moonless night, where not a single blemish marred the breathtaking dark of the night. I have stood (with Timothy Good) on a balcony in Brazil, watching for one vestige of movement from that vast bejewelled panorama above São José do Rio Preto. Nothing stirred: no huge starship hovered dramatically above me, and no one attempted an abduction of either of us! And still, I believe.

What is it then that drives us? Is it faith in humanity; that so many people cannot all be lying? Is it a conviction that somewhere there must be other better beings, other knowledge greater than ours? Or is it because subconsciously, I know *something*, like Leo says, that has not yet manifested itself in my conscious mind?

I am not growing younger, but I am growing wiser and more experienced, more questioning, ever seeking. There is bound to be a time when it will all pay off, one way or another.

6

The Soviet Scene 1988

NIKOLAI LEBEDEV

Nikolai Lebedev was born in Valday, USSR, in 1950. He studied at the Institute of Mechanical Engineering in Leningrad, 1968–75, at the same time studying developments in aeronautics and astronautics. He now specializes in irrigation engineering and lives in Leningrad, where I had the pleasure of meeting him in January 1989.

His interest in UFOs was stimulated in 1983, when he read a book about unexplained mysteries by Helmut Höflung.

I am indebted to Cyril Darbishire for translating the majority of the following reports, which are mainly from the Dalnegorsk, Dalniy Vostok area (on the East coast). I have also made use of material supplied to me in English by Mr Lebedev, including some sketches.

Sightings in Dalnegorsk, Dalniy Vostok

Liudmila Moxunova, Hostel Manager
12.02.88

'On 12 February 1988 I was walking home from the shop at 8.00 p.m., along with other women carrying their shopping, when I saw a big yellow sphere, half as large as the moon, and after it followed a smaller one, keeping pace with the larger one.

'The spheres moved slowly from Svetliy Klyuch, then stopped and remained stationary for several minutes. Inside the spheres you could make out a sort of unevenly spun network. There was no sound and the intensity of the light did not change. The spheres were travelling 300–400 metres above the hills and were identical in colour.

'From the big sphere came rays as if from the sun, but there

117

were none from the other one. The length of the rays was such that they seemed to reach the roofs of the buildings, their colour identical with that of the spheres. The distance between them was about ten or twelve metres, and movement was from west to east.'

Vitya Zinchenko, School No. 21, 7th Class
14.03.88
'On 14 March 1988 a large sphere a quarter the size of the full moon flew straight through the village, in the direction of Goreloe. When it was approximately in the centre of the village, a dark pink sphere of smaller dimensions split off from it and flew off to the north. There was no noise during its flight and its colour changed at regular intervals from fully white to having a grey sphere in its centre.'

18.03.88
Black-and-white photos were taken at 20.45–20.51 hrs of a large glowing sphere with a trail in the Beriozovsky area between Yugo-Aleksandrovka and Bolshaya Zlatogorka. The photos were analysed at the Geographic Institute of Dalniy Vostok with a French computer, and showed the object to be solid.

Alexei Rodion, School No. 10, 3rd Class
1.05.88
'On 1 May 1988 at 6.00 p.m. I was mending my motorcycle in the garage on Engineer Street. There weren't yet any stars in the sky. I saw a high-flying sphere, orange in colour, about one-sixth the size of the full moon. When it had flown approximately to the centre of the village it stopped and hung for five or six seconds, then turned off sharply at an angle of 90°, heading in the direction of the chemical factory.'

V. Pavlov, computer engineer
7.05.88
'On 7 May 1988 I was returning home from the garage, and at 10.30 p.m. saw a bluish sphere at a height of 600 or 700 metres, making no sound and with a dove-coloured trail behind it, flying parallel to the Earth. It was flying to the south-west, intersecting the centre of the village. The length of the trail was about 200 metres. In certain defined sections it flared brightly, in pulses.

When it reached the approximate vicinity of Sakharnaya it again flared and I didn't see it anymore, possibly because of a change in course or because of the distance between us.'

Observation by A. Ya over Partizanskii
25.07.88
'A large sphere-shaped object went by at 11.09 p.m., one-sixth of the full moon, lower than the clouds, at about 3,000 to 5,000 metres altitude, at a speed half that of a jet. The intensity of illumination became extremely strong.'

25.08.88
On this day there were three reports of sightings.

I. Yu. Sleptsova
'We had returned from the cinema with the girls at 11.00 p.m. and were in our room when we saw a hemisphere of dull white rise from behind the house opposite. It was foggy, like a cloud, and close to the Great Bear. It began to grow, then from the hemisphere came a ray of the same colour – long, narrow, and steady. We watched all this for about two hours.'

G. B. Karandashov, veterinary surgeon
'On 25 August I was on a business trip and was returning by official car from Vladivostok, together with a chauffeur. There was a bright moon to the right. To the left hung a huge sphere ten times larger than the full moon. It hung there motionless, dull and dense, with round, even edges. It was slightly paler than the moon. Then it began to grow, touched the Earth and quickly began to grow until it was the size of the firmament. Then, just as quickly, it dispersed, melting away like a rainbow. Above the Earth where the sphere had been, a black body seemed to be suspended. We watched all this for three minutes, as did people from a service bus standing beside us.'

Yu. Grankin, head of a photographic laboratory
'On 25 August 1988 my wife and I were at our datcha when at 11.08 p.m. we saw a huge sphere, six or seven times bigger than the moon, flying across the forest and the taiga from the direction of Krasnorechen, towards Dalnegorsk. There was no

sound. It approached at a tremendous speed, during which time we noticed that it was spinning and there were spots on it, but I couldn't make out what sort of spots. . . . Then it began to go down behind the hill not far from Dalnegorsk, and began to spread very quickly. . . . The sky was black, but where the sphere had gone down it was milky-white. My wife and I were very frightened, thinking it was a nuclear explosion.'

[These three sightings seem to me to be more probably due to Strategic Defence Initiative (SDI) tests, or barium gas experiments, but Nikolai Lebedev is sure they were not – Editor.]

Pavlik Pavlov (graduated from the 10th Class, 1988)
27.08.88
'On 27 August at 10.43 p.m., as I was getting off a bus in the centre of Dalnegorsk, I saw a large sphere descending just above the Party Committee building, white, yellow, and orange in colour. Its size was approximately one-fifth of the full moon. It hung for a short while over Dalnegorsk, then moved off in the direction of the quarry. I watched it for two or three seconds. Its speed was about 80 k.p.h. As it moved it emitted several bright flashes, as if at one-second pulses.'

Workers from the Automatic Telephone Exchange, Anuchino
4.09.88
'On 4 September at 11.15 p.m. a triangular-shaped object, a quarter the size of the full moon, was observed hovering near the village. It shone brightly and hung there for twenty minutes. We saw the same sort of object over the same place on another occasion (Figure 6:1).

Pasha Gladkov, School No.4, 9th Class
15.09.88
'On 15 September between 8.10 and 9.00 p.m., my friends and I were at a little shop not far from the "Khimik" cultural centre, talking among ourselves, when we suddenly saw an object, disk- or plate-shaped, flying slowly and evenly from the direction of Lyubov hill. Round and flat, it shone brightly. Its height was 400 or 500 metres as it flew low between the hills. Behind it came a shining whitish trail some tens of metres long, and fading away.

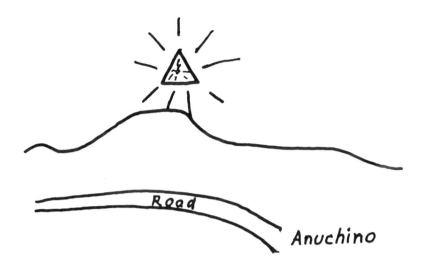

Figure 6:1. Sketch of the 'shining triangle' seen by workers at the Automatic Telephone Exchange at Anuchino. September 1988.

When it had completed a half-circle it passed over the hill where the road runs to Nikolaeskiy. It hung there for about a minute, and after hovering for a while over the north-western slope, disappeared behind the hill in the direction of the chemical works. In all, we observed it for three to four minutes.'

I. A. Sabanin, cinema mechanic
16.09.88

'On 16 September I was in a fishing-boat on the River Listvenno together with my friend V. I. Pristavko, in the Ternevskiy region. At 9.15 p.m. we both saw an unusual phenomenon which we watched for between forty seconds and a minute: a series of bright, fluorescent dashes flying in one group with a diameter of five metres, parallel with each other, dying out and lighting up at strictly defined intervals like tracer bullets, at a height of about 3,000 metres and an angle of incline to the Earth of 20°.

121

They were flying in the direction of Dalnegorsk from north-east to south-west.'

At the same time, Sabanin's wife Elvira observed a large cylindrical object flying from the direction of the sea, from the TV tower to the north, towards Upper Rudnik. It was about 200 to 250 metres long, and shining brightly, with a glowing trail.

V. F. Morozov, worker
24.09.88

'On 24 September I came out of my house into the street in order to bring our Siamese cat home. It was about 8.00 p.m. but not quite dark yet. I looked at the sky over the Bruderovskiy Raspadok and saw something quite incomprehensible – a fiery body of cylindrical shape was flying past, leaving a stripy white trail behind it. It was flying in a horizontal position. The body was unlike any aeroplane, and it was about 400 metres long. There was no sound. It was not flying very high – just below the hilltops, and it was flying in the direction of the hill where an object had fallen on 29 January 1986.'

A group of children from School No. 27, 7th Class
25.09.88

During the holidays a group of schoolchildren on Lake Dukhovo saw a ring-shaped light, yellowish-red in colour, hanging motionless over the mountainous area on the mainland side nearer to Dalnegorsk. The time was 4.00 a.m. According to the witnesses, the ring-shaped light had a shining object in the centre. A few minutes later the ring dispersed and the shining object began to make agitated movements in a circle.

From IZVESTIYA
18.09.88

WHAT'S HAPPENING IN THE HEAVENS?

In Japan last Friday, from 6.30 p.m. onwards, telephones at police stations and observatories were overwhelmed with calls from people reporting that they had witnessed a unique phenomenon; a huge fiery sphere, several times larger than the full moon, flew over the largest Japanese island Honshu from north to south-east at the speed of a jet-plane, without leaving any traces on radar screens.

In various parts of the island descriptions of the unknown object varied: different colours were named (ranging from milky-white to orange and

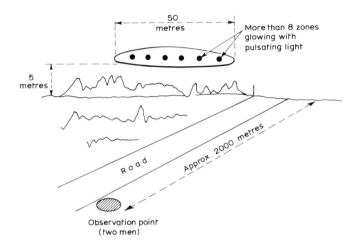

50 metres

More than 8 zones glowing with pulsating light

5 metres

Road

Approx. 2000 metres

Observation point (two men)

Figure 6:2. At Lomonosov, Leningrad, the object shown here was seen by two men on 16 October 1988.

gold), different time parameters (visibility of the UFO was from 2–3 to 40 seconds). At the same time it remained apparent that the heavenly newcomer could not have been imagined by dozens of people simultaneously. Consequently, something really is happening in the heavens . . .

There is no doubt in my mind that the same object flew over the territories of both the Soviet Union and Japan, making several landings in remote, unpopulated regions of the USSR. Unfortunately, no landing traces have been discovered, on account of heavy rain and the subsequent fall of leaves.

Sightings in the Leningrad area

16.10.88

Two men observed the object, sketched in Figure 6:2, at an unspecified time on the evening of 16 October in the region of Lomonosov, Leningrad. At least eight circular areas, glowing with pulsating light, could be seen along its side, and points of light flew away from the object and then returned. (Figure 6:2.)

123

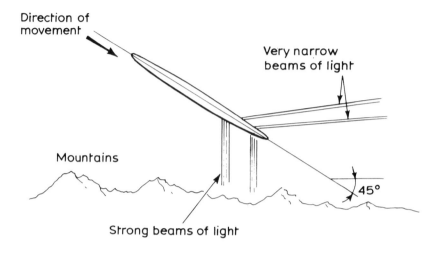

Figure 6:3. The object as seen by two observers at Alma-Ata airfield on 25 October 1988.

20.10.88

At 6.50 p.m. a witness reported seeing a bright red triangle, one-third the size of the full moon, moving slowly close to the horizon, on the road to Koporie, Leningrad state.

25.10.88

Two men on duty at an observation post at Alma-Ata airfield reported seeing a thin, cylindrical object (Figure 6:3), estimated to be 2,500 metres in length, from which very narrow beams of what seemed almost 'solid' light emerged. Sometimes the object remained stationary, then seemed to land. The men did not get permission to investigate the landing site.

UFO Sighting in Dalnegorsk

30.12.88

At 7.45 a.m. on 30 December, Pavel Ujva was driving with a bus-load of passengers on the Primorskaya–Himkombinat route. The sky was clear with only a few high clouds. As he approached a bus-stop, he noticed a bright, pulsating light ahead of the bus. At the next bus-stop he could see that the light had become brighter and he could make out a shape, which was in the form of either a parachute or a triangle, hovering above one of the high mountains, opposite the buildings of the Passenger Auto-transport Association.

The driver announced the presence of the UFO over the intercom, and the passengers disembarked and watched it for one minute.

The object appeared to be half the size of the full moon, and was stationary and noiseless, hovering about 500 metres above the mountains. At the base of the strange craft many points of light could be seen, flashing at intervals of a second, and things like 'aerials' were visible (Figure 6:4).

Beams of light then came down from the object to the aerials on the PATA buildings, and these aerials began to glow with blue-yellow 'hemispheres' (Figure 6:5). A moment later the beams of light disappeared, together with the glowing 'hemispheres'. The driver ordered his passengers to return to the bus, and he drove off. While approaching the next bus-stop, the UFO could be seen ascending and flying in the direction of the sea. (From a report by V. V. Dvujilniy in *Labour World*, 21 January 1989.)

I do not yet know why the Dalniy Vostok area appears to be the focal point for recent sightings in the USSR.

In concluding this report, I would like to point out that the vast majority of the population of the Soviet Union remains woefully ignorant of the facts regarding UFOs. Newspaper articles continue to spread false information, and there is a lack of unity among even like-minded ufologists, which leads to considerable confusion. The Commission for the Investigation of Anomalous Atmospheric Phenomena was disbanded recently, although the local research teams have been regrouped into a new umbrella organization known as 'FACT'. Regrettably, the approach of this group is far from objective, and stories of actual encounters with ufonauts are largely dismissed as nonsense.

To my mind, the only weapon against ignorance is truthful and factual information. It is absolutely clear to me that our planet

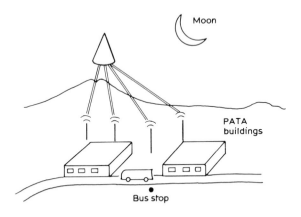

Figure 6:4. Nikolai Lebedev's impression of the object seen on 30 December 1988.

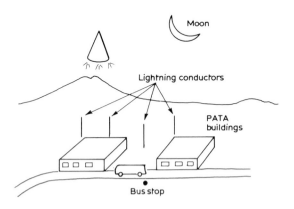

Figure 6:5. Further impressions of the object in Figure 6:4.

is being visited by extraterrestrials. The main task, as I see it, is to establish this fact on an official basis. Alas, I doubt that this will happen until such time as the aliens land beside the Tsar's cannon in the Kremlin . . .

7

UFOs in China
1987–88

PAUL DONG

Paul Dong was born in Canton, China, in 1928, but now lives in Oakland, California. He has been studying the UFO phenomenon for many years and has written over fifty articles for newspapers and journals in China, a number of books, including *The Four Major Mysteries of Mainland China* and *UFOs over Modern China*.

In 1981 Paul Dong lectured on UFOs throughout China, speaking to packed audiences at the Peking Ching Hua University Students Union, Canton Science Museum, and Canton Jinan University, etc.

Paul Dong is an editor of the Chinese language magazine *Journal of UFO Research* (see Appendix).

UFO research has continued for forty years, but has yet to reach any satisfactory conclusion. Because of its mysterious nature, bordering between fact and fantasy, it has attracted the interest of researchers from all countries to track it down, hoping it will some day give us a 'signal'.

Because China was closed to the world for thirty-five years, it only came to recognize UFOs in 1978. This immediately generated much interest, and in the short span of the past ten years, China has compiled over 6,000 UFO cases, including those from ancient times. Of course, among these are many false reports. The percentage of clear-cut cases which cannot easily be explained away was found to be twelve per cent, over twice as high as the rates found by English and US UFO researchers (Dr Allen Hynek, for example, estimated that five to six per cent of UFO reports cannot be explained away). However, because China's researchers were lacking in scientific methodology, further analysis explains a half

128

of those cases, so those which cannot be explained away are also six per cent.

Considering that UFO researchers from other countries have continued to study UFOs with undiminished interest for forty years, while China's UFO researchers started just ten years ago, it is only natural to expect that the Chinese would have a stronger interest in UFOs than researchers from other countries. Just look at our *Journal of UFO Research*. When it came out in 1981, it sold just 150,000 copies. Since then it has been on a steady rise, and its 1988 circulation was 325,000 copies. Isn't that an excellent indication? A further indication is that when people all over mainland China first became interested in UFOs, there were no more than twenty-eight UFO research associations, while today the number has increased to thirty-six.

China's UFO researchers lack funding, communications, photographic equipment, instruments, and scientific techniques; otherwise, China would have even more UFO students and our UFO magazine would have even wider circulation (an initial estimate would be 500,000 copies). To mention a few examples, at the second National UFO Convention, held on 24 February in Guangzhou (Canton), the number of delegates giving presentations was no more than 121, from a base of thirty-six local branch UFO associations. Thus, each organization sent only three delegates. Afterwards, I inquired why they had so few speakers. The answer was that they were unable to buy train tickets – China has a population of one billion, and it usually takes one month to buy a train ticket!

It was ten years on 30 July 1988 since the founding of China's UFO associations, and they held a 'Ten Year Commemorative Exhibition', also in Guangzhou. Because participation was not limited to UFO association members, it attracted UFO amateurs, journalists, and television film teams from all over the country. An estimated one million people saw the exhibition. The display showed UFO photography from around the world, books, magazines, slide shows, UFO postage stamps from many countries, special publications of all the local branch research associations, and so on. Our *Journal of UFO Research* sold 36,000 copies during the week of the exhibition.

UFOs over China, an eighteen-minute colour documentary film shot five years earlier, was also shown at the exhibition. Since it came out, theatres all over the country have clamoured for it, because the film's length does not interfere with the time for the main feature film, and also because China has about ten million UFO enthusiasts. As a result, this film has continued playing for a long time.

In view of the large number of UFO followers, some people might wonder why the *Journal of UFO Research* sells only 325,000 copies. [Even allowing for China's huge population, this is an enviable figure compared to Western UFO magazine sales – Editor.] Permit me to explain. Since everybody there has a low income (on average, 120 *yuan* in Chinese currency per person per month, equal to 30 US dollars), one magazine or book is usually passed along and read by more than ten people. Everyone lends books to one another. Also, many people do not buy books but do go to the library to read them.

Sightings in 1988

There were not very many UFO cases in China in 1988, but there were still over twenty reports. Some of them had rather low levels of credibility. What follows is a selection of the two best cases and a separate description of each one.

Xinjiang Airlines Sighting

The New China News Agency of 20 March reported that at 9.35 p.m. on 18 March, Xinjiang Airlines flight 2606 from Beijing to Urumqi was flying above Qijiaojing, Hami County, at an altitude of 11,000 metres, when suddenly somebody discovered that a ball of light the size of a basketball, radiating intense beams of light as though from a flashlight, and flying in the opposite direction to the aircraft, had appeared on the aircraft's front starboard side. The crew immediately contacted Urumqi air traffic control, who replied that there was no other flight activity. Members of the crew turned on the plane's navigation lights as a signal. There was no response.

Three minutes later, the ball of light changed course and flew off to the north and meanwhile turned into two shapes of light, one above the other. The upper part was a small circular shape, and the lower part appeared as bean-shaped. The two parts were both revolving rapidly. A green halo appeared outside the circle of light.

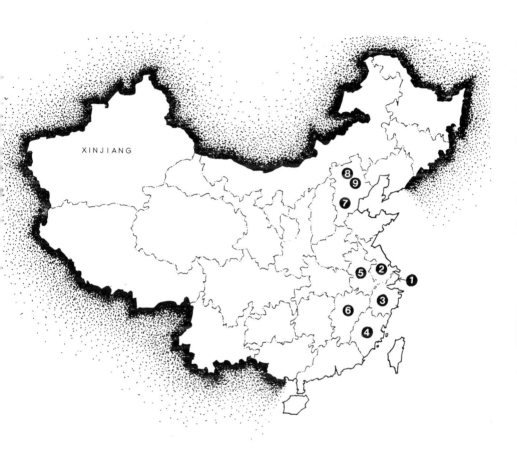

Figure 7:1. China. 1 – Shanghai: 2 – Jiangsu: 3 – Zhejiang: 4 – Fujian: 5 – Anhui: 6 – Jiangxi: 7 – Hebei: 8 – Beijing: 9 – Tianjin.

At this moment, the lights on the plane went off and the passengers on the plane saw this scene before their eyes and followed the two forms as they went into the distance and gradually got smaller. At 9.48 p.m. the unidentified flying object disappeared northward into the night.

Half an hour after the event, when flight 2011 was returning from Guangzhou to Urumqi, flying close to the Hami region, other people saw this UFO.

Corroboration

With regard to this event, Hami Television Broadcasting Bureau Vice-Chairman and head of Hami Television, Fan Chengliang, submitted a report to the *Journal of UFO Research*, which appeared in the journal in the fourth quarter of 1988, and is a more detailed account:

> At nine o'clock in the evening on March 18th 1988, I left the office building to return home. When I had reached a point some 10 metres from the building, I suddenly saw a very large ball of light surrounded by a hazy glow in the north-western sky before me. At the time, my first impression was that it was a solar eclipse, because a partial solar eclipse was scheduled on that day. However, I immediately realized that was wrong, because it was past nine o'clock in the evening, and the solar eclipse had occurred 12 hours ago. A lunar eclipse? That was not possible, either. The 18th was the first day of the second month on the lunar calendar, a new moon, so there was no moon out that night. Just then, several students came over. I pointed it out to them and asked them what it was. After looking at it a while, they said it was a disc rotating in a ball of light. I became aware that this might be one of those UFOs which people often speak of.
>
> I gave a quick glance at my watch, and the hands showed precisely 9.36 p.m. By that time I had been watching the UFO for about two minutes, which means that the UFO must have appeared at 9.34 p.m. Suddenly, a child shouted, "It is flying, it is flying!", and when I looked again, the ball of light, which had been hovering motionlessly, was indeed rapidly moving eastward. In an instant, it had flown from the west of the first antenna to the second antenna of our bureau's station 7601. Also, changes in its shape had occurred, beginning as an elongated, upright circular shape, and then making a somewhat smaller circle of light, and in a little while, it formed into a horizontal cigar shape (this may have been an illusion caused by the sideways flying motion of the object). Nevertheless, the yellowish-green halo it produced and the hazy glow surrounding it remained the same throughout.
>
> At this point I realized the need to take a picture, so I rushed back the approximately 80 metres to the television station office building. Before I got there I heard a commotion from the building. Several workers on duty for that shift had run out and were looking at the flying saucer. It turned out

that they had also received calls from viewers. I ran up to the editing room but failed to find a photographer, so I just stood on the second-floor balcony and watched. The ball of light was still in the field of vision, but apparently its brightness had weakened, and it was getting further and further away. At 9.46 p.m. the flying object flew off to the east-north-east and suddenly disappeared. By this time the sky was full of stars, and there was silence everywhere.

In my judgement, the unidentified flying object flew from the north-west to the east-north-east, at times hovering motionlessly, at times moving rapidly, and it could fly straight up and down. It remained in my field of vision fully 12 minutes. The flying saucer appeared about 15 to 20 kilometres from the city of Hami, at a height of about 2,000 to 3,000 metres.

Before dawn on March 19th on Xinjiang People's Radio News, and on the 20th on the Central Television Station's evening news, it was promptly reported that two passenger planes (Beijing–Urumqi flight 2606 and Guangzhou–Urumqi flight 2011) encountered an unidentified flying object in the airspace above Qijiaojing, Hami County (located 200 kilometres from the northern end of Hami, and 130 kilometres from Hami). The times of their encounters were from 9.35 to 9.48 p.m., one minute off the time of my observation.

Among those in the television broadcasting bureau who had seen this flying object were: television shift workers Wu Wanjun, Ahmed Jiang (Uigur ethnicity), Mi Xiuchun (female, Hui ethnicity), anchorman Ming Aijun, security guard Xu Yongchang, technical engineer Cheng Jingchun, technician Ju Hang. Among the students were: Zhang Gaofeng (Hami High School 4, high junior), Ding Zhipeng (H.S. 2, starting sophomore), Zou Dongjiang (H.S. 5, starting junior), Fan Nanjia (H.S. 4, high sophomore), Wang Xiaofeng (H.S. 4, starting freshman), Liang Yong (Elementary School 4, sixth grader), Cheng Gang (Railroad Technical High School 2, high sophomore) – over 10 people in all.

The event described above not only caught the attention of UFO researchers in China, but also the Civil Aviation Commission and the Air Force.

Important Sightings in August 1987

Another sensational UFO event took place from 27 to 31 August 1987. Although this story does not belong to 1988 news, there was a recurrence of it on 22 January 1988, therefore the following report, from the *Journal of UFO Research*, is relevant.

From 27 to 31 August 1987, an unidentified flying object was observed simultaneously in the areas of Jiansu, Zhejiang, Fujian, Anhui, and Jiangxi provinces, with China's largest industrial city, Shanghai, as centre, and also in Beijing, Tianjin (Hebei

Province). Many thousands of people were witnesses to the spectacle, including workers, peasants, People's Liberation Army men, technical engineering specialists, university students, high school students, graduate students, workers in the news media, university students, high school teachers, and so on.

According to incomplete figures, the editorial department of the *Journal of UFO Research* received 600 eyewitness accounts. The reputable news media organization New China News Agency, *People's Daily, Literary News, Liberation Daily, New People's Evening News, Zhejiang Daily*, and Shanghai television and radio stations, all reported this incident from different perspectives.

Shanghai

Zhang Zhengyong, a teacher at Shanghai's Guanghua High School, reported:

'It was a cloudless sky with excellent visibility on the evening of 27th August. Around 7.55 p.m., Beijing standard time, an unidentified object flew from the north-west toward the south-east. The flying object was orange, and consisted of a ring of light revolving around an extremely bright focal point. Surrounding it was a hazy glow in the form of a spiral with three twists, spinning in a clockwise motion about once every two seconds. The glow was a pale earthen orange colour, and the flying object was noiseless and flying very rapidly, disappearing in probably half a minute . . .'

Wuxi City

Three aviation engineers at Wuxi Aviation Bureau Convalescent Hospital No. 738 reported that at 7.57 p.m., an unidentified object flew across the sky. 'At first, it covered a diameter of observation of about 300–400 millimetres,' they said. 'It was flying across the sky on a spiral course, leaving a trail of red and orange light behind it. At the centre was a circular point of light.'

Hangzhou City

On the evening of 27 August, the busy airport was quiet after the 10.15 p.m. flight had left. Ping Xiaojun, an Air Force air controller, was leaning on the fence outside the control tower, looking into the clear night sky. 'Suddenly, I noticed an unusual

134

glowing object hovering about 900 metres from the end of the runway,' he said. 'It was giving off an orange glow. Because of its rather small size and the dazzling brightness of the light, I cannot describe its shape precisely.'

New China News Agency
28.08.87

Our correspondent in Shanghai reports that quite a number of Shanghai residents observed an unidentified flying object yesterday evening. Eyewitness descriptions of the shape of the object varied. Some said it was a spiral beam of light scattering sparks behind it, some said it appeared to be an oval disc of light, while others said it looked like a comet with a tail shaped like an umbrella.

According to reports, the unidentified flying object was orange, spinning clockwise, and moving rapidly from west to east, with only a few seconds from the time of its appearance to its disappearance. According to another report wired in from Shengsi county, Zhejiang Province, when the UFO flew over that area, the Shengsi county electric generator was suddenly cut off, even though the switch for its turbine was set as normal, and the island was instantly thrown into darkness. *The majority of people's wristwatches stopped* [Editor's italics]. Just then, the object, shaped like a coiling snake, was seen to spin across from the north-west towards the south-east. Its trail was as bright as day. Because the electricity was cut off, the majority of military and civilian residents on the island noticed the spectacle.

Air Force pilot's sighting

According to the *Liberation Daily* of 30 August, Mao Xuecheng, an Air Force pilot stationed at Shanghai, pursued a UFO for nearly three minutes on the evening of 27 August. As he related to reporters:

'I had orders to fly at 7.35 p.m. on the 27th, and to return to base after completing air patrol duty. As I was approaching the airspace above the Yangtze river, I suddenly observed that ahead of me to the right, above Jiading county, was a very bright, dazzling flying object. I immediately hit the throttle hard and pursued it closely from an angle of 110 degrees at a rate of 900 k.p.h. At that time, the clock was showing a little past 7.57 p.m.

'I observed carefully and noticed that the unidentified object was descending, the focus of light was an orange spot, and the spiral tail it was trailing was also orange. At 7.59 p.m. it went from descending to ascending, and its speed was now much faster than when it had been descending. After 45 more seconds I was unable to keep up with it, so I requested permission to land.'

Following the 27 August incident, a spokesperson for the Chinese Academy of Sciences observatory expressed the following opinion:

'Judging from the shape and mode of movement of the UFO, we may be certain that it was neither an airplane, nor a shooting star, nor a comet. It is also extremely improbable that it was an alien visitor. It is possible that UFOs are man-made flying objects, because they come in many different shapes and sizes, and perhaps while spinning at a height of a few hundred kilometres, they can shine by reflecting sunlight. In addition, we cannot rule out the possibility that UFOs are a natural phenomenon produced by the earth and the air.'

James Oberg of NASA was equally convinced that the sightings had a rational explanation. 'The UFO which appeared in the sky around Shanghai on the evening of August 27th was actually a large quantity of fuel released by a rocket launched by the Japanese,' he commented. 'Three hours before the incident, Japan launched an H-1A rocket 600 miles east of Shanghai, which flew over the Shanghai vicinity twice.' This explanation was quoted by *People's Daily* in September, and newspapers everywhere quickly spread it.

The mystery of 27 August appeared to have been solved. 'Was the UFO which appeared on August 27th a carrier rocket launched by Japan?', the newspapers asked. 'Was it mass hallucination? To put it differently, have the UFO phenomena observed all over the world up to now all been discarded carrier rockets or other aerial objects created by human ingenuity, or figments of the imagination? There are different schools of thought on these questions. Investigation and research is continuing, and the controversy is far from finished.'

Lu Feng, in a submission to the *Journal of UFO Research*, stated that the Japanese rocket explanation was invalid, for the following reasons: Out of the 112 eyewitness reports collected from Shanghai, two said they had seen portholes on the object,

场跑道东大约900米上空处有一特殊发光物。它悬在空中，散发着桔红色的光华。由于发光体较小和光的耀眼，我无法确切地描绘它的几何形体……" 这是驻杭州空军飞行管制员平小军的观察记录。

据新华社北京8月28日电讯稿载："本报讯上海记者报道，咋天晚上不少上海市民观察到天空出现不明飞行物体。目击者称，发现不明飞行物的时间大约是晚7时50分到8时30分之间。目击者对飞行物的形状描述不一，有的说是'螺旋形光束，后散为光点'，有的称似'椭圆形光盘'，还有'象望远，尾部光圈似伞形'的说法。据报告者说，不明飞行物呈桔黄色，顺时针旋转，自西向东快速移动，从出现到消失仅数秒钟。另据一通讯员自浙江嵊泗县来电称，这一不明飞行物经过当地天空时，嵊泗县发电厂在机器运转正常并未关闭的情况下，突然停电，瞬间岛上一片黑暗。人们戴的手表大部分都停止走动。只见一形如旧螺，若直升飞机需要众大小的物体由西北向东南旋转运行，所经之处如白昼。因为停电，岛上大部分驻军和居民都睹了这一景象。

据《解放日报》8月30日报道："驻沪空军某部飞行员毛学成8月27晚驾机追踪不明飞行物达2分45秒。毛学成向记者叙述道：'27晚7点35分，我奉命驾机起飞，执行空中巡逻任务后返波。当我飞临长江上空时，突然发现有前方嘉定县上空有一个很亮、刺眼的飞行物体。我立即加大油门，以900公里时速与它成110度夹角紧紧追赶。此时，时针指在7点57分上。我经过仔细观察，发现不明飞行物在下降。亮点部分颜色为桔黄色，后面拖着的螺旋形尾巴也呈桔黄色。7点59分，它突然下降为上升，速度比下降要快得多。又过

了45秒，我未能追上它，于是请求者随去了。

8·27事件后，一些权威人士回答了记者的提问。中科院上海天文台发言人认为，"根据不明飞行物的形态和运动方式，可以肯定，这个物体不是飞机，也不是流星和彗星。'天外来客'的可能性也极小。不明飞行物有可能是一人造飞行体，因为它们的形状多种多样，大小不一，且有可能旋转运行，高度约为数百

公里以上，它们靠反射太阳光而发光。另外，也不排除不明飞行物是地球及大气本身产生的一种自然现象的可能性。"

美国得克萨斯州航天工程师詹姆斯·奥本格接受记者电话采访时说："8·27晚出现在上海附近上空的不明飞行物体实际上是日本发射的一枚火箭释放出的大量燃料。在那之前3小时，日本在上海以东600英里处发射了一枚H—1A火箭，并两次飞临上

海上空。"他认为上海附近人们看到的不明飞行物却这枚日本发射的火箭有密切关系。这一说法被《人民日报》在9月份的报纸中引用，各地报纸纷纷转载，8·27之谜仿佛已拨到汗。

8·27出现的不明飞行物是日本发射的运载火箭吗？是人们的集体幻觉吗？换句话说，世界上迄今发现的UFO现象，都是废弃运载火箭或其它人造飞行工具的杰作或都是人们的幻觉的产物吗？对于这些问题，仁者见仁，智者见智，探讨和研究仍在进行，争论也会由之迭起。

如同地球人必须摆脱地球人生命的模式去研究其它星球上智慧生命的模式一样，地球人也必须摆脱地球人的物理法则，去研究隐藏得更深的宇宙法则。或许，8·27之谜仅仅是人类固有的哲学观、宇宙观未一次大革命中的一个小小前插曲。

《荆铁 图》

Figure 7:2. Air Force pilot Mao Xuecheng pursued a UFO for 2 minutes 45 seconds on 27 August 1988 (with acknowledgement to the Journal of UFO Research*).*

and several had seen the object stop in mid-air. Most importantly, a pilot with many years experience reported that he saw the object gradually lower an auxiliary object, and from the way the object rose straight up, he further surmised that it was self-propelled. As an afterthought, he added that the way the electricity was suddenly cut off while the generator mechanism was working normally when the object passed through Shengsi County, Zhejiang Province, was a typical case of an electricity blackout when a UFO passes. Many such incidents had occurred throughout the world.

This incident was discussed for months in the Chinese press. Just when discussion was dying down, at 11.30 p.m. on 22 January 1988, a similar object flew over Shanghai. The sighting lasted half a minute. This time, however, there were not many witnesses. It was seen only in Shanghai and all the events were the same as before except that there was no electricity blackout. Commented Zhang Yunhua of the Shanghai UFO Research Association: 'Spiral UFOs over China are not rare. Since 1977, flying objects have passed over a number of provinces on many occasions. There have been three cases when the objects were seen by thousands of people [including the 27 August case]. The first case took place on 26 July 1977, and the second on 24 July 1981.'

The Future

In the period from the beginning of UFO research in China ten years ago to the present day, a greater competence in dealing with the subject has developed. For example, seven years ago I was appointed Editor-in-Chief of the *Journal of UFO Research* (the only UFO magazine in China). Six years later they replaced me, and five local people are now able to handle all editorial duties. Six years ago I wrote a feature called 'Questions & Answers on UFOs', and today I note that researchers have begun to write similar articles. In addition, they have discovered sixty examples of UFO reports in ancient Chinese books. And with the rise of psychic research in China in the past few years, they have discovered that there is some kind of relationship between UFOs and the paranormal.

Practically all developments in Chinese UFO research parallel the experience undergone in such Western countries as the USA,

UK, France, and Australia. Even more fascinating, the Japanese have been enthusiastically seeking out and collecting Chinese UFO material.

In another ten years, perhaps, Chinese UFO research will begin to display its own unique features . . .

8

UFO Encounters along
the Nullarbor Plain

PAUL NORMAN

Paul Norman was born and educated in the United States. With
the exception of six years in the US Navy and a short period
as a publisher's representative, he has been employed in various
positions, including superintendent in hydro-electric stations and
engineer-in-charge of thermal-electric stations.

He became interested in UFOs in 1953, after observing a strange
object approach and hover over a power station in Tennessee. His
interest was intensified when Major Donald Keyhoe was cut off a
coast-to-coast TV network while attempting to tell the public about
official UFO investigations – an incident that prompted him to join
the fight to end the cover-up.

In 1963 Paul Norman emigrated to Melbourne, Australia, where
he continues his research with the Victorian UFO Research Society
(VUFORS) as Vice-President and Investigations Officer. In 1979 he
joined MUFON as State Director for Victoria. He is also a member
of BUFORA.

He opted for early retirement in 1976 in order to devote his time
to UFO research. Since then he has travelled the world in search of
answers to the phenomenon, spending summers in both the northern
and southern hemispheres. He has contributed several articles for
various UFO publications and organizations throughout the world.

January 21 1988, commenced as a routine day for me. After
awakening, I switched on my bedside radio for the morning news
broadcast. There was mention that some sort of a UFO incident
had occurred on the Eyre Highway near the remote Mundrabilla
roadhouse about midway across the Nullarbor Plain in Western
Australia.

After shifting from one station to another the story began to emerge as a significant case worth a follow-up investigation. A Perth woman, Faye Knowles, and her three adult sons, Patrick, Sean, and Wayne, had claimed that an unidentified flying object had picked up their 1984 Ford Telstar and given it a shake before dropping it back to the ground.

I dressed hurriedly and rushed to the news agency for copies of the Melbourne newspapers to see what was being published about the incident. What made the story more interesting was that policemen were taking the report seriously because of physical evidence to support the claim – *and* there were other witnesses.

The Nullarbor Plain is a dry limestone, almost featureless landscape with little rainfall occurring during the year. The plain extends to 180 miles west and 150 miles east of the state border between South Australia and Western Australia. The width from the Great Australian Bight is about 150 miles. The name Nullarbor means no trees. Only bluebushes and saltbushes survive the harsh desert climate. Underground, there are many caves with only a few having been explored. The openings to the caves are usually very small and hard to find. Some were formerly inhabited by Aborigines.

After reading the newspaper versions about the event, I finally got a telephone call through to Judith Magee, President of the Victorian UFO Research Society (VUFORS), in Melbourne. She had been tied up all morning answering calls concerning the fast-breaking story. Judy passed on the information and said John Auchettl, VUFORS investigator, was already in contact with Mr Frank Pangallo, Chief of Staff at the Channel 7 TV Station in Adelaide, who was interested in contacting some one who knew something about UFO investigation.

Meanwhile, more details were coming to light concerning the incident. The family had stopped at Mundrabilla before the restaurant had opened for business. Three truck drivers were waiting to have their breakfast. One driver, Graham Henley, from Melbourne, was the first person to talk to the family about thirty minutes after they had left the scene where the highlight of the activity had taken place.

Mr Henley said that all four were distressed and in a state of shock. Two dogs were cowering inside the car in a state of fright as well. The car was covered with a black sooty substance, which was described as a fine silicon-type material. Later, reports

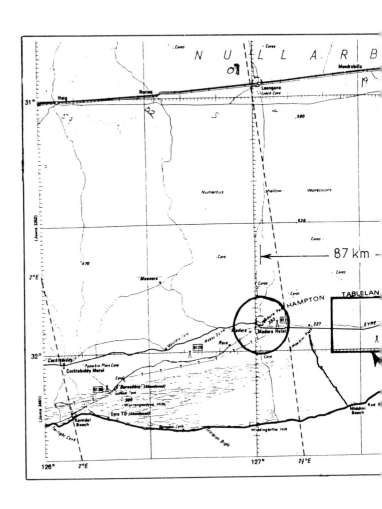

Figure 8:1. Maps showing the 'Encounter Location' in the Nullarbor Plain with inset indicating the position of the area concerned (© Commonwealth of Australia 1977).

142

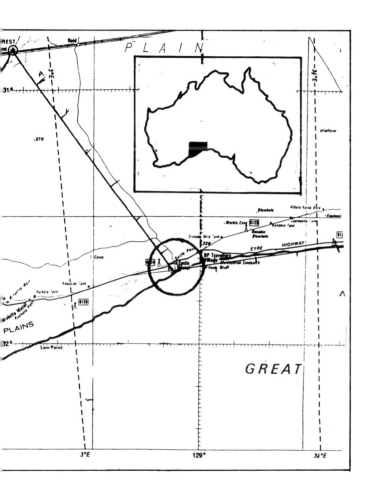

came from the police station at Ceduna, in South Australia, where the Knowles stopped to make the report. The Ceduna police confirmed the excessive amount of black dust and said it was unknown material and that a forensic policeman had taken samples for analysis. Policemen at Ceduna confirmed that the occupants were visibly shaken as well. One officer said that calls had come in from other people claiming to have seen flying objects within the same week, including another truck driver who reported that his vehicle was being paced about the time of the Knowles' encounter and near the same location.

Debunking Attempts

As the story began to spread through the press, radio, and TV, the sceptics (armchair experts) increased their debunking attempts, even before investigations had commenced. Within forty-eight hours five 'explanations' came in rapid succession from the scientific community; all contradictory, none satisfactory. This was the type of mysterious event that makes ufologists out of academics and clowns out of sceptics.

One of the first 'explanations' came from a professor of impossibility, Ph.D., EtC, EtC, as being consistent with a meteorite, in spite of the fact that the object landed on top of a motor car before flying away moments later. Following this attempt another 'solution' was put forward by a second gentleman of learning: 'The description of the event was consistent with dry lightning', even though other motorists were driving along the highway and viewed the manoeuvring object and confirmed that no electrical storm was in the vicinity.

After that amusing interpretation, another spokesman from the scientific community came up with the 'solution' that the occupants were fooled by the rising sun, even though motorists travelling in the opposite direction saw the manoeuvring object fly away in the other direction.

Another expert said it must have originated at the Woomera Test Range. That statement was followed by another spokesman who said that could not be true because it would not be allowed. My own opinion is: of course not, unless it was out of control. But even so, how could a missile strike or lift a motor, and drop it back down to the ground with only minor damage?

144

Prior to the arrival of the car in Adelaide, where the first debunking efforts were made, the Knowles' experience was being treated seriously until the dedicated debunkers got into the act. The first samples of dust alleged to have been analysed were done by employees of a laboratory in Adelaide. The statement released to the press was: 'The dust was mostly iron oxide consistent with residue from worn brake linings.' The large amount of dust was ignored. The report was distributed in Australia and overseas as if it were God's gift to the sceptics. Apparently the first analysts did not realize the matter would be taken further afield.

Whether the report was an effort to cover up or some other reason, I am not prepared to state. The opinion of other analysts is that the dust from the brake linings was mixed with dust from other parts of the car. Naturally, the result would show predominantly brake dust. VUFORS samples taken were kept separate and analysed accordingly. With comments being made by dedicated debunkers from various sources such as: 'The family was mesmerized by a light in the sky; had been driving all night, dozed off and had overturned the car'; or 'UFO experiences occur during dozing-off stage and while awakening (dreamtime ufology)', made the situation urgent that ufologists should begin investigations.

The facts are: Dreams do not leave holes in the ground. Dreams do not lift motor cars off the road. Nor do dreams lift helicopters hundreds of feet as experienced by Larry Coyne and his crew while flying over the American state of Ohio in October 1973.

Meanwhile, the first person to have spoken to the family after their terrifying experience, Melbourne truck driver Graham Henley, broadcast a statement that theories aimed at debunking the encounter, 'were a lot of rot'. He said he had felt the sooty material and it was not brake dust. He had been around the car-racing scene as well as being a truck driver and knew what brake dust was like, and added that the substance on the car was a fine silicon-type material with an incredible feel to it. Brake dust only gets on the wheels, not on the roof. Furthermore, the brakes were not even hot (it was the coolest part of the morning). Besides, he was convinced when the Knowles first told him what they had experienced earlier that they had seen something frightening when he saw the terror on their faces. Even the dogs were scared.

145

The Encounter in Detail

By 25 January, John Auchettl had made arrangements for an interview with the Knowles family, who had arrived in Melbourne. Interviews were to be conducted by himself, Judith Magee (VUFORS President), Mark Sawyers (Secretary), and myself. We arrived at the address of a relative with whom the family was visiting and found the Knowles still in a state of distress and suffering from an assortment of symptoms, including the swelling of Faye's right hand and arm.

We learned that the incident occurred before daylight after the family had left the Madura Roadhouse and were heading east towards Mundrabilla, when they sighted a group of lights. They thought at first that these were street lights but then realized that there were no street lights in that part of the outback.

During the three-hour interviews with the mother and her three sons we were told several details of the encounter. Although it was difficult to determine the sequence of the different phases of the activity, some of the highlights were clear in the memory of one or more members of the family. Beginning about a quarter of an hour before the lights were first spotted, the car radio started malfunctioning, with a lot of static and other noise which continued for the entire period of the encounter.

At another stage Sean saw another light ahead. He thought at first that it was a truck with one headlight, but as he got closer he saw that it was not a truck but a strange brightly glowing light either on the road or hovering slightly above the ground. It was on his side of the highway so he had to swerve to the wrong side of the road, and looked up just in time to see an approaching car pulling a caravan. They almost collided.

Soon after the near collision, the Knowles met another vehicle, with a light flying at the same speed above it. By this time Sean's curiosity got the best of him and he made a U-turn and sped back towards the west to see what the light was. After chasing it for a few moments the light changed course and headed back towards the Knowles' car. Sean then made another quick turn, and as he was speeding towards the east again, the object overtook the car and landed on the roof with a thud (see Figure 8:2). Patrick said that the object seemed to grab the car and began to pull it up. At the same time he yelled out, 'Why us?'

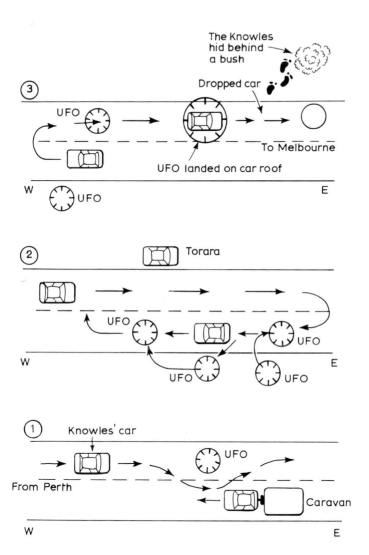

Figure 8:2. This diagram (not to scale) illustrates how the UFO attacked the Knowles family around 0500 hours (W.A. time) on 21 January 1988 (adapted from a sketch by a sister of Mrs Knowles).

Figure 8:3. The Knowles family. Left to right: Faye, Patrick, Sean, and Wayne.

'We did not know what to do,' said Patrick. 'The dogs started to go crazy.' All four felt as if they were about to die. Patrick said that he felt as though his brains were being pulled from his head.

Sean did not realize that the car was in the air until it dropped back to the ground, bursting the right rear tyre. He thought he was doing 200 k.p.h. (120 m.p.h.) to escape from under the UFO. While the object was on the roof, Faye rolled down the window so she could reach up and touch the object. It felt like a warm sponge and she thought it might be a suction pad. She began to scream. Patrick, who was in the front passenger seat, rolled down his window, and dust started pouring into the car. When Faye pulled her arm back inside the car her arm was covered with this dust. She said there was an odour that she thought smelled like decayed bodies. [Abductee Alfred Burtoo reported a smell of 'decaying meat' during his encounter in Aldershot, England, in 1983, as described in *Above Top Secret* – Editor.]

Sean reported that at one stage he was 'out cold' and could not remember some of the details related to us by other members of the family. During the time the car was in the air their voices sounded as though they were talking in 'slow motion'.

When Sean brought the car to a stop, all jumped out and hid in the bushes along the side of the highway until the UFO flew away. The family described the object as a white light about the size of the car, with a yellow centre, 'like an egg in a cup'. The sound was similar to a humming transformer. They changed the tyre as quickly as possible before speeding on to Mundrabilla, where they talked about the frightful experience with three truck drivers. One of the drivers had been driving some distance ahead and saw a bright, white light with a yellow centre through his rear-view mirror.

The Investigation Begins

After the interviews we realized that the case required urgent follow-up investigation on a priority basis. This prompted John Auchettl and I to go to Adelaide and check out the car first-hand. On 30 January we arrived in Adelaide and did some preliminary work. Three days later John flew in from Melbourne and joined me at Channel 7 TV station for the appointment with Mr Pangallo, who arranged for us to begin inspection and test of the car. Dust in sufficient amounts for several laboratory analyses was vacuumed from inside and outside the car, and was also scraped from the brake linings, to compare with samples taken from inside the car.

We found the radio which had malfunctioned during the encounter to be operating satisfactorily. The dents on the roof were found to be just as the family had described: they were very slight with the largest one about the size and depth of an ordinary saucer. Reports of a rack or baggage strapped to the roof were false, as we learned from the family. A story being told both locally and abroad was that the damage was caused by the roof rack and the owner was trying to collect insurance money by telling the story. Philip Klass, America's foremost UFO debunker, offered that story as an explanation. So much for his methods of scientific investigation – there never was a roof rack!

The tyre was found to be damaged from a blow-out and was ripped all the way around the circumference (see Figures 8:4, 8:5). The side mirror on the driver's side was broken, but Sean

Figure 8:4. The Knowles' car on 1 February 1988. It was inspected by Paul Norman (shown) and John Auchettl.

Figure 8:5. The damaged tyre.

explained that this happened when they hit a kangaroo while driving in the dark.

Sean had reported that he had been going 200 k.p.h. (120 m.p.h.) to escape from under the UFO. The 1984 Ford Telstar, a four-cylinder front-wheel-drive automobile, will not go that fast while on the ground. To check Sean's story, the wheels were jacked off the ground, and in a test documented by Channel 7 on video, it was shown that the speedometer will register 200 k.p.h. under those conditions.

After some of the tests were televised on the news programme on the night of 1 Feburary, we understand that some of the sceptics made adjustments to their earlier comments. The story was being treated seriously again.

On 20 March I left Melbourne for San Francisco, arriving there in time for the Bay Area branch meeting of the Mutual UFO Network at Mountain View, where I gave a set of the samples to Dr Richard Haines, a scientist from NASA's Ames Research Center. A few days later Dr Haines submitted the samples to the 'state-of-the-art' Philips Laboratory. Since this laboratory is one of the most advanced in America, with many people using its facilities, we had to wait our turn.

In a letter from Dr Haines, dated 12 July 1988, he enclosed a report entitled 'Scanning Electron Microscope Results of Mundrabilla Dust and Other Samples'. The interior dust was *not* from the brake system of the car, he reported. This was in direct contradiction to the original findings reported by the analysts in Adelaide. The Philips Laboratory analysis also revealed the presence of '. . . oxygen, carbon, calcium silicon, potassium, and others. The analyst found fibres typical of pipe insulation but it is not asbestos. Many of the fibres contained carbon and oxygen only (cellulose fibres). Atomic element 85 (At; astatine) is also possible in the sample as is a relatively long fibre of NaCL which is unusual. However, NaAT does combine in fibre-like form . . .'

On 3 July I returned to Melbourne. Due to briefings with the VUFORS committee and the necessity of catching up with accumulated correspondence and other matters, I was delayed until 22 July before going to the Nullarbor Plain and other areas in Western Australia. Priority for the trip was due, of course, to the fact that the Knowles' experience had emerged as the foremost mystery case of the decade in Australia.

Further Corroboration

The highlight of the itinerary was without doubt a visit with a resident of Norseman who was in the Nullarbor area at the time of the Knowles' encounter and had a report of his own experience. Not only did this key witness provide me with accommodation and hospitality in his home, but spent many hours driving me to the spot where the car had skidded, and over several miles around the Nullarbor Plain.

The witness reported that soon after daylight on the day of the event, fibre-like substance was scattered in places along the bitumen highway for about three-quarters of a mile from where the Knowles' car was dropped. At that time he did not realize that the material was associated with the UFO. As he picked up some of the fibres, they crumbled into a powder or dust between his fingers. The dust was similar to graphite, only much lighter.

A few days later this man began to suffer an illness similar to the Knowles family, only his symptoms were more severe. He was admitted to a hospital but did not report the mysterious experience because he feared ridicule. Nevertheless, efforts are now being made to determine whether or not the illness was related.

It now appears that dust samples vacuumed from inside the car were the best samples, free of contamination from outside sources. The apparatus used to analyse the dust was a scanning electron microscope with an EDAX analyser and ECON detector. Some of the particles were magnified 5,000 times.

The mention of possible astatine in the samples aroused my curiosity, since I had suspected some sort of radiation that did not show up by the time the car had reached South Australia, where it was checked for radiation but found to be negative. My reason for thinking radiation was involved was due to the swelling of Faye's arm, hair falling from the dog in patches, and other symptoms.

Astatine is a radioactive chemical element that has no stable isotopes. It was synthetically produced in 1940 at the University of California, where scientists bombarded bismuth with accelerated alpha particles (helium nuclei) to yield the element 85 Astatine. After the reaction, it has a half-life of only seven to eight hours before decaying. The Knowles did not arrive in Ceduna, South

Australia, until 1.00 p.m. after the pre-dawn encounter. Naturally, the astatine, if that is what it was, would have decayed by that time.

One hour after the Knowles left Mundrabilla, they stopped at the Border Village Service Station to enquire about the cost of a tyre. The service station attendant with whom I spoke said, 'I thought at first the four were trying to be funny when they were telling me about their experience. They were excited and scared. When I got near the car I noticed an odour similar to that of hot insulation, and there was definitely a scent like ozone.'

The Police Report

The first police station to receive a report directly from the Knowles was the Ceduna station in South Australia. At that time they were still in a state of fright. They had passed two police stations, one at Eucla, in Western Australia, and one at Penong in South Australia. The station at Eucla is well hidden behind small trees in that vicinity, although there is a sign on the opposite side of the road from the station. At the early stage after the experience the Knowles did not know what to do or who to report to. The following report was taken down by a policeman at the Ceduna station and was given to me during a visit there on 23 July:

At about 1.00 p.m. (S.A. time) on Wednesday, 20th January, 1988, I was approached at the Ceduna Police Station by two male persons (Sean Knowles and his brother Patrick Knowles). They reported to me that while driving on the Eyre Highway at a point between Madura and Mundrabilla in Western Australia at about 5.30 a.m. (W.A. time) this date they were confronted by an extremely white light about 50 to 60 feet in front of their vehicle. They described the light as being extremely bright, was white with a yellow core. They further stated that their vehicle, a Ford Telstar, had been damaged by the object when it landed on the roof of their vehicle while they were travelling at a speed of about 110 kilometres an hour. They further stated that the object while on the roof of their vehicle had showered the vehicle with a black ash-type dust.

They displayed great anxiety and were visibly shaken by the ordeal. I asked why they had not reported the incident to the Police Station at Eucla in Western Australia prior to leaving that state, and they informed me that they had not sighted a Police Station at Eucla. Neither did I receive from them a completely satisfactory explanation as to why they had not reported the matter at the Penong Police Station, being the first Police Station in

South Australia which they had passed. This may have been a double-sided question therefore receiving the one answer.

The vehicle was parked in Poynton Street, Ceduna. I attended at the vehicle in company with the two persons and made an inspection of the damage to the hood of the vehicle which they indicated to me as having been caused by the object when on the vehicle. I found that there were superficial dents to the four corners of the hood although the remainder of the hood appeared undamaged. The exterior of the vehicle was covered by a fine black/grey dust similar to a road film left on a vehicle in need of washing. That same dust was obvious on the upholstery within the vehicle. An inspection of the complete vehicle indicated that it appeared quite well looked after and did not display any noticeable damage consistent with having been involved in an accident or collision of any kind. All tyres on the vehicle were in good condition and showed at least $3/4$ tread.

They told me that whilst attempting to escape from the object, the rear right-hand side tyre on the vehicle had blown out. I asked to see the tyre which was produced from the boot of the vehicle. The tyre was of the same make as the other tyres on the vehicle and has the same tread wear. It was in good condition. However, the complete outer side of the tyre was fractured at the base of the tread. I asked for the vehicle to be conveyed to the police station where I could speak further with the occupants of the vehicle and make further examination.

On return to the station I spoke with Mrs Faye Knowles and her son Sean together in a location where we were out of earshot of the other occupants. Mrs Knowles was visibly shaken by the ordeal and insisted her honesty in the belief that police were sceptical at the report they were making. It was stated that they had been on the Eyre Highway as before stated at about 5.30 a.m. when they were confronted by the brilliant white light in front of the vehicle. The light remained a short distance ahead of the vehicle and began to 'zig-zag' from side to side across the road. They stated that the object was about 3 feet in width but were unable to estimate the height except to say that it blocked their view of the road ahead of the vehicle. At this time a second vehicle approached their position travelling in a westerly direction on the Eyre Highway. They state that the object gave chase to this vehicle and in fact they lost sight of it to the rear of their vehicle as it circled around their right-hand side in apparent pursuit of the other vehicle. At this point I asked Sean to draw a sketch of the object which he did. The sketch resembled an egg in an egg cup. The ground was indicated at the base of the cup.

They stated that the object then came from behind their vehicle and their vehicle began to shake violently on the road from side to side. Both state having been extremely scared at this time and Sean states that he increased speed to the vehicle in an attempt to escape from the object. Mrs Knowles then stated that she wound down the rear side window and reached toward the hood of the vehicle. She stated that she felt something on the hood of the vehicle and made her distress known to the other persons in the vehicle. Both Sean and Mrs Knowles could not recall any indication of light at this time from the object on the roof but Mrs Knowles states that it felt soft, spongy and rubbery and was hot, although she did not burn her hand. On retrieving her hand however she found it was covered in black-grey dust. Both state that at this time they were aware of a high-pitched whirring or hissing noise but which was of normal intensity. Both stated that they felt disorientated and that they noticed that their voices had become slow and deep when they spoke.

They were unable to say how long the object was on the roof of the car but during the time it was there it appeared to lift the vehicle from the road and then force it back down heavily on the road. The rear right side tyre on the vehicle then blew out and Sean considered that this occurred as a result of the weight of the object forcing down on the vehicle. They state that the object then vanished and they were able to stop the vehicle. They both state that the wheel was changed hurriedly and they were about to move off again when they noticed the object again glowing bright white ahead of the vehicle. The object appeared to be in the centre of the road. They were extremely concerned and scared and in fact drove the vehicle behind roadside bushes, vacated the vehicle and hid themselves separately from the vehicle. They remained hidden for a short period until they could no longer see the object and then drove from the location to the Mundrabilla Roadhouse where they spoke with persons at that establishment shortly prior to 6.00 a.m. (W.A. time).

I then spoke with the passenger who had been indicated as sitting in the front left side of the vehicle, Patrick Knowles. I spoke with him separately from Sean and Mrs Knowles and before he had an opportunity of conversing with them. His indication of the situation which had occurred was similar to that as told to me by the others although his description of incidents differed. He stated that his impression of the object was about similar in size to that indicated but appeared to him to have a brighter light at the top and at the bottom. He described it as being bigger than the car and that the light which it gave off was brilliant white. He also stated that after the object was apparently on the hood of the vehicle and his mother had felt it and remarked, he had opened his left side front window and had been showered with black powdery dust. He was also aware of a foul smell. He stated that he began speaking with a deep voice which was obviously sluggish and he gained the impression that the object was 'taking over' his body!

His impression of the object on the roof of the vehicle was that it was heavy and was pushing down on the vehicle and concurred that at that point while driving faster to escape the object the rear right tyre blew out. His impression of the noise which apparently emanated from the object was a deep whirring sound but he made no mention of any light being emitted from the object whilst on the vehicle. He stated that they had driven from the location to the Mundrabilla Roadhouse where they had spoken to persons including a semi-trailer driver who they believed had made observations of the white light as it was travelling on the Eyre Highway in the same location at that time.

I have checked with Eucla Police Station and ascertained that they received a similar report to that given by the four persons at the Ceduna Police Station. Their report had been received early on the morning of 20/1/88, apparently from the driver of the semi-trailer. Eucla Police were aware of the report made by the four persons to the Mundrabilla Roadhouse and were looking for the Ford Telstar vehicle to obtain particulars of the incident. They have conducted enquiries in the Mundrabilla area, particulars of which I am not yet conversant.

During my visit to the Nullarbor, I learned the details about the missing jack that the Knowles forgot after changing the damaged tyre. Truck drivers and other interested motorists stopped at the spot where the Knowles had changed the tyre after the UFO flew away. These people found tracks where the terrified family had run into the bushes. In addition, dog's tracks were found, as well as a print left in the ground by the jack. Police and other searchers had returned to the spot looking for the jack. Our contact from Norseman said that one of his employees had found the jack and had left it in Norseman for the owner to retrieve.

Fishing Boat Encounter

That same night of the famous encounter, the tuna fishing boat *Monika* was buzzed by a strange manoeuvring light. The sighting was confirmed by police at Port Lincoln, home of the Australian Southern Bluefin fleet. The skipper was requested to report to the station when he arrived in port, for an interview, but due to the ridicule already being dished out by armchair debunkers, the crew declined. (The owner of *Monika* told me that the crew only saw an unexplained light. A newsman invented the story that the crew spoke in slow-motion voices during the incident.) However, witnesses from another vessel of the same fleet did respond to the police request, and later a report from one of the observers (name in VUFORS files), given to me by the policeman who conducted the interview, follows:

I am a resident of Canada, and at present I am having a holiday on my relative's vessel, *Empress Lady*. I reported an incident which I saw whilst on watch on the fishing vessel. What I saw was not a usual sight. I am used to looking into the night sky and looking at stars and have seen aircraft flying overhead at night. What I saw on this particular night was none of these.

It was about 12.30 a.m. I was walking around the vessel, on watch. At the time we were positioned on the Australian shelf, in the Great Australian Bight. I had been looking into the sky, and around the horizon . . . using binoculars to assist my vision. My attention was drawn towards the north about 20° off north, to starboard. I saw a bright light; at first I thought it

156

was a star, but on looking and concentrating on it, I saw that it was much brighter than the stars. I used the binoculars to view this light and could clearly see several green lights just above the edge of the light and several red lights just below the edge of the light. The light remained stationary. I observed the light for up to thirty seconds and then went below and called out another deckhand, who also viewed the light.

We watched the light for another ten seconds, and it then moved off at a fast rate and went out of sight over the horizon. It travelled towards the north. I do not know what caused the light – it was much brighter than the stars. The sky was crystal clear. In my own mind it was something other than a star, but I do not know what. This event occurred several days after the sighting in Western Australia, and I was not aware of that sighting until the next day when I read it in the papers.

Further Incidents

About two weeks after the Knowles incident, a bus driver told me that he had been travelling west along the same stretch of highway when he spotted a cigar-shaped object ahead and to his right. The time was before dark and all passengers on the bus saw the 'thing'. The driver did not report the sighting because he did not want to get into the spotlight of ridicule.

Yet another bus driver reported a strange experience to me. A bright light appeared about a mile ahead of him and his CB radio began to 'squeal' and the static became unbearable. At the same time his headlights dimmed. By the time he arrived at the spot the light had gone. He said he was much concerned about the experience and was at a loss to explain it.

During October 1988, another bus driver was paced by a bright, glowing light along the same highway near Mundrabilla, just after midnight. The driver, who was concerned about the safety of those on board, was able to arouse seven passengers from their sleep. After the incident was made public, the witnesses were ridiculed by debunkers from Adelaide.

Earlier Incidents

The Knowles encounter resulted in some earlier incidents being reported. An example is that of two motorists (names on file) who never intended to talk about the incident because they did not want to be thought crazy. The event occurred on the Eyre Highway, near Balladonia, west of Mundrabilla. Suddenly a big, bright light appeared on the horizon in front of their car. The driver and his companion thought it was a truck, so moved over. The light, which seemed to be hogging the middle of the road, approached at about the speed of a truck. As it got closer the driver cursed him for not dipping his lights and gave a blast of full beam as a warning. This had no effect. With the light blinding them, the driver slowed down and waited for the 'truck' to pass. When the light came to within about 100 yards, everything conked out – car engine, lights, and radio.

The light slowed and made a couple of slow passes over the car. In no time at all the two were perspiring and the metal of the car became hot to touch – it was like an oven inside. The witnesses could do nothing but sit there. The object made a humming sound like a vacuum cleaner. The driver said that he was too curious to be scared, but did admit to being 'rattled' by the experience. The whole incident lasted only a few minutes, then the light turned and took off at a fast speed in the direction in which it had been headed.

Another witness came forward with a report that his car had been picked up on the same stretch of road before being dropped back to the ground. This occurred about five years prior to the Knowles event. The witness decided not to report it at the time because he thought he would be ridiculed.

Just two weeks before the Knowles' experience, the owner of the Eucla Roadhouse, about sixty miles from Mundrabilla, sighted strange lights when he was looking for a plane, the pilot of which was booked to stay at his motel. When the plane did not turn up at the airstrip at 7.00 p.m., as expected, he went home. Later that night the owner's wife said she could see a plane coming in so assumed it was the expected guest. She saw what looked like navigation lights moving over the west of Eucla towards the airstrip. The lights came down slowly like a plane preparing to land, but then hovered at an elevation of 20° for about a minute. The owner said the lights moved lower, then slowly east, before vanishing over the horizon. He reported the incident to the Eucla police because he feared the plane might have crashed, and then reported it to Air Traffic Control in Perth, who checked with Adelaide Airport. No aircraft were in the area at the time.

The Roadhouse proprietor, who described the sighting as two twinkling lights on top of an 'ultraviolet light', was mystified by the incident until the Knowles story became known.

One month prior to the Knowles case a former resident of Eucla reported a sighting. At that time she was living in a house on a hill with an overlooking view of the Great Ocean Bight. She was in bed looking at the stars when a bright light appeared and came towards the house, then zoomed away at high speed.

Aftermath

On the evening of 2 August I arrived in Perth for another visit to the Knowles, including Mr Knowles, who had not accompanied them on their trip to Melbourne. Mrs Knowles and her sons had by then – six months after their frightening ordeal – settled down to normal routines, but were still eager for more information and results of tests, so that they could have a better understanding of their experience.

All members of the family expressed appreciation for help from the VUFORS committee; the only people, other than relatives, who had shown concern for their welfare. While in Melbourne they had received independent medical and psychiatric examination and care, including hypnosis to sort out the sequence of events during the running encounter with the unknown object.

There were certain aspects which caused us some anxiety, such as the swelling of Faye's hand and arm, the patchy loss of hair from one of the dogs, and the general reaction on the family. Our concern stemmed from knowledge of other cases where close encounters had caused similar symptoms.

During my visit, the Knowles family mentioned several instances when they had been mistreated by the media, as well as individuals interested only in making money out of their predicament. During the course of events following the UFO episode, their car was repossessed and sold at an auction. Mrs Knowles had requested previously that I drive the car from Adelaide, when returning to Melbourne on 4 February, where they were visiting relatives at the time. They considered the vehicle to be 'jinxed' after the alarming experience, and wanted to sell it because they needed the money. I was interested in buying the car myself, pay off the mortgage, and give a fair price to help relieve their burden. In addition, I wanted to drive the car to Melbourne, where the Ford Motor Company was very interested in conducting tests on it.

About an hour before I was due to leave Adelaide on 4

February, a man knocked on the door of my hotel room to tell me that the owner had given him authority to keep the vehicle in Adelaide for an exhibition. When I arrived back in Melbourne, I learned that the Knowles family had been told that I did not want to drive the car to Melbourne. During my August visit I learned additional details with regard to the transaction, that is, authorization had not been signed until 10 February, six days after my return to Melbourne.

The family mentioned several other examples illustrating how they had been mistreated. Their hopes had been encouraged by promises of looking for Australian and overseas markets for television commercials, and of making a documentary dealing with the encounter. Also, the Ford Telstar was to be placed on exhibition and all expertise would be used to promote and market the vehicle to its fullest advantage. The agent stated that the venture would be costing him a considerable amount of time and money in phone calls, faxing, staff, telegrams, travel, and arrangements for transport of the vehicle. The family was to receive sixty-five per cent nett and the commission to the agent was to be thirty-five per cent nett. The promises were altogether different from the reality suffered by the family. A loss of nearly $20,000 resulted. Most of the money was tied up in the car, plus the costs of six weeks away from home and airline tickets to fly back to Perth. The family had relied on money promised by the agent. In addition to these troubles, the Knowles suffered from the ridicule dished out by the debunkers, reinforced by comments from individuals in the scientific community who, knowing little about other well-documented cases, were unable to ask even sensible questions, let alone knowing how to deal with the problem.

Another disappointment suffered by the Knowles was a promise for an overseas trip to Japan, with all expenses paid. This was the incentive for a television documentary by a Japanese company. A camera crew came to the Nullarbor where the drama was re-enacted. Two of the witnesses were put under hypnosis and were obliged to live through the ordeal again, all for the benefit of vested interests. The documentary was completed and later shown in Japan. Faye and Patrick had been looking forward to their first trip out of Australia, but at the last minute the company cancelled the trip.

Meanwhile, interest among some Australian scientists began to manifest, due to the tireless efforts of John Auchettl. John submitted a set of dust samples to a Monash laboratory in Melbourne, where a scientist made further unusual discoveries. He isolated the potassium particles and noticed that they had identical straight edges, unknown to occur naturally. The scientist's conclusion was that an artificial reaction had taken place, for some unknown reason.

A third laboratory is conducting follow-up analysis, but has yet to present a report on its findings. Other samples are being held in reserve for additional tests if necessary.

While the scientific community, on the whole, makes one debunking attempt after another, yet a further encounter has occurred which indicates that the mysterious objects have a strong magnetic, gravitational, or similar capability. There is reason to believe that this was an abduction attempt that failed. The Knowles incident is the fourteenth case that we know about, where cars have been lifted and dropped back to the ground. There are perhaps other cases that we do not know about.

There are also twenty known encounters involving aircraft, such as the well-known case involving a four-man crew aboard a helicopter that was flying at 2,500 feet over Ohio in the United States, when the crew chief spotted a light which he at first thought was a radio-tower beacon. To his surprise, the light was approaching on a collision course. As the UFO came closer, the pilot, Larry Coyne, saw that it was cigar-shaped and metallic. Thinking the object would collide, he put the controls into the descent positon. After reaching 1,700 feet, Coyne looked up and realized that the helicopter was being pulled up to 3,500 feet in a matter of seconds, with the controls still in the descent position. At that altitude Coyne regained control and flew on to his destination.

Australia's most outstanding case of the last decade, the Frederick Valentich encounter, when the young pilot and his aircraft disappeared without trace while being paced by an unidentified flying object, and an unexplained sound disrupted his radio transmission with Melbourne Flight Service, leads me to suspect that this could have been a successful abduction, and the helicopter incident was another attempt that went wrong. At least Larry Coyne and his crew returned to tell the story, as did the Knowles family. Frederick Valentich did not. [Both the Coyne and Valentich cases are examined in detail in *Above Top Secret* –Editor.]

Before we know for sure what is happening, there are more reports to check out, and much more research remains to be done. Meanwhile, the UFOs that have terrified motorists on the Nullarbor Plain have not as yet been satisfactorily identified.

9

UFO Crash/Retrievals: Is the Cover-Up Lifting?

LEONARD STRINGFIELD

Leonard Stringfield served in intelligence (S2) and counter-intelligence with a unit in the 5th Air Force in the Southwest Pacific Theatre for thirty-one months during World War II. During this period an aircraft he was flying in encountered three UFOs near Iwo Jima, en route to Japan.

He is the author of two books and a number of monographs on UFOs. *Inside Saucer Post . . . 3-0 Blue* (1957) reviewed, in part, his close liaison with the Air Defense Command of the US Air Force, 1953–57, screening and reporting UFO sightings. *Situation Red: The UFO Siege*, was published by Doubleday & Company in 1977. Since then he has concentrated on UFO crash/retrievals, and is widely considered to be the leading authority on this most controversial aspect of the subject.

This chapter contains most of the information privately published in his *Status Report V* (1989). A full list of Mr Stringfield's status reports is given at the end of this chapter.

Leonard Stringfield was formerly Director of Public Relations and Marketing Services for DuBois Chemicals, a division of Chemed Corporation. He retired in 1981 and lives in Cincinnati, Ohio.

Prologue

At the time of writing, many issues of controversy hang over UFO research. Some have caused bitter differences between team members; some can backfire and smear the image of objective research itself. In the middle zone, trying to avoid the 'people' problems, I feel the urgent need to continue my probes into one basic issue – UFO crash/retrievals.

In this endeavour, once we can see through the spectre of

disinformation and find convincing evidence – or proof – that UFOs are nuts-and-bolts vehicles with an alien crew aboard, I believe that serious researchers can then go forward to disregard all the other wispy issues and maybe even put a stop to the disruptive noises coming out of the woodwork from the far-out fringe.

Ideally, with the media supporting the demands for 'bottom line' facts from a strong phalanx of the scientific community, and perhaps some politicians, the UFO cover-up lid might melt or at least be lifted a little, allowing for some admissions and disclosures.

Confirming any one case of an alleged UFO crash and recovery – such as at Roswell, Aztec, Kingman, El Yunque, or even Brown County, Ohio – could, in itself, alarm the world public or even demolish some of its cherished traditions and philosophies. It could also lead to an eventual sharing of alien technologies – a new propulsion system for inner and outer space travel or new 'metals' and many other marvels – and certainly it would bring public support for NASA and a bigger budget for vital space probes. More importantly, we might learn about the alien entities themselves; their intent for being here and an explanation for some of their incursive actions – to name one, abductions!

Even at this short-of-proof stage the UFO crash/retrieval (C/R) story, still unfolding, I believe, should be public information, unless it, and the full UFO story, is too exotically grim to tell. In that case, I reserve judgement.

Feeling confident, I submit new data, based on research and the co-operative work of others, for open review. *Veritas vincit.*

Part I: The Quiet Of Dusk . . .

As we close out the decade of the eighties, new public interest in UFOs, it seems, is surging. Some of it is probably the trickle-down from new books on the market, but for the most part new and old researchers alike are being spurred by recent revelations of official cover-up amid some sobering reports of human encounters of the first, second, and third kind.

Perhaps already an established fact is the climactic close encounter of the fourth kind: contact with an alien race. Because of rumours contending that a covert human–alien relationship has been in operation and, of late, more rumours that tell of a ruptured 'alliance', we must not only pause and wonder about the magnitude of a colossal cover-up but also the implications of an eventual *open* contact – even if it were on terms of peaceful co-existence. Any other alternative staggers the imagination! But getting down to Earth, as we once knew it, we must also pause and ask in all seriousness: where is the *proof* that alien spacecraft exist or, for that matter, that there is a cover-up?

A seemingly stupid question, when we hear so many lurid tales about abductions, alien underground installations, genetic manipulation, animal and human mutilations, of American and Russian satellites exploding in space, of alien artifacts on the Moon and Mars, of dire predictions of the world's end and, yes, to a lesser degree, UFO crash/retrievals. Once a blockbuster to research in the late seventies and early eighties, a crash story in 1988 was no longer big ufological news.

As I weigh all the reports, or rumours, mindful of mis/disinformation, I still maintain that it is in C/R research that we may find our elusive proof. Once the hardware and the crews, cadaverous or alive, are forced into public view, then we may find credibility for some of the other postulations, and be in a better position to espouse endless hypotheses.

Since presenting my paper, *The Fatal Encounter at Ft. Dix–McGuire: A Case Study*, at the Mutual UFO Network (MUFON) Symposium, St Louis, in 1985, and pursuing some leads in that case to little consequence, I have remained relatively quiet on the literary front. New C/R reports have surfaced from time to time since 1985, but most were second-hand or of the 'Cheshire Cat' variety, providing scant information. What I had, with a few exceptions, were not up to Roswell calibre, and these could wait until . . . August and September of 1988.

Then, in the quiet of dusk, the valley of my research suddenly hit a peak. As Richard Hall, author of *Uninvited Guests*, commented, the 'thermostat' seems to have been turned up (by official operators). During this time ten new sources emerged, each promising that useful information about UFO crash/retrievals would soon follow.

By the end of November most promises were fulfilled. Some were first-hand reports, others second-hand, but more importantly, some provided new back-up information for cases cited in my previously published status reports. Most rewarding was the timely emergence of persons serving in covert positions with substantial information in key areas of my work. Reflecting back, I see in them parallels to the medical sources who surfaced in 1978 and shared graphic descriptive anatomical details of the alien for release in *Status Report II: The UFO Crash/Retrieval Syndrome*. As a matter of record, this prototype information remains to this day analogous to most reports of alien encounters and is much like the computerized rendition shown in October 1988 on the TV documentary, *UFO Cover-Up? Live*.

Proof? Of course not. Getting close to it? Perhaps. And, yes, I am aware of the adroit arts of disinformation. While I see no evidence of devious game-playing in my current input, nor in some of the material received in the later seventies and early eighties, I am aware of another recent suspect annoyance, where my name was in blatant public view in a tabloid, the *Weekly World News*. In its 20 September 1988 issue I was headlined as an 'expert' having the inside scoop on an alleged alien underground facility in Dulce, New Mexico. Bunkum! The fact is, I have no such scoop, although I have heard the rumours about Dulce as well as the one in Nevada, and others.

Alert to the risk of tabloid exploitation and official machinations that try to maintain secrecy, those handling a sensitive subject like crash/retrievals must also expect the unexpected from even 'friendly' quarters. And, most often unexpectedly, from out of the rank-and-file of research, comes the sudden strike of a cobra or a 'loop' of such snakes-in-the-grass who try to take one's work and credibility to task and make a big stinking mess of it. The reasons may be many. Is it simply arrogance, a thirst for fame or power, or is it the work of the orchestrators who pick and choose their lackeys? Whatever the reasons, I have felt their sting since I presented my first paper, *Retrievals of the Third Kind*, at the MUFON Symposium in Dayton, Ohio, in 1978. While most of these early adversaries have faded away, little loops persist who employ subtler ways to undermine my work.

Haunting me still is a remark by a loop kingpin averring that all my case histories, published in my series of status reports, were 'fairy tales', thus of no substance. Drawn into his loop is a pundit, a prominent writer in the UFO media who, having belittled my work since 1978, has worked well into the scheme.

In later years, through his editorial controls, whenever C/R was an issue, my work was simply snubbed. More recently, yet another in the loop told a mutual correspondent that my investigations have no depth and that I am a good subject for disinformation.

Sad to say, these loopers have obviously not done much 'investigation in depth' about my *modus operandi*, nor have they taken into consideration the lack of funds at my disposal to follow up hundreds of leads, coast-to-coast. Also, it is beyond my comprehension how some of my contemporaries can entertain the notion that I have gullibly accepted as valid, or *bona fide*, every item of C/R material published in my papers. For the record, the purpose of my status reports is to draw in *new* sources with *new* information that could either strengthen a case or give reason for dropping it in the circular file.

It is true that some of the best-made plans go awry and true that some entries in my monographs have obvious weaknesses and that some, based on new information, have become questionable. An example is Case A-2, *Status Report III*. However, the mainstream material from early sources remains solid. One that I thought deserved a full investigation was the Ft. Dix–McGuire case, which has become stronger as a result of *new* information from *new* sources. Someday, perhaps, I may write a special paper updating the *status quo* of my published case histories.

While the mid to late eighties period did not yield any substantial C/R case histories worthy of a monograph, except the Ft. Dix–McGuire affair, it was not devoid of high points.

The Pentagon, 1952

While attending the MUFON Symposium in St Louis in 1985, Raymond Jordan, a MUFON investigator, gave me a confidential lead to follow up involving a lady who had worked at the Pentagon in 1952 who, he said, had seen an alien body 'pickled' in a glass tank in an 'Off Limits' room. By mistake, she had entered the room and was promptly nabbed and forced to sign papers swearing her to secrecy.

When I reached the lady, who was still employed by a government office, she said, 'I know what you're talking about,' then added, 'but I can't talk.' I suggested that she communicate by other means, to which she replied, 'No. I don't want to talk about it at all.'

Recovered Disk, 1963

Thanks to Michael Johnstone, a California researcher who did some good spadework, it was arranged for me to talk with a former marine who claimed that in 1963 he had stood guard at an undisclosed military base which houses a 'disk-shaped vehicle with ovoid cross-section, 40 feet across and 13 feet thick at the centre'.

A more detailed description appears in my article, 'The Chase for Proof in a Squirrel's Cage', published in the British book, *UFOs 1947–1987* (Fortean Tomes, London 1987). The marine, who signed a security oath, said that he had guarded the premises for two weeks while a technical crew, speaking in code, tried every known means to gain entry into the craft, including a laser device. Once, he said, he observed that it deflected off the curved side of the craft into the rafters, causing some damage. 'The public should know the truth about UFOs,' the ex-marine told me. I felt that he knew more than he had cautiously related, but he refused to disclose the name of the base.

McClelland AFB, 1973

Former military sources with information about witnessing a special movie showing deceased alien bodies surfaced in the late seventies. These were published in my *Status Report II* (see cases A-4 and A-9). The viewing of the film was always behind closed doors and the viewers were few. Then in 1985 Chris Coffey, of Cincinnati, who was a close friend of astronaut Ellison Onizuka, revealed to me that she had asked him about his interest in UFOs when they met after one of his visits to Wright-Patterson AFB. Onizuka admitted that he kept an open mind on the subject and added that his curiosity was aroused when he and a select group of Air Force pilots at McClelland AFB in 1973 were shown a black-and-white movie film featuring 'alien bodies on a slab'. In his state of shock, he said he remembered saying aloud, 'Oh, my God!'

Chris, knowing my work in C/R, had arranged for me to meet Onizuka to discuss UFOs after his scheduled flight on the space shuttle *Challenger*. As it turned out, fate intervened tragically when the shuttle exploded.

Mexico, 1948/49

With the confusion among researchers over the number, loca-tions, and dates of several alleged UFO crashes on the Texan border with Mexico – and in Mexico – Tom Deuley, who heads the MUFON team in Texas, wrote to me in February 1988 saying that his group had been challenged to look into the El Indio–Guerrero case that is briefly mentioned in the Majestic-12 document. Could I give any details, or rumours, beyond what I had already published? he wanted to know.

I responded that in recently sorting some old correspondence I had found a letter dated March 1985 on which I had noted 'Follow Up'. I noted also that I had tried to reach the sender, seeking more information, but got no reply. So I tried again in January 1988. Fortunately, this time I was able to reach the son-in-law of the source. Co-operatively, he gave me the phone number – Mr JA, in California. Having a friendly chat with JA, I found no reason to question his sincerity. He was no UFO buff, having no knowledge of current affairs.

According to JA, he was aboard the USS *McKinley*, cargo class, the commandship for amphibious operations, docked at San Diego, with many admirals aboard, when the incident took place. His job: messenger. The date: late 1948 or early 1949. It was winter and he remembers a quick cruise to Alaska in between those years.

JA was on deck when he learned from the top brass that a small task force was assembled and ordered to go to a certain location (unknown to him) in Mexico to retrieve a crashed 'flying saucer'. They departed by vehicle, but he was not certain if they drove to the site or used other means to reach what was described as a 'remote region of Mexican desert'.

The task force was gone for several days and when they returned, JA said, everything was hushed up. He did, however, hear one of the officers on the mission say that they recovered some dead bodies but some had managed to get away. 'They were able to move at great speed,' he recalls the officer saying. JA never heard more about the saucer or the bodies, but he did remember reading a brief item in a San Diego newspaper about the crash in Mexico.

St Geniez, France, 1972

Something unidentified crashed into the rocky slopes of a mountain in the township of St Geniez, France, on 18 March 1972. According to witnesses it caused brush fires over a forty-acre area. Significantly the incident occurred during a flap of UFO reports in that south-eastern part of France.

The story was originally obtained by researcher Olivier Rieffel in 1986, during a meeting with Leon Visse, the person identified in Dr Jean Gille's papers published in *Status Report III* (see Case B-8). With Visse's disclosure that the crash occurred near the Durance River, Rieffel informed his colleague Jean Sider, who found in his records that the time and place coincided with a reported crash of a 'space object' into a mountain near the town of Sisteron. According to most witnesses, the UFO was described as a 'red ball' of fire and one informed source, who prefers anonymity, stated that it was 'red-orange, shaped like a disk'.

While the investigations continued, through the well-co-ordinated teamwork of Sider and Rieffel, extensive records of their findings were sent to me for appraisal in April 1988. Included was a fragment from the site of a ceramic-like substance appearing to have been baked by intense heat, and three pages of first-hand reports from witnesses who saw the descending red object, among them farmers in the region, the son of a mayor, a newspaper reporter on the scene, and members of the police and fire departments. Of note was an astronomer whose investigations ruled out a meteorite and meteorological and atmospheric phenomena.

'The facts of the case remain classified in the files of the military and the Gendarmerie Nationale archives,' Sider reported, and added, 'Confirming all the main details was a member of an intelligence agency who stated that "something" was received by the Gendarmerie and shipped in a truck to a location near Paris.'

Sider emphasized that his report was not conclusive and that investigations were still in progress. Listed were many more names of people, directly involved, who he hoped to trace and interview.

Kentucky, 1987

Far more spectacular, but affording far less supportive evidence than the St Geniez incident, is the first-hand report from a retired medical doctor who alleges that he accidentally found the skeletal remains of two humanoids, possibly of alien origin, on his farm in western Kentucky in March 1987.

When informed of the story, I was eventually able to reach the doctor through his friend Bill Boshears, who first aired it on his radio talk show in Cincinnati. Having been warned to 'shut up' since the show, the doctor none the less entrusted me with his name, but would not reveal the location of his farm nor give me his unlisted phone number. He also advised that some of the details he shared with me about the Air Force investigation should be kept confidential.

The doctor, when he talked with me on his friend's phone, was cordial but brief. He said that it was during a routine evening stroll on his farm property of 400 acres that he discovered the extraordinary evidence. Next to a burned-out circle, about four feet in diameter, in an open, grassy field, he found the skeletons of two humanoid entities about four feet apart. Without a trace of clothing, some of the bones showed residual ligament, he said, with evidence that predators had been at work. As a doctor, he was certain that the bones were not of animal origin and on closer examination he was shocked, he said, to find that the structure was bipedal, about four feet tall, with a large skull and cat-like jaw, and a barrel-like rib cage with long arms and three fingers.

The doctor's next move was to call the sheriff, who immediately called the Air Force. The next morning at sunrise, the doctor was surprised to see three helicopters land in a clearing and many people, some in uniform, being deployed over a wide area. Greeting him was a colonel (name known to me) who cordially introduced himself and stated his mission: remove the bones and undersoil, test and remove the burned circular soil, and comb the area for any other evidence. Later in the day fresh soil was filled in the excavated areas, and the doctor was told that the soil in the circle had been baked at 3,000 degrees.

When asked about the time factor of body decomposition (allowing for predators), the doctor estimated that, according to cursory examination, the aliens had been exposed for less than a hundred days.

Reminding me that 'they put the fear of God' in him after his trip to a military base for further interrogation – and where he was shown photos of other alien corpses – the doctor expressed interest in my research, so I suggested that we lunch together soon. He agreed, but never called.

Ohio, 1987

News of a UFO crash on a farm in Brown County, south-western Ohio, in the spring of 1987, looked promising at the outset, but as I tried to put the pieces of raw information into some order to make the next move, mainly to reach the principal source, I ran into every conceivable roadblock. A year later, after 'giving up', information surfaced from a new source to give credence that something did crash at the farm site. Whatever happened, I could now see through some of the bizarre diversions that blocked me from contacting the farmer who claimed that he saw the crashed disk, *three small female non-human bodies* strewn in the field and, above all, had some unusual metallic fragments from the debris to prove it.

My initial informant was JD, a gemologist and a persevering UFO buff who, in getting many packages by United Parcel Service, learned from the driver on her rural route that the farmer 'down the road' had pieces of metal from a UFO that had crashed on his property. When JD tried to learn the farmer's name and location, the driver became scared, and I was later told that to avoid the issue he even changed his route. Undaunted, JD then opted to go to the local police office near the site, hoping to locate the farmer. There she got the run-around and was advised by one officer to forget the matter. But according to JD, the officer later visited her home and for some unexplained reason gave her a photo of the farm property.

At this point, JD suddenly showed signs of confusion and fear, claiming that her house had been entered, that the photograph of the property had been taken, which she had used as a bookmark in a library book (by Major Keyhoe) and that the book was found on the hood of her car in the garage. Next came word that she had been injured in a fall into a sewer hole between her house and the garage. The lid had been loosened, she said. Investigating, my son-in-law and I could find nothing abnormal in her manner of housekeeping, but we did begin to wonder about her going off the deep end, and if she had become obsessed to a degree of fantasy. Or was it all a hoax, or a ploy of disinformation?

Time went by without further contact. I felt that something was amiss about the case. Concerned, I got in touch with a former Air Force intelligence officer who had the 'right' connections, and asked if he could help throw light on the affair. Two days

172

later he called back to relate that he had been in touch with the 'right' person and was told that there had been 'no significant UFO sightings in that area for the past year'. He added that my informant would soon be visited by two investigators in an official capacity.

Several weeks later I received a surprise call from JD, who simply said, 'I'm not supposed to talk with you, but here I am.' She went on to explain that she had had *two visitors* who, on learning that she had no hidden metal artifacts, debunked the crash as well as my crash/retrieval research, and advised her in so many words that she should not contact me again.

Not long after that, JD called me again, admitting that she had met the farmer, had visited the farm, saw the newly added soil over the crash site and, moreover, gave me the farmer's name, and had even arranged for him to visit me the following week. He never came, as expected, and when JD called a few days later she regretted to tell me that he had been moved, expenses paid, to Virginia. This, if true, I suppose, was his reward for being a good citizen, a real patriot.

In April 1988 a researcher, joined by a person knowledgeable of military intelligence operations, visited my home to discuss an abduction case. Inevitably, the conversation drifted to crash/retrievals and I mentioned the alleged crash in Brown County. 'Oh, yes,' said my knowledgeable guest, 'I heard that a jet crashed on a farmer's property.' She added, 'It was in an inaccessible area and they had a hard time getting the wreckage out.'

A jet? Certainly there had been nothing in the news about a jet crashing the previous spring in that locality and, as we all know, airplane crashes, of any kind, always make news. Significantly, my guest also stated, 'I heard from a good source that the government came in and bought the farm and moved the owner out of town.' Amen!

Much can be said about this case, pro and con. I have also omitted some details that might compromise the positions and activities of certain people involved.

Part II: . . . To the Burst of Dawn

From my perspective, the official cover-up and the ways to control it seem as effective as ever up to the Fall of 1987.

Both the Kentucky and Ohio incidents, described in Part I, which involved civilians, show that anything goes, from trickery to threats, to keep the facts hidden.

Then, throughout 1988, like the burst of dawn, something changed. Whether or not the iron lid had loosened, more people, and concerned people, suddenly became more vocal. Of concern were the implications of MJ-12, the meaning of abductions, the flap of low-level UFOs in the Blue Ridge Mountains of Virginia, the Gulf Breeze affair, and what was said and left unsaid on the TV documentary, *UFO Cover-Up? Live* about alien–human relations by two disguised informers, 'Condor' and 'Falcon'. (The identities of both 'birds' are known to me. Condor was an Air Force officer stationed at Wright-Patterson AFB in September 1985, during which time he called me on several occasions. Expressing interest in my research and my sources, he claimed to know a colonel with sensitive information relative to my work, but his proposal for me to meet with this source fell through and I heard no more. Later I learned that he confided with a member of the Fund for UFO Research and after that with Bill Moore, etc.)

Yes, things have changed: this is reflected in my volume of mail and the phone calls I get at all hours. Is the cover-up, then, in a 'calculated' countdown from ten to a three, two, one, and lifting?

Frankly, I do not think the time is right for a sudden *formal* announcement of alien 'visitors' by the world powers, which would have unpredictable effects on society. If the press were suddenly to wake up and demand the bottom line on all the UFO happenings in the MJ-12 files, or were to confirm the horrors described in an exposé of the alleged secret Project Grudge Report #13, released by a former Air Force officer, Bill English, then we would have more to worry about than just the stock market.

But maybe the cover-up is loosening a little because of new pressures, or guilt, or leaks, or the fear of more Falcons and Condors. Maybe we are being spoonfed in various ways, and the masqueraded Falcon and Condor are only doing their job. But, while the media still sleeps, amid all the UFO 'noise', I have seen a change on my thermostat. For whatever reason, I am suddenly getting more C/R input.

Pennsylvania, 1965
Thanks to the in-depth research of Stan Gordon, Director of the Pennsylvania Association for the Study of the Unexplained (PASU), the Kecksburg crash/retrieval case of 9 December 1965 may now find recognition as a classic in the annals of ufology. Considering the number of witnesses tracked down by the PASU group, it may even rank with Roswell.

As Case B-1, the incident was originally reviewed in *Status Report II* by Clark McClelland, but at that time, save for knowing that something had crashed and was retrieved, there was some uncertainty about the nature of the object. The Air Force, of course, explained it away as a meteorite; others suggested space debris. Gordon, however, accepted neither explanation as more information and Freedom of Information Act data surfaced. In the spirit of co-operation, he kept me informed.

Then in 1987, by good fortune, Stan met 'Pete', who showed up at a PASU UFO exhibit at a local mall. Having feared ridicule for twelve years, he finally decided to tell his story. It began at the age of nineteen, as a fireman, when his unit in a nearby village was summoned by the Kecksburg authorities to help in the search for something that had crashed in a wooded area – possibly an aircraft. But the shocker came, he said, when the crash site was located. Instead of an aircraft, they found something else – a large acorn-shaped object embedded deep in the ground.

Armed with Pete's new information, Gordon published the full Kecksburg story in the final quarter issue of *Pursuit*, in which he reports the UFO's flight pattern across several states, tells of the first-hand experiences of local residents who saw the 'fireball' crash and of others who witnessed the sudden, incursive 'take-over' by the military to perform the retrieval operation. According to Gordon, many of the local citizens viewed the action as constituting a state of martial law, and he comments, 'Many were influenced enough by their contacts with military or local authorities to the effect that they refused to discuss what they saw or were told, even to this day.'

Before being chased from the crash site by the retrieval team, Pete and companions had a close-hand look at the semi-submerged mystery object. To them, it appeared that the object had descended at about a 30° angle and had broken tree limbs and knocked down a fifteen- to twenty-foot-high tree before impacting. The trench was about twenty-five feet long and at the greatest depth was about seven feet. It was puzzling that there were no signs of fire. The size of the acorn-shaped UFO (which had no windows or seams) could not be determined because of its submerged position, but it was estimated to have been about seven feet high and wide.

In trying to give a better description of the craft, Pete said that it gave him the impression of a deflated beach ball pushed in, and towards the bottom there was a ring or bumper-like structure about eight to ten inches wide that seemed to cover the circumference of the object. He said that on this bumper, which was raised up off the surface, was a writing that looked like Egyptian hieroglyphics. He remembered the characters of broken and straight lines, dots, rectangles and circles. As a machinist for twenty-five years and familiar with metals, solid and liquid, he observed, 'Never in my life have I seen the colour of that metal in any shape or form.'

Pete said that he will never forget the excitement on his return to the Kecksburg firehall, which had been set up as a command post. It was swarming with military personnel – mostly Air Force – and a lot of equipment was being carried in. Soon guards were at the front entrance and the firemen, before being dismissed from the building, were told to use the outside toilets.

There is much more to Gordon's article, like his learning later that Air Force records showed that NORAD's Space Detection and Tracking System (SPADATS) did not have any space junk re-entering Earth's atmosphere that day. Thanks to Gordon, I was privileged to interview Pete on the basis that I would not use his name. Once this was agreed, Pete gave me his complete story, confirming Gordon's version.

I asked Pete about the hieroglyphics, wondering if they could be Russian. 'No way!', he said. 'I'm of Russian-Polish descent and can read Russian. It was not Russian, nor American.' He added, 'I'll stake my life on it: the object was not man-made.'

New Mexico, 1947

The crash and recovery of an 'alien' object near Roswell, New Mexico, in July 1947, so well-documented by Bill Moore and Stan Friedman and others, is a case that should cause sceptics to think twice before they impugn the existence of UFOs or the plausibility of the extra-terrestrial hypothesis.

Though most of Roswell's first-hand witnesses were civilian, the overall evidence supporting this 'nuts-and-bolts' incident is massive, and of significance, ironically, is the report that news of the UFO's discovery at the base slipped out in an 'uncleared' press release by the PIO, 1st Lt. Walter Haut. Had it not been for a fast and effective cover-up, the full story, once in the public domain, could have re-written what we know as history. Having been informed, perhaps mankind in his philosophical and geopolitical pursuits would have chosen a wiser course.

Except for rumours, the truth about Roswell did not surface until 1978, when the late Jesse Marcel told a NBC radio newsman, Steve Tom, in Chicago, about his official role as the intelligence officer assigned to the crash site to retrieve the scattered debris. On 7 April 1978, Tom called me and linked me up with Marcel in Houma, Louisiana, to get his story first-hand. This led to other calls to Marcel, and upon learning that we had both served in the 5th Air Force during World War II, in the same combat areas in Leyte, Philippines, we developed a feeling of camaraderie and talked about meeting together for a UFO discussion in the near future.

Marcel confirmed that the debris he combed from the crash site on the Brazel ranch was *not* the remains of a balloon and that he had observed on a fragment of metal beam a row of symbols looking like hieroglyphics. (See *Status Report II*, case A-10, and the foregoing Kecksburg case.)

Regretfully, I never got to meet Jesse Marcel. Stan Friedman did conduct an interview which appears in *The Roswell Incident* (see Appendix), and the following extract is a statement by Marcel that left some questions unanswered:

'. . . that afternoon, we loaded everything into a B-29 on orders from Colonel Blanchard and flew it all to Ft. Worth. I was scheduled to fly it all the way to Wright Field in Ohio, but when we got to Carswell at Ft. Worth, the general nixed it. He took control at this point, and ordered me not to talk to the press under any circumstances. I was pulled off the flight and *someone else was assigned to fly the stuff up to Wright Field . . .*' [Author's italics]

177

My status reports do pay off. Thanks to one reader, John August, in Hawaii, I got the 'missing link' referred to by Marcel as his replacement who flew the Roswell remains to Wright Field. August followed up his initial phone call with a letter, dated Labor Day 1988, which states in part:

'. . . Confirmation of the Roswell crash reached me through a Maui resident, who claimed that her father, Captain O. W. Henderson, flew the retrieved spaceship from Roswell to Wright Field on a B-29. According to Henderson's wife who was reached by phone, a news officer reported the incident but it was quickly quieted down. On February 17, 1981, the story appeared in the tabloid, *Globe*, and Henderson admitted to his wife and daughter that the story was true. The crew, she said, were little people with exceptionally large heads.

. . . At the time, Henderson was stationed with the 509th Bomb Group at Roswell . . . an élite group for which all involved required high-security clearances. Besides being a highly decorated pilot during WWII, with over 30 combat missions, Henderson was in charge of the movement of all passengers and freight transported by air for organizations participating in the atomic bomb tests and the Manhattan Project . . .'

Enclosed, as a result of August's attentive spadework, were copies of photos showing Captain Henderson and flight crew, and a letter of commendation for an 'excellent job accomplished' from Carl Spaatz, Commanding General, AAF, forwarded to Colonel William Blanchard, Commander, 509th Bomb Group.

For verification, August footnoted his letter with Mrs Henderson's address and phone number. Calling her on 1 October 1988, I explained my work; asked many questions to which she cordially responded, and got approval to publish her name in this report. She said that her husband, known as 'Pappy' among his buddies, passed away in 1986, and stated unequivocally that he transported the Roswell wreckage to Wright Field and kept the secret faithfully until 1981. She remembers his comment, 'I've been dying to tell you for years, but couldn't. It was top secret.'

When I asked Mrs Henderson if her husband had ever described the object he transported, she replied that all he said was that 'It was strange', avoiding details.

Avoiding details, it seems, goes with the business of covert work if one must talk at all. And so it was with another source who revealed some information about his stealthy activity at Roswell in 1947.

The source, Bev, is British; her father a former American serviceman, a staff sergeant who took up residence in England following duty in the Pacific theatre, World War II, and notably with the 509th Bomb Group at Walker Field, Roswell. According to records, he was at Roswell during the same time as Major Jesse Marcel and Captain O. W. Henderson.

Bev, referred to me by Timothy Good in 1988, is, by the tone of her letters and phone calls, sincere in trying to verify her dad's alleged participation in the Roswell retrieval case. She sent me copies of all his military records, which confirm his assignment at Walker Field in Roswell, such as medical records, one with orders 'cut' for hospitalization at the base for both he and Jesse Marcel, and his pass to the base's Non Commissioned Officers' Club, dated July 1947. [These records are also in my files. I have had several meetings with Bev, her sisters and mother, and am convinced that they are telling the truth – Editor.]

As a child, Bev recalls her dad talking about his hush-hush work at Roswell, and whenever he described the nondescript bodies, her response was to giggle. The subject never came up much, she said, until she was a teenager. Once, she recalls, he had read a feature story in a newspaper about a UFO crash and, looking grim, he told her about his experiences of standing guard where the wreckage was stored and during the retrieval of the bodies, and cautioned his family to keep it quiet lest he get into trouble. According to Bev's letter, she recalled the following:

'. . . he stood guard once outside a hangar where a crashed saucer was stored. He couldn't see anything as it was all packed up and ready to be flown out to Texas the next day. . . . We disagree on the number of bodies he saw. I'm sure he said two, but one of my sisters said three . . . All available men stood guard duty around the site where a crashed disc had come down and they couldn't understand why [the bodies] had to be kept cold, as there were trucks of ice . . .

Although he and others were told they would get into trouble if they saw too much, they did look under the cover and saw two small dead bodies. He said they were like us, but not like us. They were smaller than a normal man with large heads and slanted eyes. He also said they looked yellowish, a bit Asian. . . .

I remember when I got older and asked for more information, he got angry and said, "That's all I know and I shouldn't have told you that much." Whenever he talked about it, he always looked worried. . . .'

His last words, according to Bev, were about Roswell, before he died in hospital in February 1986.

Fort Dix–McGuire AFB, 1978

When I last made contact in January 1987 with Jeff Morse, the former 'Blue Beret' who lifted the lid off the Ft. Dix–McGuire affair, I felt that my chase for more supportive information, at least through him, had ended, and I was back on the treadle of the proverbial squirrel's cage.

As agreed, Morse met with Dick Hall, his brother William, Dr Bruce Maccabee, and myself in a busy mall near Washington, DC. Over lunch, he openly answered any questions about the incident, but grimaced over the tangled and costly prospects of his current legal pursuits in Federal Court involving an incident of harassment (see *MUFON UFO Journal*, June 1987). On departure, he said he planned to return to his work overseas. I wished him well and thought of the seven years I had spent investigating his case. There has been no word from Morse since, but his words that day left the four of us believing that he was telling the truth about the ill-fated alien interloper.

Since I presented Morse's story in *Status Report IV* at the MUFON Symposium in St Louis in 1985, there was a spark of hope in 1986 of getting a new source as back-up; a former master sergeant who was stationed at Ft. Dix in January 1978. According to Pat Marcattilio, a MUFON investigator in New Jersey, the source, 'Mr S', whom he knew at a place of previous employment, told him that he heard the rumours about the incident and, in his own time, tried to round up the facts. But he got nowhere and learned that all records, tapes, etc., had been destroyed. He was also advised to stop snooping. When Marcattilio later tried to get more details from 'Mr S', he said, 'He seemed very nervous and refused to talk about it.'

In September 1988 a new source with convincing credentials called me about the incident. As a MUFON state section director in New Jersey, presently serving as Vice-President of the Air Force Association, he had been an intelligence officer with the rank of major at McGuire AFB in January 1978. Although not a witness to the retrieval operations, he had been in a key position to put the twos-and-twos together enough to give credence to the story told by Morse. His letter of 6 September, in part, follows:

> . . . I attempted to recall as best I could the report of the alien being shot on the base back in January 1978. My job was Deputy Director of the 21st Air Force Intelligence 438th Military Wing Intelligence. In this dual role, we were responsible for briefing both the 21st Air Force Commander, who controlled all military airlift aircraft in half the world over to India, and the Wing Commander at McGuire AFB.
>
> I remember walking into the 21st Command Post and most people were talking about an incident that had occurred on the base during the night. The report was that an alien, a short little guy, had died from a gunshot wound. No-one seemed to know where he came from or what he was doing on the base. At first it was treated as a joke and that the Security Police must have meant an alien from another country, like Mexico.
>
> Usually, I would brief the Commander, Major General Tom Sadler, on anything important that occurred during the night. We were concerned about acts of terrorism, hijacking, and Soviet movements that could be a threat to our aircraft. Normally, if something was felt to be important, I would either brief the General in a stand-up briefing in the Command Post, or if it was classified above "Secret", in his office.
>
> . . . Later in the morning I was told that Intelligence would not brief the General on the alien; that the Security Police Commander or a Liaison Officer was handling it. Later in the day I saw the officer, who was a Lt. Colonel (name unknown), coming out of the General's office. He looked tired and somewhat under pressure. He said 'Hello'. I expected the Lt. Colonel to fill me in on the situation, but he avoided saying anything . . . Assuming this was an alien, I wonder how he got lost from his craft?

The answer to my source's question comes from still another officer, allegedly on the scene in *early* January during a phase of significant UFO activity over the two large military compounds. During this phase, I was told, one of the craft had malfunctioned and crash-landed. One survivor of the crew, lost and starving, managed to reach the outer perimeter near a guard post at Ft. Dix and was shot by an MP. My source said that the interloper, mortally wounded, was later found dead at McGuire. Here (relying on Morse's testimony), the 'alien' was retrieved from an abandoned airstrip.

The Lt. Colonel who briefed General Sadler (referred to by the intelligence officer in his letter) had been previously identified by Morse as his commanding officer, whose name was made known to me. His name, rank, and serial number, as well as the officers who interrogated Morse at Wright-Patterson AFB following the incident, had all been authenticated by the National Personnel Records Center, St Louis, in 1985.

Also of interest is a letter of 12 September 1985, from the New Jersey State Police, in response to a letter from Robert Bletchman, an attorney in Manchester, Connecticut, asking about accessibility to their records of alleged involvement in the incident. They replied:

'. . . Please be advised that it has been, and continues to be, the policy of the New Jersey State Police, that the records, radio logs and other documents maintained at our stations are privileged and are to be kept confidential. We further advise that we do not consider them to be within the public domain in conjunction with general disclosure, etc. . . .'

This information should answer those who queried the State Police about its involvement and were told that they have no such records.

For me, the evidence collected over eight years of investigation into this case may not prove that UFOs are real or extraterrestrial, but it does show that such incidents, if true, would be difficult to explain to a benighted public. Thus, the cover-up.

Norton AFB, 1973

John Lear, an airline pilot who is MUFON State Director for Nevada, undaunted in his pursuit of people, anywhere, to get UFO facts, has lectured extensively and broadcast on radio and TV in Las Vegas. Listening on one occasion was 'Mike' (real name withheld on request), who surfaced in September 1988 to tell Lear his first-hand story.

Admittedly troubled by his experience, Mike explained that in 1973 he had been an Air Force photographer stationed in

182

Hawaii, following duty in Vietnam. His prime duty there was processing gun-camera film. One day, he said, he was notified that his security clearance had been upgraded, and several weeks later he and another photographer in his unit were flown for a temporary duty assignment to Norton AFB in California.

Lear's letter to me, dated 21 November 1988, recounting briefly his interview with Mike, is paraphrased as follows.

On landing at Norton, Mike and his companion were taken by Air Force vehicle with windows blacked out on a two-hour drive. During the drive, Mike was told by the driver, 'So you guys are going to photograph the UFO, eh?'

The vehicle came to a halt on a platform which was then lowered into a large underground installation. Escorted to a briefing room, they were told that they were to photograph a flying saucer and the autopsy of three dead aliens. Ordered to disrobe, they were issued white smocks and combat boots for security purposes. Mike was then escorted into the installation where he saw a disk-shaped craft about thirty feet in diameter, contained in a heavy net suspended from a large crane.

Mike was boosted into the opening of the disk (there were no stairs or ramp) and proceeded to crawl inside. He was shocked, he said, to find that the inside looked to be about ten times the size of the outside. 'I could have thrown a football as hard as I could and not hit the other side', he commented. Disorientated, Mike poked his head back outside to check the size, which appeared to be about thirty feet in diameter as before. Once inside, he met two persons similarly clothed who showed him what they wanted photographed. He shot many photos of control panels and various other fixtures, and was later asked to photograph the exterior from different angles and distances.

Mike was later taken to a room in which there were three dead aliens. He described them as approximately five feet tall, with almost normal human heads, except that the eyes were more rounded. The skin texture was like baking dough, and very white. Before the autopsy the aliens had been dressed in blue uniforms, like flight suits.

As the initial incisions were made for the autopsy, Mike saw green fluid and black innards. At this time he became ill and called for the other photographer to continue the assignment.

Later that day they were driven back to Norton, where they spent the night before being flown back to Hawaii the next day. About two months later Mike's companion disappeared, and neither Mike nor his family have heard from him since.

The year 1973 brings to mind Case A-2, *Status Report II*, where three humanoids were examined at Wright-Patterson AFB. While the head sizes described in each case differ, and the body heights also differ by a foot or so, the description of the skin is strikingly similar. According to the sergeant in Case A-2, who stood guard in the underground facility, the colour was 'off-white or cream'. Both observers, it should be noted, were admittedly traumatized by the sight of alien bodies, which could account for visual differences of anatomical sizes and heights.

Suspicious Deaths

For those of us in research who wonder or worry about the rigours of the cover-up, so effective for a long time, there is the suspicion that the reason for it must be compelling; in fact, so compelling that it may explain why it is maintained at any price – even at the price of sudden death for those having sensitive information who may talk too much.

Evidence of such thinking finds support in the recent disclosure of a retired police officer, with twenty-two years of service, in an eastern state. Through the co-operation of John Ford, head of the Long Island UFO Network, I first received word, on 5 August 1988, that his source had information concerning a crashed disk and the recovery of seven bodies in a western state, which in some way also involved the FBI.

Fulfilling Ford's request for a notarized statement, ensuring his source's anonymity, I then received his videotaped interview with him. After viewing this, which firmly established the former officer's credentials, I reached him by phone for his first-hand story.

It was in 1973, he said, that he was joined by two FBI agents in a special three-day training programme for cadets on 'behavioural science' at the police academy. One evening, after a long day's work, he and the two agents went out to dine and relax, and the subject of UFOs came up. To his surprise, one talked about a crashed disk in Colorado and the recovery of bodies. 'What

184

he said next', added my informant, 'I could tell by his "body English" [body language] that he was disturbed.' His concern was the means used to ensure the cover-up, stating that a doctor, who had been called upon in the night for urgent medical needs, died suddenly of 'cancer' three weeks later. At that point, according to my informant, he observed that the talkative agent was booted under the table by his companion. The subject was dropped and nothing was said about the FBI's role in the affair.

Sudden and accidental death stories I have heard before. Never finding any substantiation, I relegated them to a quirk of orchestrated propaganda; probably a scare tactic to intimidate potential whistle-blowers.

Reports of suspicious deaths, darkly and deeply linked to UFOs, persist, however, and continue to cause speculation. Word comes from Gordon Creighton, editor of the informative *Flying Saucer Review*, who notes a possible deathly tie-in with the US 'Star Wars' programme. He wrote to me in November 1988 as follows:

'. . . here in Britain 22 scientists have recently either taken their own lives or died in very strange or mysterious circumstances. And it seems that most . . . were engaged in British work on behalf of, or related to, the US "Star Wars" programme. The British government, it seems, was trying to hush it up. But press statements here say that the US government had put our government on the spot and demanded a full enquiry. So, quite clearly, it is either the Russians or THEM . . .'

As many researchers have surmised, 'Star Wars', ostensibly conceived as a defensive system against Russian missile attack, may have had from its beginning a 'defensive' UFO connection. Whatever the case, a 'mock test' in September 1988, of an earth-shattering warhead – much like 'Star Wars' in reverse – was conducted at the Tonopah Test Range in Nevada. Announced as a proposed super-weapon designed to destroy Russian under-ground command centres dug in solid rock down to 1,000 metres, some UFO analysts believe that the real target is not Russian but another adversary deep down in cavernous installations in Nevada and New Mexico.

According to the Pentagon, the proposed earth-penetrating

185

warhead is 'urgently needed'. According to the rumour-mills, an alien race – the 'greys' – in their fortressed underground laboratories, are genetically experimenting with the human race. Even more ominous, rumours say that their intransigence today may lead to new perils tomorrow.

It is beyond the scope of this paper to speculate on all the sinister machinations attributed to the alien super-race, but news of the British death syndrome and my awareness of other suspicious deaths and disappearances, allegedly connected to UFO crash and retrieval events, must be reckoned with. They may, indeed, have at least a peripheral pertinence to fears, causing suicide, or extreme security measures to maintain a monstrous cover-up.

At the time of writing (December 1988), I have four other sources with UFO crash/retrieval information not included in this report. Most, as far as I know, are in positions to throw strong light on the humanoid factor and other phases of retrieval operations, which could confirm information already cited in my previous paper. But at this stage, and in some instances being dependent on intermediaries, I find the material to be either too fragmentary, or too sensitive, to even hint at as to its nature.

LITERATURE BY LEONARD STRINGFIELD

Retrievals of the Third Kind, revised edition, July 1978, MUFON, 103 Oldtowne Road, Seguin, Texas 78155-4099.
UFO Crash/Retrieval Syndrome, Status Report II, 1980, MUFON.
UFO Crash/Retrievals: Amassing the Evidence, Status Report III, 1982, available from the author: 4412 Grove Avenue, Cincinnati, Ohio 45227.
The Fatal Encounter at Ft. Dix–McGuire: A Case Study, Status Report IV, 1985, available from the author.
UFO Crash/Retrievals: Is the Cover-up Lid Lifting? Status Report V, 1989, available from the author.
Inside Saucer Post . . . 3-0 Blue, 1957, available from the author.
Situation Red: The UFO Siege, Doubleday & Co., 1977; Fawcett, 1978.

10

The Gulf Breeze (Florida) UFO Encounters

DONALD WARE

Donald Ware became interested in UFOs when he witnessed the highly publicized lights over Washington, DC in July 1952. He served for twenty-six years in the US Air Force as a pilot, teacher, staff scientist, test manager, and programmes manager, and flew F-105 Thunderchief jets for seven years, including 125 missions during the Vietnam war. His Air Force decorations include the Distinguished Flying Cross and Meritorious Service Medal. He obtained a B.S. degree in Nuclear Engineering from the Air Force Institute of Technology in 1970.

After retiring from the Air Force in 1983, with the rank of Lieutenant Colonel, he joined the Mutual UFO Network that year as a field investigator and state section director, and was appointed state director the following year. In addition to UFOs, he has an active interest in ornithology.

In July 1988 I was Donald's guest at his home in Fort Walton Beach, Florida, where he introduced me to a number of his team of investigators, including Charles Flannigan and recently retired USAF Colonel Robert Reid. We visited many of the sites where UFOs had appeared, and I was introduced to several key witnesses, including Ed and Frances Walters, who impressed me with their sincerity, courage, and strength of character.

For copyright reasons we are unfortunately unable to reproduce any of Ed's remarkable series of photographs, which are due to be published in his book *The Gulf Breeze Sightings* (William Morrow & Co., New York) in 1990. These photographs have generated a great deal of controversy, as do all photos which show a structured craft, rather than a fuzzy blob. Yet Dr Bruce Maccabee, a US Navy optical physicist who has devoted much of his time to studying them, is convinced of their authenticity.

The Gulf Breeze UFO encounters have involved many people and produced over sixty photographs of objects that appeared

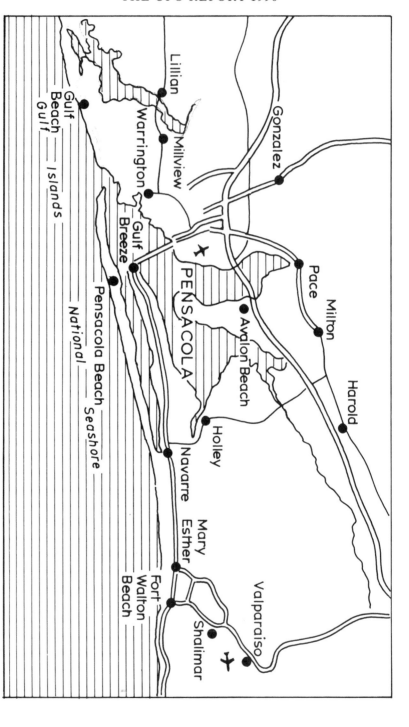

Figure 10:1A. Map of the Pensacola/Gulf Breeze area.

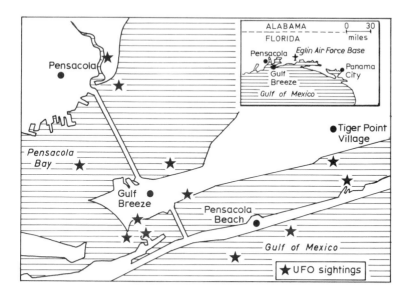

Figure 10:1B. Map showing places of UFO sightings with inset showing location of area detailed (from a 'Tribune' map by Vaughn Hughes).

to be under intelligent control. Between 11 November 1987 and 1 May 1988, one couple had twenty-two encounters, including eighteen separate photographic sessions, and through most of this period they maintained a close co-operative association with several highly trained investigators. The resulting photographs and related experiences were reported by the national media.

The primary investigation was run by the Florida division of the Mutual UFO Network, Inc. (MUFON), of which I am State Director. I appointed Charles D. Flannigan as State Section Director for Escambia and Santa Rosa counties, where most of the encounters took place. Flannigan is the chief investigator for Northwest Florida MUFON Case #15 involving most of the photographs. He has been involved in UFO research since his daylight encounter with two convex disks in 1952.

When it became evident that this case would receive national attention, three internationally known UFO investigators, were brought into the investigation. These were Walter H. Andrus, Jr., MUFON director; Dr Bruce S. Maccabee, MUFON consultant in photo analysis; and Budd Hopkins, experienced researcher of UFO abduction cases. Other investigators who contributed significantly to the on-scene investigations were Gary A. Watson, president of the Pensacola Board of Realtors; Robert E. Reid, a recently retired Air Force Colonel; and Vicki P. Lyons, part-time school teacher and co-chairman of the local abductee support group.

The town of Gulf Breeze (see Figures 10:1A, 1B) is rather unique in that it is like an island community, surrounded on three sides by water and on the fourth by a wooded park, the Live Oaks Reservation. As a bedroom community of Pensacola, the population of fewer than 3,000 is rather prosperous and well educated. A large population of retired military people residing in the area probably contributes to the apparently broadminded perspective of the people. A 1987 Gallup poll showed a direct relationship between education and acceptance of extraterrestrial intelligence. Consequently, *if* the purpose of the photographic sessions was for large numbers of people to see the pictures, this was more likely to happen in Gulf Breeze than most other places.

Between 1983 and 1987 many people of Gulf Breeze and the neighbouring communities had been exposed to the UFO subject through my forty-three lectures, seven newspapers articles, six television appearances and four radio programmes. These emphasized three points: that UFOs have been here for a very long time; some UFOs are controlled by a more advanced intelligence; and, a select few in our government know a lot more about UFOs than they will admit. Because of this publicity, I was notified the day the first picture appeared in the weekly Gulf Breeze *Sentinel*.

The First Encounters

In 1987, Florida MUFON received several UFO reports from Florida locations outside the Gulf Breeze vicinity, but these did not involve photos. On 1 January, a lady reported red lights hovering low over Highway 6 in north-central Florida. On 8 January, a couple reported a large vertical cylinder above their house in Lakeland. On 15, 16, and 17 June many witnesses reported UFOs near Ocala, and following one three-hour series of sightings by many witnesses including two police officers,

190

fourteen dogs in the neighbourhood were reported missing. On 23 July, several people saw six spherical objects make 90° turns over West Pensacola during daylight hours. On 5 August, a huge silent, circular object with coloured lights stopped 100 feet above a witness near Gainesville. On 19 October, a lady reported a UFO hovering beside a bridge near Arcadia in daylight and close enough to see beings through a window. And, on 25 November, a lady in Destin reported the apparent temporary abduction of her five-year-old son.

11 November 1987

It was 11 November 1987 when the Gulf Breeze encounters first attracted attention, and they would continue through most of 1988. About 02.30, Mrs Zamitt, wife of a retired Navy Captain, was awakened by her dog and led outside where she observed a silent, hovering object shine a 'pathway' of bluish light on to her dock. Several blocks to the north, at 08.15 on 11 November, Jeff Thompson observed a circular object with two rows of dark spots and a small dome on top hover silently 350 to 400 feet away. As two Air Force jets flew directly towards the object at low level, it quickly moved up about 200 feet, and just before the jets arrived, the object departed straight up 'very fast' as a flash of light appeared to engulf the whole object. The jets immediately turned north over East Bay. Thompson described the object as being approximately thirty feet in diameter, about fifteen feet high with a dull silver top, light tan middle portion, and a dark beige bottom.

The next reported sighting was at 17.00 that day by Charles Somerby and his wife, Doris, as they walked their dog about five miles to the east. They described a circular greyish object with bright white lights on the bottom and a dome light on top. Sunset that day was at 16.55. They said the object seemed to drift like a balloon towards the west (which was against the wind).

Then, at about 17.05, ten miles to the west, a 41-year-old father of two teenagers, Ed Walters, saw a light approaching through a window of his home office. Curious, he stepped out of his front door and realized it was a very unusual object. Ed is a builder who often uses a Polaroid camera in his work. He grabbed his camera, went to the front porch and took a picture. He stepped down one step and took three more pictures as the

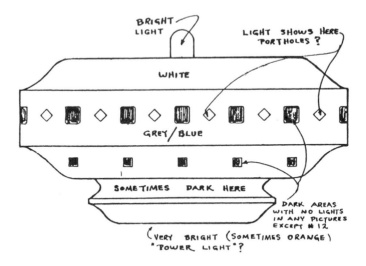

Figure 10:2. Ed's composite drawing of the 'Type–1' vehicle which he photographed many times between 11 November 1987 and 1 May 1988.

object approached. Then he went into the house for a new pack of film and took a fifth picture from the porch. The object changed course towards him, and as he walked into the street for a close shot, he was frozen in a blue beam. During the approximately ten seconds while in the beam, Ed described the following physical sensations:

(1) Eyebrows and eyes would not move;
(2) He could not expand his chest;
(3) He felt like he was going to die;
(4) He could breathe, barely, but there was a nasty smell like ammonia; and
(5) He started to pant when breathing became difficult.

The beam lifted him three feet off the ground and as he tried to scream a voice in his head said, *'Stop that! You will not be*

192

harmed. Be still. Stop that! We will not hurt you.' He also received a mental image like someone was flipping through a book showing him dog pictures! Then he was dropped to the street, and the UFO departed as a distant airplane flew past. A few minutes later, Ed's wife, Frances, reported a smell like ammonia and cinnamon coming from Ed. Photo 1 shows an object partially behind a pine limb thirty-seven feet away, decreasing the possibility of a double exposure.

Four later sightings that day were reported. An anonymous couple wrote to the Gulf Breeze *Sentinel* that they saw a silent object bob up and down at about 17.30. They were afraid it might 'zap them up' if they got out of their car. Linda Lube said that at 17.50 she saw something that looked like 'it was from another place'. Diane Hansen reported that her seven-year-old daughter saw an object at 19.30 with 'different coloured light falling down from it'. A Pensacola executive reported an object that arched downward with a bright white light that lit the entire wooded area around his home at about 21.30.

The events of 11 November 1987 are just some examples of the kind of activity that continued around Gulf Breeze for many months. Ed and his wife decided to give the five original photos to the editor of the weekly Gulf Breeze *Sentinel,* Duane Cook, while pretending to be only an intermediary rather than the photographer. Ed was known by the editor for his large charitable contributions in support of high school activities and the youth of the community, so Cook decided to publish the pictures. Cook was quite surprised to learn that his mother, Doris Somerby, had seen the same object a few minutes before the pictures were taken.

Personal friends of mine who live in Gulf Breeze notified me on 19 November when the pictures were published, and the investigation started. As soon as Ed was suspected of being the photographer, these friends, who co-incidentally were long-time friends of Ed and his family, provided an excellent character reference for Ed. The investigative team had three major concerns throughout the investigation. These were: protection of anonymity for those who desired it; getting all the facts while helping to minimize the stress level in Ed's family; and encouraging responsible reporting of the events so that other witnesses would be encouraged to come forward.

193

Ed's Further Encounters

20 November 1987, 16.00 hrs

Ed heard a 'humming' sound in his head while sitting in his home office, which reminded him of a sound he heard while in the beam. His family left the house and he was alone. At 16.45 he heard a sound like air brakes . . . 'Whoosh', followed by an unintelligible voice with incredible consonants. Then at 16.58 an object, like before, 'came down with incredible speed like it knew where it was going'. A deep computer-like voice said, *'Be calm. Step forward'*. Ed took picture 6. A female voice told him in Spanish that photos were prohibited, but he then took pictures 7–9. Photo 7 showed the object partially behind a small cedar. Then he got a flashing of 'disgusting' nude women pictures in his head before the object departed. (Ed understood Spanish because he had spent five years in Costa Rica.)

2 December 1987, 03.00 hrs

Ed was sleeping peacefully when he heard a humming sound, but he assumed it must be his swimming pool. When the 'hum' was followed by the sound of a baby crying, his brain could not justify this since there were no babies in his household. He became wide awake. He then heard a conversation in Spanish between a male and female that made little sense. He quietly slipped out of bed with his 38-calibre pistol and, picking up his camera, went out back and took photo 10 of the same type vehicle.

At 03.30, while back in bed, he heard his Spitz dog bark just once. He went to the French doors and raised the blind, finding himself 'eyeball-to-eyeball' with a large-eyed being peering in through the window. The being had a partially transparent helmet, shields in front of his body, and a silver rod in his right hand (see Figure 10:3). Ed jumped back and saw the creature run. He then went out back in pursuit, and as he moved from under the roof an 18-inch-diameter blue beam 'nailed' his right foot to the wooden deck. After struggling with his foot trapped, he slowly pulled his foot out of the beam, went in for his camera, and took photo 11 of the object shining the blue beam into the school yard behind his house.

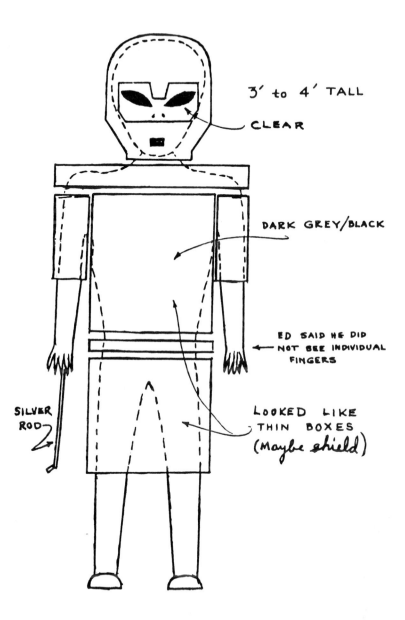

Figure 10:3. Ed's drawing of the alien that peered into his bedroom window on 2 December 1987.

5 December 1987, 05.45 hrs
Ed woke up normally and saw a UFO twenty to thirty feet above the field behind his house. He got his camera and took photo 12 as the object moved higher.

17 December 1987, 01.00 hrs
Ed was awakened by a sound like a waterfall, both in his head and his ears. He got his camera, went outside and got photo 13 of an object quite close. This appeared to be the same object which would later be designated a 'Type-1' by Dr Bruce Maccabee, the primary photo analyst. The light emanating from the bottom ring was changing from orange to pale orange repeatedly. Ed thought the object was having some kind of trouble, as a greyish-looking smoke or fluid was falling from the bottom, and he could hear something like liquid hitting the ground. After momentarily disappearing, the object reappeared very close to the ground across the school yard, perhaps 400 feet away. He took photo 14. This was an especially important photo because, although the original appeared quite dark and distant, it would later be intensely illuminated, re-photographed with high quality film and pushed to show great detail in a blow-up. There was sufficient light reflected from the ground to make the entire vehicle visible. Bob Oechsler, a MUFON State Section Director from Annapolis, Maryland, managed this effort.

After about three minutes, the light source on the bottom of the vehicle became brighter and it took off, flying very fast directly towards Ed. His wife had joined him with a new pack of film. He took photos 15, 16 and 17. Photo 16 was taken when the object was nearly overhead, and 17 (from the new pack) showed the object close to the roof of the house. The image was twenty-two millimetres wide on the Polaroid picture. There was some confusion about the sequence of these photographs. This confusion would lead eventually to hypnotic regression that indicated Ed had been taken on board, while his wife had somehow been incapacitated with no memory of the abduction.

22 December 1987, 17.15 hrs
Ed heard a hum in his head which lasted nine or ten minutes. When he looked out the back and front of his house, he saw no object. The next day Ed speculated that this humming might have

been associated with the three UFOs photographed by 'Believer Bill', whose nine coloured prints were put in the Gulf Breeze *Sentinel* drop box at 08.00 on 23 December. The toy 'Hot-Shot' camera that exposed the film was also provided. A public appeal in the 21 January 1988 edition of the *Sentinel* for 'Believer Bill' to provide the date, time, and location of his sighting was answered. He said they were taken at about 17.15 on 22 December, near Shoreline Drive, which is just on the other side of the high school from Ed's home. Two of the nine grainy photographs showed two identical Type-1 vehicles.

23 December 1987, 05.55 hrs

Ed told investigators that he went out of his back door to turn on the pool pump when the sky was just beginning to lighten in the east (sunrise was 06.39). He saw three UFOs that appeared to be over an apartment complex just beyond a row of trees. All were at low level. While he was in the house getting his camera, he said one moved to a higher level. He took photo 18 showing three similar objects. 'As soon as I lowered the camera,' he said, 'the top one brightened and went up faster than I could raise my head to follow it.' A second or two later the other two did likewise. He got the impression they had waited until he took the picture.

27 December 1987, 20.15 hrs

A close family friend, Patrick Hanks (pseudonym), aged twenty and a junior college student, had visited Ed's home on numerous occasions during the latter part of December, hoping that he would be present if the object reappeared. When he rang the bell on 27 December, he was greeted by Ed's wife who quietly announced, 'It's here!' Patrick walked straight through the house to the family-room window where he simultaneously observed Ed by the pool and the object hovering perhaps 500 feet away. Ed came into the house for his camera, and at the instant Ed's face indicated that he saw Patrick, the UFO blinked out. This sequence of events implies that the UFO reacted to Ed's thoughts. Patrick Hanks' account was later recorded by Charles Flannigan.

28 December 1987, 20.00 hrs

Ed was sitting on one of his porches writing in his UFO log book, with his back towards the pool when he observed a glow over the field in his peripheral vision. It came towards the house with no humming noise present. Since he was out of Polaroid film, he got his Sony Model CCD M8 camcorder. He sneaked around the bushes in his back yard and tracked the vehicle for one minute and thirty-eight seconds. It passed behind a tree fifty feet away and another about 100 feet away. Then it 'blinked' out in two frames (1/15th of a second), while a schoolyard light was readily visible. Bob Oechsler would later do a detailed computer analysis of each frame and said that something on the bottom of the vehicle was cycling 7.5 times per second.

6 January 1988, 17.10 hrs

Ed heard a hum for approximately one minute. He went to the front and back of the house, but observed nothing unusual. The next day Ed made a full disclosure of the above events – except that involving Patrick Hanks – to the MUFON investigators.

12 January 1988, 17.10 hrs

While at home, Ed heard a hum of short duration. He excitedly called my home, hoping that an investigator nearby could respond. My son took the call in my absence, and he later told me that one of my friends was *very* excited. Ed observed nothing unusual then, and a few minutes later he remembered that he needed to check the power meter installation at one of his houses scheduled for inspection. So at 17.25 he drove seven miles east of Gulf Breeze to highway 191-B. When he was about one-half mile south on the deserted black-top road, the object came over his pickup truck and emitted a white flash through the windshield that partially immobilized his forearms and hands. He managed to stop the truck on the left shoulder. His hands and forearms were stinging, like many pin-pricks.

The object then moved very fast to a point 180 feet in front of the truck and hovered two or three feet left of the double yellow centre-line and three feet above the ground. He tried reaching for his shotgun behind the driver's seat, but could not feel it due to the lack of sensation in his fingers. After retrieving the camera from the floor, he took photo 19 of the Type-1 object through the windshield. The glow emitted from the bottom of the object illuminates the road very distinctly in the photograph. Ed said the object brightened up and came towards him. With his camera, he slipped out of the truck and clumsily tried to crawl under the pickup for protection from the object's white flash. Before he could get completely under the truck, the white flash struck the back of both legs from the knees down. The object then hovered a bit closer over the road in front of him. As he peered between the front wheels of the truck, he tried to take another photo, but he apparently did not have the camera aimed at the object.

The object then started to turn or rotate. To Ed's amazement, the blue beam deposited five aliens on the road, one after the other, less than a second apart. All five aliens, each wearing a shield and carrying a silver rod as before, started walking towards him. A thought flashed through his mind: 'If they can't get me with the white beam, they are sending aliens after me.' This prompted Ed to get back into the truck. He tried to start the engine, grinding the starter motor in his excitement because it was still running. He shifted the automatic into reverse, made a hurried U-turn, and departed the area rapidly.

16 January 1988, 02.00 hrs

Ed was awakened by a very soft hum, but of a higher pitch than the previous experiences. He took his camera to the semicircular front driveway and stood beside his pickup truck scanning the sky. He saw a red glow in the southern sky about the size of a star, which became larger, and in about ten seconds a UFO was nearly overhead. It looked entirely different and has been designated a Type-2 vehicle by Dr Maccabee. It was not as thick vertically as Type-1 and had a thin reddish 'veil' hanging below the lighted ring on the bottom. The underside of the body looked blue. When Ed lifted the camera to take a picture, he heard a very loud hum with the same tone or pitch as on previous occasions. A bright white UFO 'winked' into the sky. It hovered close to the reddish one, and Ed snapped photo 20 showing both objects. Then the red object moved to the east and disappeared, followed immediately by the white one.

21 January 1988, 22.30 hrs

By this time, Ed and two of the investigators had two-way radios. All-night stake-outs were being conducted nearly every night by Bob Reid and Gary Watson. On this night, Bob Reid was in his van across the field from Ed's house near some apartments with his camcorder ready. I had asked Ed for a negative of a particular photo for the MUFON UFO Journal, and Ed told Reid, by radio, that he would walk over and deliver it so Reid could take it back to Fort Walton Beach. Half way over, while walking through the woods to skirt the intervening fence, Ed heard a hum and got very excited. He saw a starlike object in the southern sky (beside Sirius), but Reid, still several hundred feet away in the dark, was watching what turned out to be an aircraft's landing lights to the north. The pinpoint of light that Ed recognized as a UFO blinked out before Reid could locate it. (Perhaps the UFO occupants did not want to be photographed by the investigators. Ed had no camera.)

24 January 1988, 17.30 hrs

While at home, Ed heard a faint hum. He immediately called on the two-way radio to see if an investigator was present. When he did not get a response, he got his Polaroid and camcorder and drove to the *Sentinel* office to have Duane Cook accompany him for verification. They drove east in Ed's truck in a light rain, followed by Dari, the newspaper's business manager, and her friend Ann. Dari said that 'Ed looked like he was in a trance'. While driving, Ed told Cook that he felt as if his face was falling off, the hum was in his right forehead, and that he felt like they wanted him out of the truck. Ed said, 'They are communicating with me,' and added that he received the following message: '*In sleep you know.*' Ed was being video-taped all the while showing great stress.

After reaching a deserted part of the winding Tiger-Point-East Road going south off highway 98, Ed stopped, and he and Cook got out. (Ed felt, at that time, that the aliens had on 11 November somehow given him the ability to hear them, but that their mission had been interrupted. He wanted to give them the opportunity to remove that capability, and he wanted someone else to record it.) Ed was standing in front of the truck being tormented by pain in his head and stomach. Cook scanned the sky but saw nothing in the dark misty rain. He got back in the truck with the video camera still running. Ed expressed his displeasure at the hum, and he had earlier asked the aliens to get rid of it. The torment and hum stopped. Ed thought it was over, but as he was about to open the truck door, he said, 'Oh s——, there it is.'

Ed raised the camera about 55° and snapped photo 21. This picture shows the railing on top of the truck and parallel light streaks going vertically from the UFO bright spots to the top of the picture. The UFO was gone after the camera flash. The total time it was visible was probably two or three seconds. Cook's view was blocked by the truck roof, and the ladies, parked around a bend in the road, had a tree between them and the object's location. They did, however, report seeing a flash, thinking it was just the camera, but later recalled some light coming from above the road. Photo 21 is important because it appears to show the object motionless for most of the time the camera shutter was open and then depart vertically before the shutter closed. This departure, in a fraction of a second, indicates acceleration well above 20 Gs.

26 January 1988, 21.30 hrs

Two days later Ed was taking a shower when his wife called to him, 'It's back.' She then got the camera, ran to the kitchen door and took photo 22, showing their Spitz in the foreground. The dog had been nervously looking back and forth between her and the UFO. Ed, still dripping wet, came on to the back patio with a towel wrapped around him. With the memories of the 24th still fresh in his mind, he shook his fist at the UFO while his wife took photo 23. The pictures show a Type-2 object. The main difference is what appears to be a 'wave' in the 'red veil' hanging below the bright bottom circle, such as is often seen in the aurora borealis. Also, there appears to be a tinge of blue at the bottom along with the red and some bright yellow-orange. The 'windows' are thin and triangular shaped, unlike the round or squarish ones in previous Type-1A and 1B images.

7 February 1988, 20.30 hrs

Ed's wife was out by the pool feeding the dog when a blue beam was seen coming down from a UFO above the house. It struck the ground between her and the house, and she screamed. After her twelve-year-old daughter looked and saw the beam, she ran to the front office and said, 'Daddy, Mommy needs you.' While Ed got his camera and ran to the kitchen, the daughter held the back door open for her mother who was coming around the beam towards the back door. As Ed was about to exit, the beam came down immediately in front of the doorway partially blocking it. Ed backed up and got a picture of his wife ducking around the approximately eighteen-inch-diameter beam to enter the door. The beam appeared brighter on the outside than the middle, and it seemed to rotate clockwise (looking up). The dry leaves in the spot where the beam first struck indicated that the beam caused a vortex action.

Following this event, the family began to think the creatures were entering the house. Every creak, whether a natural house noise or not, caused concern. After a while, they went to the garage and climbed into the van where they spent most of the night. This last photo was not given to the investigators immediately, because Ed wanted to avoid publicity involving his family. However, on 21 May, 1988, he was persuaded to allow the *Pensacola News Journal* to publish a cropped version in full colour on the front page.

26 February 1988, 21.30 hrs

Ed was given a Nimslo 4-lens sealed camera provided by Tom Deuley of the San Antonio MUFON group. I asked Ed to please use the camera on the next opportunity so he could convince the sceptics he was not photographing a small model at close range. After eighteen days with no photographs, Ed was feeling much pressure. However, the next night he and his wife went to the secluded Shoreline Park area where they took exposures 25–34, each with four images. This was designated a Type-3 object (Figure 10:3), and it looked entirely different from the others. It was a horizontal cylinder with a bright light on the rear and three rows of lights down the side. A few days earlier, Ed had reported seeing this light pattern while driving down Florida Route 87 towards Navarre, but he thought it might be an airplane. The object later proved to be only about three feet long at a distance of about forty-seven feet.

After Ed made drawings of what he saw, the investigators decided to make a media event out of the opening of the sealed camera. Walt Andrus was again invited to Pensacola to manage this event. The first frame contained a signed letter assuring that the film could not be switched, and the second was designed to test the sensitivity of the film. The small images that appeared as the reporters waited were almost identical to Ed's drawing.

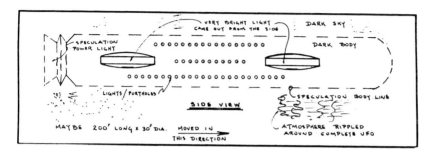

Figure 10:4. Ed's drawing of the 'Type-3' vehicle he photographed on 26 February 1988 at 21.30 hrs. This was drawn before the photographs were developed, showing it to be only three feet long.

(If he had this to do over we would put a diffraction grating on the two inner lenses.)

7 March 1988, 18.00 hrs

While eating dinner, Ed heard a hum in his head, lasting only five to eight seconds. He told his wife and continued eating. Later that night, while in bed, he heard another hum. He wanted to go out and use the new Polaroid Sun 600 LMS camera he had bought that day, but his wife persuaded him to stay in bed.

8 March 1988, 17.45 hrs

While his wife was fixing dinner, Ed again heard a hum. This time he took his new camera out back without telling her. It was raining a little. Soon he saw a glow between the pine trees, and he took photo 35. As he lowered the camera it was gone. This photo again shows the object departing vertically after providing a clear image and before the shutter closed. (Perhaps their motive system is keyed to the camera flash.) If a constant acceleration is assumed and the vehicle left the frame in 1/10th of a second, about 1/3rd of the shutter open time, then the acceleration was about 150 Gs.

17 March 1988, 20.05 hrs

The investigators were anxious to determine the precise size of the objects, so Dr Maccabee designed a self-referencing stereo (SRS) camera rig. Ed mounted two new Polaroid SUN 600 cameras on a heavy tripod two feet apart. A parallax reference point was fixed on a broomstick four feet in front, so as to be visible by both cameras. These cameras automatically flash and eject the film each time the lever is activated. On 17 March, Ed and his wife were in the *Sentinel* office discussing with Cook the UFO sightings reported by others. About 16.00, Ed heard a hum. They got excited, but Ed decided not to pursue it. He went home, and after Cook and Dari finished work on the paper, they went to Shoreline Park. After a while, they called Ed and talked him into coming over with the SRS camera rig. Ed had promised to call Peter Neumann, WEAR-TV manager, and Buddy Pollak, a close friend, when he went out, so Cook called them on his car phone. When they arrived, Ed asked Neumann to open and insert two new film packs. Test photos of those present were made. Carlos Hill and a young friend showed up. The cameras were set up in a secluded part of the park to avoid unknown people, and the time passed with a cold wind blowing.

At about 20.00, Ed had not heard a hum for about an hour. Cook and Pollak suggested there might be too many people around. All but Ed and his wife left. Neumann and his wife went home, but the rest did not go far. According to Ed, about forty-five seconds after they departed he heard another short hum. Then, three or four minutes later, the object appeared in the direction opposite where Pollak and the other had gone. Ed swung his cameras around and fired both, although not simultaneously. These were labelled 36L and 36R showing a Type-1 object well over 100 feet distant. Three or four seconds later the object departed. Ed's wife said they had to lean forward in order to see it. Cook, Pollak, and the other two saw the flashes and returned in time to see Ed watching the pictures develop in the illumination of his headlights. At this time, Brenda Pollak, a Gulf Breeze councilwoman, was coming to the park to find her husband. On her way, she saw a UFO twice, once at the apparent time and location it was photographed. Ed immediately sent the photos to Dr Maccabee for photogrammetric analysis.

20 March 1988, 20.45 hrs

Three days later, Ed heard a hum while at home. He grabbed the SRS camera rig and went to the back yard. While waiting, he heard a voice in his head that seemed to say, '*Zeehaus,*

Zeehaus . . . sleep and know'. In a few minutes, the UFO appeared to the north. He viewed it clearly through the right lens and took photos 37L and 37R. The left camera did not flash simultaneously with the right, but it was within a fraction of a second. The left photo showed an obstruction between the camera and the bright light that appears to be the bottom of a Type-1 vehicle. Daylight photos from the same location show the obstruction. Analysis of the photos also shows divergence rather than convergence, indicating the object was moving to the left at several miles per hour. Possibly, the instability in the broomstick caused by activating the cameras one after the other was also a factor preventing accurate distance measurement. Consequently, Ed spent much time practising the activation of both camera levers simultaneously.

21 April 1988, 22.30 hrs

Ed and his wife, at this point, had not received a full analysis of the Nimslo camera photographs, so there was still some disagreement as to the size of the Type-3 object. Ed, almost constantly looking through the camera lens on 26 February, thought it was a large distant object, while his wife, who constantly viewed it with both eyes, thought it was a smaller object rather close. On 21 April they were out for an evening walk in the neighbourhood when the Type-3 object flew nearly overhead, stopped briefly at what appeared to be sixty feet away, and then moved out of sight towards the school yard. They both measured its angular size to be one inch at arm's length, indicating it was a small object, not large enough to carry the aliens previously witnessed.

1 May 1988, 01.10 hrs

At Dr Maccabee's request, Ed had stabilized the parallax reference of the SRS camera rig to provide more accurate measurements of the vehicle size. He and his wife took the cameras to Shoreline Park on several nights after their daily duties were over, but found nothing to photograph. He had been asked to photograph the UFO with the SRS cameras while his wife photographed him and the UFO with the camcorder. (Some critics are hard to satisfy!)

The next night Ed went alone, as his wife was acting as chaperone on a school trip. At about 23.30 he set up the improved SRS camera rig along with a set of coded poles, each 60° around an arc ten feet from the tripod centre. This would provide a second set of parallax references and more accurate distance calculations. He waited in his van for nearly an hour and a half. At 01.00 he got a short hum and manned his cameras. At 01.10 a bright UFO popped into view towards Pensacola Beach, and Ed flashed both cameras simultaneously (photos 38L and 38R). He looked up and saw the Type-3 object to the right of the bright one, but when he looked back through the right lens he did not see the objects. When he looked up again, the large bright one was about thirty feet above his head. At this point he said he got a 'white out' in his head.

Ed thought that the next instant he was lying face down on the beach, disorientated and with a sore head. After picking himself up, he saw his cameras twenty feet away, and as he walked to them noticed that it was 02.30. He was missing about one hour and fifteen minutes. He suddenly had great concern for his daughter, grabbed his cameras and two of the six poles, and rushed home. After seeing her sound asleep, he sat on the floor in front of her door until 06.00. When he went to the bathroom and turned on the light he saw a dark reddish mark between his eyes, and another on each temple. There was 'black smelly stuff' under the three longest fingernails of the right hand. He wrapped his hand in a towel and slept until 11.30. The black stuff was frozen in a jar and later found to have a silicon base, but the black impurity has not been identified as of this writing because the processes available near Gulf Breeze would be destructive-analysis processes. The next day the investigators could easily see the three reddish marks, and there was a bump on the back of Ed's head.

This last set of Ed's photographs is probably the most revealing. The SRS system worked as Dr Maccabee had hoped. The photos show the Type-1 object to be about 475 feet out over the water with a bottom light 14.8 feet in diameter. It was also about 14.8 feet tall. The Type-3 object was 132 feet away and about 2.5 feet from the 'tail' to the right-most portion of light. Since this object was similar to the object photographed with the Nimslo camera, it appears to be about three feet long, which is consistent with analysis of the Nimslo camera data.

Time-regression hypnosis of the 1 May event was done by Dr Dan Overlade, a highly experienced clinical psychologist. It appears that Ed was captured by a group of aliens like those he saw on 12 January. They used their wands like our police use stun guns, and during a struggle, apparently projected telepathic images of his daughter, as if to distract him. After being subdued, he found himself lying in an empty room where the bright, white light seemed to be coming from no particular source, but from the air molecules. When Ed had an aggressive thought as the leader came in, a blue beam came from the ceiling and hit him in the head. Almost immediately he got the smell of ammonia and a stinging in his throat. (Perhaps the energy in the beam disassociated the hydrogen from the oxygen in the moisture of his breath, and the hydrogen re-combined with the nitrogen of the air to form ammonia.) The beam physically picked him up and set him on a bench where his emotional memories were apparently transferred to immature aliens. Further time-regression hypnosis indicates Ed was on board a UFO when he was seventeen, twenty-five and thirty-three years old, and each time a similar 'emotional transfer' was accomplished.

Other Events

On *17 December 1987* a liquid fell from the UFO into the school yard, and some was apparently caught in a plastic butter container. The liquid, mixed with dirt and algae, was determined to be diluted seawater by Pioneer Laboratory Inc., in Pensacola, and by the Guadalupe-Blanco River Authority in Texas. For an unknown reason the fluid in the plastic container bubbled for nearly a month.

The same night the UFO had been photographed near the ground in the school yard. Nearby, the grass died in a circular area fourteen feet in diameter, and it did not grow back in the spring. Extensive tests by the Florida Cooperative Extension Services three weeks later could not determine the cause, but they suggested that exposure to a short-lived toxic chemical or to an energy source could have killed the grass. An investigator from Mobile, Alabama, was previously provided funds by MUFON for the Alabama Forensic Sciences Department to do a soil sample analysis, but he refused to provide the report to the investigative team. Another visiting investigator, Dr Willy Smith, said he definitely could smell petroleum products at the circle, although the other investigators could not. The extensive testing showed no petroleum residue.

On *13 January 1988*, at about 08.30, two men in an unmarked white American-made sedan came to Ed's home and knocked on his door. They wore civilian suits and visually exposed large pistols under their coats. One of them said, 'Are you Ed Walters?', to which he replied in the affirmative. They introduced themselves as agent McKathy and agent — of Air Force Special Security Services. Agent McKathy said, 'We have a Material Seizure Warrant. We understand you have some photographs of UFOs. It is against the law to withhold them.' They came in and looked around his office. He told them he had given the photos to the *Miami Herald* reporter, Dave Barry. Ed said, 'If you call Dave he's going to say he does not have them; because, he told me he would deny having them.' One man said, 'You know if you are lying to us you are in big trouble, because this is a Material Seizure Warrant.' Then they left.

On *18* and *23 February 1988*, Ed submitted himself to a polygraph examination by Harvey McLaughlin, Jr. The purpose of the examination was: 'To verify the authenticity of the photographs, personal sightings, experiences, and general information supplied by Mr Walters concerning his experiences with UFOs since November 1987.' After over five hours of working with Ed, the examiner stated his opinion: 'With the information that is available to this examiner at this time, it is felt that Mr Walters truly believes that the photographs and personal sightings he has described are true and factual to the best of his ability.'

Later Michael Kradz, of Dector Counterintelligence and Security, Inc. in Glen Burnie, Maryland, processed two of Ed's tape-recorded interviews with a psychological stress evaluator (PSE-101). He said Ed '. . . is being truthful about what he saw and what he did, and does not show any reactions to cause this examiner to doubt his answers.'

Also, psychological tests given Ed by Dr Dan Overlade prior to his ten hours of regression found no evidence of any psychopathologies. These tests included the Wachsler Adult

Intelligence Scale (Revised), the Minnesota Multiphasic Personality Interview, the Thematic Apperception Test, the Draw-A-Person Test, and the Rorschach 'inkblot test'.

Ed and Frances Walters have documented their story for a book entitled *The Gulf Breeze Sightings*, due to be published in 1990.

Shortly after the Gulf Breeze UFO encounters got their first publicity, three low-level radar vehicles were moved into the area: a ship named the *Jan Tide*, an Army Division Air Defense vehicle, and a NASA long-range tracking ship. Several witnesses reported fighter planes or light fixed-wing aircraft coming directly towards a UFO at low level. Also, strange helicopters were seen orbiting the school yard where the circle of dead grass had been found.

Other incidents indicate some kind of government knowledge of some of the UFO activity.

On *21 November 1988*, an eighteen-year-old boy reported that he and his friends were evicted from a public national seashore area east of Pensacola Beach by the Air Force Security Police. The boys were told they could not stay there because there was an incident in progress. At 20.45, about thirty minutes later, James Larkin saw a UFO low over the trees about two miles north of where the boys were. Some investigators wonder if there is a connection between these two incidents.

Several of the sightings of late 1988 were north of Navarre towards the Eglin AFB reservation. For example, in early *December 1988*, Annette Spear and her children reported a row of red lights, each appearing slightly larger than the full moon, moving towards the reservation as if they were attached to a large silent vehicle. A helicopter also seen in the area at the same time must have been aware of this object.

Other photographs submitted to the investigators by individuals, or by the Gulf Breeze *Sentinel*, show objects that have not been identified. These include:

the nine photos of 23 December 1987, showing the Type-1 objects reported by 'Believer Bill';

two prints from a 35-mm camera showing Type-1 objects that the anonymous photographer, 'Jane', said were taken in June 1986 [see cover photo];

209

Figure 10:5. Donald Ware and Robert Reid at Shoreline Park, Pensacola Beach, scene of one of Ed's dramatic encounters (© Timothy Good).

a roll of 110 film with five photos of orange balls taken by 'Mike' at Pensacola Beach on 2 April 1988 (one glowing ball appears to be about twelve and a half feet in diameter);

two 35-mm negatives taken on 6 April 1988, by 'Milli', showing orange ovals that appear to be glowing or reflecting sunlight some distance up (the image was only 0.001 radians);

eight suspicious photos later submitted by 'A Believer', which were probably faked.

Most other sightings near Gulf Breeze are too numerous to include here, but a few will suffice. A neighbour a few doors from Ed saw a glowing object the size of a saucer at arm's length, over the school yard just before Christmas 1987. Ed's neighbours across the street had a close encounter of the third or fourth type on *1 April 1988*, that lasted two hours, and they reported later sightings in 1988. On *2 December 1987*, Pat McClellan, with his wife and daughter, saw a UFO jump from one spot to another and fly silently close overhead before it departed, with a military plane close behind. On *12 February 1988*, two ladies in Cantonment saw a boomerang-shaped object with many lights fly low and slow overhead. A visiting investigator, Paul Norman, said he interviewed a lady who reported an object that approached her and her friend rapidly three times, before it dived into the Gulf, on *10 March*.

Mr Truman Holcomb [who struck me as completely sincere when I met him in July 1988 – Editor] reported a close sighting of the Type-1 vehicle shining a blue beam across Highway 98 on *28 April*, as well as another sighting later in the year. On *8 July*, Dr Fenner McConnell and his wife, Shirley, saw a Type-1 vehicle hover near the water beside their pier for two or three minutes as they were about to go jogging at 04.54. (They had earlier sent out 535 invitations to a 'UFO Watch' party to be held two days later at their home, but they were afraid to tell their guests about their sighting. Their annual party is a major social event in Gulf Breeze. Several investigators have suggested this event seemed to be more than a coincidence.)

July 8 was also the day of the abductee support group meeting in Pensacola. Since UFO investigations by newspapers, TV, and MUFON were generally accomplished without ridicule, twelve people were encouraged to tell MUFON of their experiences involving missing time or extremely strange dreams. Some of these people were having trouble coping with their experiences. MUFON established a support group, including abductees, investigators, and a clinical psychologist to help reduce the fear of the unknown. Dr Overlade has been quite successful in both recovering blocked memories and in relieving stress. In December 1988 his regression techniques were reviewed by a distinguished group of his peers at the Ericksonian Congress in San Francisco. This review of Dr Overlade's video tapes increased his confidence in his procedures and also gave the review group some food for thought.

In February 1988, WEAR-TV of Pensacola made a thirty-minute documentary, *The Sightings*, with Mark Curtis as interviewer. On

5 October, Gulf Breeze was featured on an NBC *Unexplained Mysteries* programme. Then on 14 October, the two-hour production, *UFO Cover-up? Live*, was broadcast from Gulf Breeze, Washington DC, and Moscow.

The Gulf Breeze sightings and photographs are proof of alien visitation, in my opinion. The level of technology demonstrated indicates that they can come and go at will and can reside in a variety of places; the bottom of our oceans, inside major high-altitude ice fields, in Earth orbit, on the Moon, or even on Mars.

The increasing national media coverage of the UFO phenomenon, spurred by the Gulf Breeze encounters, may cause many more abductees to gain the courage to talk about their experiences. Perhaps some will seek help in understanding what happened to them. Investigators and psychologists around the world should work together to provide this help.

Appendix

———————————— ⊙ ————————————

Some major UFO Organizations

Australia

Australian Centre for UFO Studies
P.O. Box 728, Lane Grove, NSW 2066.

UFO Research Australia
P.O. Box 229, Prospect, South Australia 5082.

UFO Research Queensland
P.O. Box 111, North Quay, Queensland 4002.

Victorian UFO Research Society
P.O. Box 43, Moorabbin, Victoria 3189.

Canada

Canadian UFO Research Network
P.O. Box 15, Station 'A', Willowdale, Ontario, M2N 5S7.

Centrale de Compilation Ufologique de Quebec
CP 103, Drummondville, Quebec, J2B 2V6.

United Kingdom

British UFO Research Association
16 Southway, Burgess Hill, Sussex, RH15 9ST.

Contact International (UK)
11 Ouseley Close, New Marston, Oxford, OX3 0JS.

Yorkshire UFO Society
15 Pickard Court, Temple Newsam, Leeds, LS15 9AY.

United States of America

Citizens Against UFO Secrecy
3518 Martha Custis Drive, Alexandria, Virginia 22302.

Fair Witness Project Inc.
4219 W. Olive Avenue, Suite 247, Burbank, California 91505.

Fund for UFO Research
P.O. Box 277, Mount Rainier, Maryland 20712.

J. Allen Hynek Center for UFO Studies
2457 West Peterson Avenue, Chicago, Illinois 60659.

Mutual UFO Network
103 Oldtowne Road, Seguin, Texas 78155–4099.

National UFO Reporting Center
P.O. Box 1807, Seattle, Washington 98111.

Journals on UFOs

Flying Saucer Review
This is arguably the world's leading journal on the subject of UFOs. Founded in 1955, it has an international team of distinguished consultants, and is taken by many governmental bodies and learned institutions including the Chinese Institute of Scientific & Technical Information and the USSR Academy of Sciences.

The Editor is former diplomat and intelligence officer, Gordon Creighton, MA, FRGS, FRAS. For subscription details, send a stamped addressed envelope to: The Editor, FSR Publications Ltd, P.O. Box 12, Snodland, Kent, ME6 5JZ, UK.

Focus
4219 W. Olive Avenue, Suite 247, Burbank, California 91505, USA.

International UFO Reporter
2457 W. Peterson Avenue, Chicago, Illinois 60659, USA.

Journal of UFO Research
A bi-monthly magazine devoted to UFOs and Science, the first of its kind in China. Write for details to: Paul Dong, P.O. Box 2011, Oakland, California 94604, USA.

MUFON UFO Journal
103 Oldtowne Road, Seguin, Texas, 78155-4099 USA.

Quest International
Quest Publications International Ltd, 15 Pickard Court, Temple Newsam, Leeds, LS15 9AY, UK.

UFO
1800 S. Robertson Blvd, Box 355, Los Angeles, California 90035, USA.

Bibliography

Berlitz, Charles and Moore, William: *The Roswell Incident,* Granada, London 1980.

APPENDIX

Blundell, Nigel and Boar, Roger: *The World's Greatest UFO Mysteries*, Octopus Books, London.

Butler, Brenda, Street, Dot and Randles, Jenny: *Skycrash*, Grafton Books, London 1986.

Delgado, Pat and Andrews, Colin: *Circular Evidence*, Bloomsbury Press, London 1989.

Devereux, Paul: *Earth Lights*, Turnstone Press, Wellingborough 1982.

—— and Thomson, Ian: *The Ley Hunter's Companion*, Thames & Hudson 1979.

Dong, Paul: *UFOs over Modern China*, P.O. Box 2011, Oakland, California 94604.

——: *The Four Major Mysteries of Mainland China.*

Fawcett, Lawrence and Greenwood Barry: *Clear Intent*, Prentice-Hall, New Jersey 1984.

Fuller, Paul and Randles, Jenny: *Mystery of the Circles*, BUFORA 1986.

Good, Timothy: *Above Top Secret*, Sidgwick & Jackson, London 1987; Grafton Books, London 1989; William Morrow, New York; Macmillan of Canada.

Hall, Richard: *Uninvited Guests*, Aurora Press, New Mexico 1988.

Hind, Cynthia: *UFOs – African Encounters*, Gemini, P.O. Box 768, Harare, Zimbabwe.

Hopkins, Budd: *Intruders*, Random House, New York 1987.

Howe, Linda: *An Alien Harvest*, Linda M. Howe Publications, P.O. Box 3130, Littleton, Colorado, 80161-3130.

Hynek, Dr J. Allen, Imbrogno, Philip with Pratt, Bob: *Night Siege*, Ballantyne Books, New York 1987.

Meaden, Dr G. Terence: *The Circles Effect and Its Mysteries*, Artetech Publishing Company, 54 Frome Road, Bradford-on-Avon, BA15 1LD, 1989.

Noyes, Ralph: *A Secret Property*, Quartet Books, London 1985.

Randles, Jenny: *Abduction*, Headline, London 1989.

Shuttlewood, Arthur: *Warnings from Flying Friends,* Portway Press, Warminster 1968.

Spencer, John and Evans, Hilary (editors): *Phenomenon*, Futura, London 1988.

Steinman, William: *UFO Crash at Aztec*, America West Distributors, P.O. Box K, Boulder, Colorado 80306, or from Susanne Stebbing.

Story, Ronald (editor): *The Encyclopedia of UFOs*, New English Library, London 1980.

Strieber, Whitley: *Communion*, Century Hutchinson, London 1988.

Stringfield, Leonard: *Inside Saucer Post . . . 3-0 Blue*, 1957.

——: *Situation Red: The UFO Siege*, Doubleday 1977 and Fawcett 1978.

Vallee, Jacques: *Dimensions,* Contemporary Books, Chicago 1988.

Walters, Ed and Frances: *The Gulf Breeze Sightings*, William Morrow, New York 1990.

Those requiring books on UFOs which are not currently available in the bookshops should write, enclosing a stamped addressed envelope, to: Miss Susanne Stebbing, 41 Terminus Drive, Herne Bay, Kent, CT6 6PR, UK or Arcturus Book Service, P.O. Box 831383, Stone Mountain, Georgia 30083-0023, USA.

Services for UFO enthusiasts

UFO Newsclipping Service

The UFO Newsclipping Service will keep you informed of all the latest United States and world-wide UFO reports, many of which are carried only in local newspapers. For subscription details, write to: Lucius Farish, UFO Newsclipping Service, Route 1, Box 220, Plumerville, Arkansas 72127, USA.

UK Newsclippings

For those requiring UK newsclippings only, a service is provided by CETI Publications in association with Quest International. For subscription details, send a stamped addressed envelope to: CETI Publications, 247 High Street, Beckenham, Kent, BR3 1AB.

UFO Hotline

The Yorkshire UFO Society has a UFO Hotline (24-hour service) for reporting sightings: telephone 0756–752216.

UFO Call

The British UFO Research Association and British Telecom run a 24-hour UFO news update service on 0898–121886.

Computer UFO Network

CUFON was established in the USA by Dale Goudie for the purpose of providing other UFO researchers with quick access to sighting data and locations, as well as documented Freedom of Information material.

Contact: Computer UFO Network, Computer line: (connect at 300 or 1200 bauds, eight data bits, no parity, one stop bit) (206) 722 5738. Information line: (206) 721 5035.

Mutual UFO Network Amateur Radio Net (USA)

Saturdays: 0800 EST/EDT–7.237 MHz. Sundays 1500 EST/EDT–28.470 MHz.

National Emergency Calling

EST/EDT	MHz
0000–0015	3.990
0400–0415	3.990
0800–0815	7.237
1200–1215	7.237
1600–1615	7.237
2000–2015	3.990

Index

⊙

217